Troubling Nationhood
in U.S. Latina Literature

Latinidad

Transnational Cultures in the United States

This series publishes books that deepen and expand our knowledge and understanding of the various Latina/o populations in the United States in the context of their transnational relationships with cultures of the broader Americas. The focus is on the history and analysis of Latino cultural systems and practices in national and transnational spheres of influence from the nineteenth century to the present. The series is open to scholarship in political science, economics, anthropology, linguistics, history, cinema and television, literary and cultural studies, and popular culture and encourages interdisciplinary approaches, methods, and theories. The series grew out of discussions with faculty at the School of Transborder Studies at Arizona State University, where an interdisciplinary emphasis is being placed on transborder and transnational dynamics.

Carlos Velez-Ibañez, *Series Editor, School of Transborder Studies*

Rodolfo F. Acuña, *In the Trenches of Academe: The Making of Chicana/o Studies*

Adriana Cruz-Manjarrez, *Zapotecs on the Move: Cultural, Social, and Political Processes in Transnational Prespective*

Marivel T. Danielson, *Homecoming Queers: Desire and Difference in Chicana Latina Cultural Production*

Rudy P. Guevarra Jr., *Becoming Mexipino: Multiethnic Identities and Communities in San Diego*

Lisa Jarvinen, *The Rise of Spanish-Language Filmmaking: Out from Hollywood's Shadow, 1929–1939*

Regina M. Marchi, *Day of the Dead in the USA: The Migration and Transformation of a Cultural Phenomenon*

Marci R. McMahon, *Domestic Negotiations: Gender, Nation, and Self-Fashioning in US Mexicana and Chicana Literature and Art*

A. Gabriel Melendez, *Hidden Chicano Cinema: Film Dramas in the Borderlands*

Priscilla Peña Ovalle, *Dance and the Hollywood Latina: Race, Sex, and Stardom*

Luis F. B. Plascencia, *Disenchanting Citizenship: Mexican Migrants and the Boundaries of Belonging*

Maya Socolovsky, *Troubling Nationhood in U.S. Latina Literature: Explorations of Place and Belonging*

Troubling Nationhood in U.S. Latina Literature

Explorations of Place and Belonging

MAYA SOCOLOVSKY

Rutgers University Press

NEW BRUNSWICK, NEW JERSEY, AND LONDON

LIBRARY OF CONGRESS CATALOGING-IN-PUBLICATION DATA

Socolovsky, Maya, 1973–

    Troubling nationhood in U.S. Latina literature : explorations of place and belonging /
Maya Socolovsky.

        pages cm — (Latinidad: Transnational Cultures in the United States) (American literatures initiative)

    Includes bibliographical references and index.

    ISBN 978-0-8135-6118-9 (hardcover : alk. paper)

    ISBN 978-0-8135-6117-2 (pbk. : alk. paper)

    ISBN 978-0-8135-6119-6 (e-book)

    1. American literature—Hispanic American authors—History and criticism.
2. American literature—Women authors—History and criticism. 3. Hispanic American
women—Intellectual life. 4. Hispanic Americans in literature. 5. Belonging (Social
psychology) 6. Identity (Psychology) in literature. 7. National characteristics, Latin
American, in literature. I. Title.

PS153.H56S63   2014

810.9'928708968—dc23

2012040277A

British Cataloging-in-Publication record for this book is available
from the British Library.

Visit our website: http://rutgerspress.rutgers.edu

Manufactured in the United States of America

THE
AMERICAN
LITERATURES
INITIATIVE

A book in the American Literatures Initiative (ALI), a collaborative
publishing project of NYU Press, Fordham University Press, Rutgers
University Press, Temple University Press, and the University of Virginia
Press. The Initiative is supported by The Andrew W. Mellon Foundation.
For more information, please visit www.americanliteratures.org.

For my children Ilan, Amia, and Gali,
and in memory of my father, Victor Socolovsky

Contents

Acknowledgments

This project has benefited from the contributions of many individuals as over the years I have worked in collegial environments that have sustained and nurtured my interests and my writing. In particular, I am grateful to Kate Flint for guiding me through my dissertation on U.S. Latina literature at Oxford University; to the late Gay Wilentz for her mentoring and support of my early scholarship; and to Marta Caminero-Santangelo, whose intellectually rigorous reading of the manuscript and astute feedback helped crystalize and enrich my ideas. She has been invaluable to this project's fruition.

Earlier versions of some chapters of this book appeared originally in various journals. An earlier version of the chapter on *Sapogonia* appeared as "Borrowed Homes: Homesickness and Memory in Ana Castillo's *Sapogonia*" in *Aztlán* 24.2 (1999), pp. 73-94. An earlier version of the chapter on *Face of an Angel* appeared as "Narrative and Traumatic Memory in Denise Chávez's *Face of an Angel*" in *MELUS* 28.4 (2003), pp. 187-205. An earlier version of the chapter on *The Line of the Sun* appeared as "Telling Stories of Transgression in Judith Ortiz Cofer's *The Line of the Sun*" in *MELUS* 34.1 (2009), pp. 95-116.

This work was supported, in part, by funds provided by the University of North Carolina (UNC) at Charlotte. At UNC Charlotte there are also numerous colleagues and friends both in the Department of English and the Latin American Studies Program who offered encouragement and support; I especially thank Tony Jackson, Jennifer Munroe, and Paula Connolly for their careful comments and advice on earlier versions of the manuscript. At Rutgers University Press, I have been fortunate to work with Katie Keeran, whose thorough reading and comments helped me vastly improve the project, and Lisa Boyajian, whose efficient and patient editorial assistance helped guide me smoothly through the publication process.

I am also grateful to my parents for exemplifying the drive and work ethic that it takes to complete this kind of project, and for embedding in me both their native and adopted tongues, Spanish and Hebrew. Most important, my gratitude goes to my partner, Gordon Hull, who read and critiqued substantial early versions of this work. His unwavering patience, generosity, and scholarly and domestic prowess know no bounds. Finally, this book is dedicated to my children, Ilan, Amia, and Gali, who bring me such joy each day, and to my late father, Victor Socolovsky, who experienced multiple diasporas in his lifetime, and must have also known something of what it means to be with, and without, a place of belonging.

Introduction: Troubling America(s)

In June 2009 the culinary magazine *Gourmet* ran a feature entitled "Fiesta Forever." Shot in real time with real people—"no casting, no script, no backup food"—the spread photographed Cuban-born cook and restauranteur Maricel Presilla's annual barbecue in Palisades Interstate Park, in Alpine, New Jersey. The event, which also promotes Presilla's two restaurants, is a giant affair where "as many as sixty people show up to cook, dance, and devour dozens of dishes," and honors Presilla, whose "all-out Latin gathering of family and friends of all ages is the ultimate outdoor party, a perfect example of why we are all in love with grilling." The editors believe that this is a rare opportunity to shoot "a grand version of el barbecue."[1] The twenty-four-page spread, offering vivid photographs and recipes with relatively little text, is presented to readers as a chance to "spend a day in [Presilla's] world, with her food." Readers are gently urged, "You're invited, too."[2] The message of the feature is clear: the magazine's readers can experience Latin America vicariously by gazing at photographs, studying recipes, and reproducing them in their own homes. Presilla, in her own words, extends the invitation: "I want to take everyone on a winding journey through Mexico, through Central and South America, to show them the artisanal cooking there, the cooking ordinary people do." The feature writers note that Presilla "effortlessly pulls guests into her own orbit, which, on this day, closely resembles a Mexican market."[3]

Of course, this orbit unfolds right in the United States. Although readers are encouraged to feel that they are on a traveling vacation in Latin

America, voyeuristically able to experience a foreign culture and its delicious cuisine with their *Gourmet* passport in hand, the event takes place within the national and political borders of the United States. This U.S. state park in New Jersey is transformed, for the duration of the fiesta, into Mexico. Two months after the issue ran, the magazine printed a perhaps predictable angry reader's response to the "Fiesta Forever" feature. This reader, a self-described longtime regular subscriber, explains why she will be "tossing out" the June issue: "Let's see . . . what will I serve my guests from this issue? How about slab bacon adobo made with four pounds of bacon? I'll serve it with refried black beans made with ten Mexican avocado leaves. I can hardly wait for the July issue. What will your staff dream up for a Fourth of July barbecue—maybe there will be some great Mongolian or Ethiopian recipes your readers can use as they plan celebrations for Independence Day. This is the United States of America, not Latin America."[4] Other than the glaring xenophobia of this response, what is startling is the way that Latin America functions as a scapegoat for U.S. anxiety about its cultural and national identification. In other words, for this reader a porous border between the United States and Latin America opens the floodgates to other foreign influences. Such Latin Americanization of the United States represents the nation's potential cultural dissolution: the sarcastic reference to Mongolian and Ethiopian influences signals the way in which the presence of Latin America in the United States spurs fears of other foreign invasions and potentially threatens the very roots of the nation's foundation. We may begin by celebrating Latinos in the United States, cautions the reader, but before we know it we will be marking the United States' most patriotic national holiday with radically foreign presences.

The reader recognizes that the magazine is not simply traveling southward, but that the expectation to reproduce such recipes in one's own home in the United States also signals the geographical border's movement northward. In such a way, Latin American cuisine enters, albeit by invitation, the domestic spaces of the United States, and threatens the dominant culture's definition of the nation. By ingesting "foreign" food, the collective, cultural body of the nation could become unrecognizably othered. Significantly, the letter also shows the United States' ambiguous and troubling relationship with Latin America. The reader, after all, takes pains to separate the United States from Latin America ("This is the United States of America, not Latin America"). In this context it would be hard to imagine a similar need to differentiate the United States from, say, Ethiopia or Mongolia; even though the reader has already cast them in our imaginations as potential cultural threats, their extreme otherness renders their presence as an almost unimaginable endpoint. But it does bear reiterating, for her, that Latin America, crouching on the edges of the United States, is a contiguous and familiar/foreign neighbor always-already within the United States itself.

Although this letter appears to be just a single xenophobic incident, the magazine's decision to print it shows the extent to which conversations about nationhood are fraught and ongoing in popular culture. The letter is an example of a much broader and deep-seated anxiety about U.S. expressions of nationhood, which depend on historical and contemporary articulations of citizenship and belonging that forge connections between cultural, geographical, and political identities. Frequently, popular articulations of U.S. identity are based on certain notions of geopolitical nationhood stemming from the late eighteenth and nineteenth centuries: manifest destiny, colonization, conquest, expansion, and the acquisition of land and property have in contemporary times allowed the nation to imagine itself as separate from, opposed to, and distinct from its Latin American neighbors. The late nineteenth-century rhetoric of nationalism within Latin America itself also historically supported this separation, exemplified by José Martí's 1891 essay "Nuestra América," where he emphasized transnational interactions rather than comparative histories of individual Spanish-speaking countries of Latin America, bringing them together through their desire to differentiate themselves from their powerful neighbor to the north.[5] This geopolitical nationalism that understands Latin America as spatially and geographically separate from the United States, however, is also part of a broader cultural separation, both perceived and real, that turns Latinos/as within the United States, almost no matter their national origins, legal standing, or historical continuity in the country, into outsiders.

What happens, then, when U.S. Latino/a writers, who occupy, as Ilan Stavans notes, "a liminal zone, a Latin America inside the United States," enter the conversation?[6] How do they challenge that rhetoric of cultural "unbelonging," and what impact might that have, for example, on current debates about immigration and citizenship, which are clearly about practices of exclusion, inclusion, and membership in the nation? In response to mainstream or popular understandings of U.S. nationhood, I argue in this book that Latino/a literary narratives imagine a collective geographical, political, and cultural presence, where Latin America becomes part of, not apart from, the political and national identity of the United States. As they imagine the United States as part of a broader

"Americas," the writings I explore clearly trouble imperialist notions of nationhood, in which political borders, and a long history of intervention and colonization beyond those borders, have come to shape and determine dominant culture's writing and defining of all Latinos/as as "other" to the nation.

That is, I show how Latina writers contest the prevailing national imaginary, constructing major revisions of national identity that de-emphasize and even at times disregard geopolitical and cultural borders in order to reimagine the United States as part of the larger Americas. The texts are all concerned with the central idea of national interpenetration, reimagining a transnational space of the Americas that is born out of an oppressive history of U.S. domination. In other words, according to these works, the United States cannot be understood separately and apart from Latin America, suggesting that the rigid national boundaries of exclusion by which nations operate are arbitrary and fictional constructs. Of course, while all the texts under discussion strongly suggest the imbrication of the United States within Latin America, and Latin America within the United States, they do so in different ways and with different foci. Some explore the national and political border between the United States and Latin America, some present the damaging effects of neocolonialism and the possibilities of resistance to it outside the geographical borders of the United States, while others attend to the psychological trauma of having a marginalized second-class status within the United States.

One of the implications of this reexamination of U.S.–Latin American relations is to legitimate Latino belonging within the United States. In a sense the texts can be read as attempts to counter current anti-immigration rhetoric, which links "illegal" presence to larger cultural "threats" posed by the "foreign" culture of Latinos/as more generally. The *Gourmet* reader's fears—that domestic and public spaces are becoming part of Latin America, that such a transformation of place will dismantle not only the nation's cultural integrity but also its political integrity, and that such cultural invasions signal the loss of stable borders—demonstrate the various ways that Latino/a cultural presence and politics intersect in conversations about national identity. This introductory chapter outlines the salient features of the broader popular and political environment of anxiety out of which many Latino/a writers write, while the book's postscript turns to recent political discourses in order to explore how they interpellate Latinos/as as criminal figures within the immigration debate. The intervening chapters do a material literary analysis of the literary texts in question, showing how they can be read as strategic interventions in these cultural moments. Such literary writing, which can of course be understood in light of the cultural context to which it responds, is in itself a practice of cultural resistance.

This study fills an important gap in our understanding of Latina literary production. While critics have generally agreed that U.S. Latina literature talks back to mainstream notions of U.S. and Latino/a identity, critical literature has not significantly explored how recent U.S. Latina literature's "talking back" has engaged with questions of belonging to the nation. Insofar as these Latina narratives demonstrate their belonging by reimagining the U.S. national and political identity as part of a collective that includes Latin America, they also encourage a rethinking of the space and "place" of the United States. Here, and for much of this book, I understand "place" broadly as referring sometimes to physical location, land, and geography, and sometimes to cultural practices and experiences. This literal and figurative understanding of place does not imply that geographic place and cultural practice/experience are the same things. It does imply, however, that they always intersect in ways that are important to our understanding of both of them.

To understand "place" in both figurative and literal terms allows the categories to constantly invoke one another, so that an analysis of physical landscape, for example, never loses sight of the cultural and/or bodily experiences that occur in that landscape. Conversely, in a discussion of bodily trauma that reads the traumatized body as figuratively "placed" or "displaced," the impact of physical landscape on that experience remains immediate. This kind of reading is particularly important because it allows us to understand the "blending" of the United States and Latin America as a process whereby geographical landscapes, cultural practices, and narrative spaces all become intersecting aspects of national identification and experience.[7] Through this broader conceptualization of place, the relational, lived, and cultural experiences of belonging to a nation-space and its geographical terrain become important sites of resistance.[8]

As the remainder of this introduction demonstrates, such imbrication of U.S. national identity through tropes of spatiality is both prevalent in contemporary discussions of Latinos/as and has deep historical roots. In contemporary discussions the threat supposedly posed by an increasing Latino population is often figured in geographical terms, constructing national identity not just in terms of attitude or birthplace but also through the location and presence of cultural and physical differences.

Many human and social geographers, then, are surprised that in the United States, place and space as hermeneutical tools for reading literature, particularly with regard to constructions of nation, have been generally understudied and "undertheorized."[9] Emphasizing the importance of reading "place," Edward Soja reminds us that life-stories "have a geography too; they have milieux, immediate locales, provocative emplacements which affect thought and action. The historical imagination is never completely spaceless."[10]

Critics of minority literature in particular have long understood how space and place are politically and ideologically determined as social constructs that must be examined for the hegemonic structures of power that often determine and shape them. Communities resisting dominant culture, of course, might use place or space for oppositional or radical practices. For example, critical attention to Chicana literature has focused on geographical displacement and recognized the possible intersections of spatial and social structures of power. Chicana writing, with its critical engagement in borderlands subjects, readily lends itself to a hermeneutics that theorizes space and interprets landscape as part of social and cultural discourse:[11] Mary Pat Brady proposes that the Chicana texts she examines are "counter-cartographies" or spatial narratives that challenge norms.[12] Looking at U.S. Latina literature under a panethnic grouping in the chapters that follow, I build on this critical interest in Chicano/a literary representations of space, asking what sorts of national narratives about land, the body, and storytelling are produced when cultural, political, and geographical experiences of place intersect, and exploring the ways that the literature creates, suggests, or reveals radical social changes.

The chapters thus show how particular examples of U.S. Latina literature, written between 1989 and 2004, respond to, counter, and trouble dominant culture's delegitimation of Latino presence in the United States and then rethink contemporary national and literary U.S. identity on that basis.[13] I examine a group of feminist texts that are representative of the U.S. Latina literary boom of the 1990s and 2000s, during which an emerging group of writers became prominent in mainstream and academic circles. My selection of women writers is intentional: as Tey Diana Rebolledo's discussion of southwestern Chicana and Hispanic women writers notes, the physical landscape of that region is inseparable from the women's sense of survival and identity.[14] Building on this analysis, I understand contemporary Latina writers to be continuing the practice of early Hispanic women writers, who "talked back"—through cultural descriptions—to the nineteenth- and early twentieth-century Anglo writers, travelers, and inhabitants who regarded the Southwest as virgin territory. Women, who historically inhabited interior domestic spaces as well as the exterior land, were perhaps particularly well positioned to imagine place—and understand their survival on it—as an infusion of cultural practice and physical geography. Thus I read, in contemporary Latina literature, experiences of the body, of trauma, and of storytelling—as experiences of and in "place," where acts of cultural and physical belonging to the nation become inseparable and collective.

This notion that U.S. Latina literature can impact our definition of the nation, and undermine popular conceptions of Latinos/as by reimagining the United States as part of the Americas, builds on critical work on U.S. Latino/a literature that has long engaged with questions of American national identity. Whether writing on Mexican American, U.S. Puerto Rican, or Cuban American literature, critics agree that the literature counters and challenges mainstream culture in various ways, and that to this end, it has become a vital component of that culture. In addition, the idea that a nation is, to an extent, an imaginary construct and cultural fiction, and that its literature—any of its literature—can thus play a role in the construction of nation, is widely recognized in critical circles.[15] Juan Flores points out that "it is becoming clear that any discussion of an 'American community' must be inclusive of Latinos and cognizant about the existence of a 'Latino community' intrinsic to historical discourses about U.S. culture,"[16] while José David Saldívar, exploring the contact zones of the U.S.-Mexico border, problematizes the notion that the nation is "naturally" there and thus questions how hybrid U.S.-Mexican borderland subjects disrupt the nation.[17] As I illustrate in more detail in the next section, nations—in particular, the United States—frequently define themselves through imagined "others," and Mexican American and other Latino communities, as longtime definitional "others" to the United States, in turn produce texts that challenge the Anglo world through their rethinking of place, belonging, and "imaginative geography."[18] There is no doubt, then, that U.S. Latino/a literature, no matter its national origins, radically transforms "the constitutive fabric of the United States" so that the boundaries and borders of the United States become stretched and "Latinized."[19] As Ramón de la Campa puts it, "it is widely known that the nation has always been an arresting point for American Latinos."[20]

Thus the ways in which all Latinas posit new versions of cultural and political identity in order to assert their belonging to the nation is, I argue, a central feature of the literature I explore in this book. The significance of these texts' re-placing of Latinos/as as members of the U.S. nation should be eminently clear: when the history of the Americas becomes, as it does in the narratives, part of the history of the United States, and when the geography of those histories—the location in which they occur—becomes foregrounded, the United States' demarcation of foreign (illegitimate) and native (legitimate) presence in the nation is undermined. The United States' troubled relationship with Latin America becomes, in these literary texts, constitutive of the entire hemisphere's transnational and collective identity.

Critical Discourses of National Unbelonging

In discussing U.S. Latino/a identity we need not only to differentiate between the various origin-groups (Mexican, Puerto Rican, Cuban) but also to consider the discourses that, in naming "Latino" communities in the United States, have to an extent homogenized them. Critics have debated extensively on the appropriateness (or not) of the terms "Latino" and "Hispanic" to convey the various Spanish-speaking national groups resident in the United States. Suzanne Oboler, for example, considers the emergence and implications of the term "Hispanic" in the context of the United States, noting that despite the historical differences between each national-origin group, "their lives are affected directly or otherwise by the use of the term Hispanic to characterize them in the United States."[21] Indeed, in using the label "U.S. Latina" myself I am aware that I might appear to be asserting a panethnicism that collapses distinct national identities. The terms "Latino" and "Latina" connote an element of transnationalism as they assimilate members of various Latin American subgroups living in the United States into "an imagined, transnational cultural and communal formation."[22]

Ultimately, though, I agree with Stavans's preference for the term "Latino" because it has "not only . . . proven to be the most neutral and the least exclusive term [as compared to 'Hispanic,' 'Hispano,' 'iberoamericano,' 'Latin,' and 'Spanish-speaking']; it is also favored by Latinos."[23] A further advantage of the nationality-derived term "Latino/a" or "U.S. Latino/a" becomes clear in David Hayes-Bautista and Jorge Chapa's description: "a geographically derived national origin group, that has been constantly and consistently viewed and treated as a racial group, in both individual and institutional interaction while in the United States."[24] For my purposes here, this understanding of the term "Latino/a" is particularly appropriate not only because of its attention to geographical origins but also because of its constructedness by the outside as a racial and national "other" in the United States. One certainty emerges from discussions: the terms, whether we use "Latin," "Latino," or "Hispanic," are made in the United States by a combination of dominant culture's acts of interpellation and acquiescence from the group in question, as part of the nation's continually evolving identity negotiation.[25]

Because of the homogeneity invoked by these terms, it is especially important to recognize the distinctions between nation-groups. Individual and group experiences among Latinos/as obviously vary not just because of national origin and history but also because of a variety of other factors, including (but not limited to) the time of and reason for migration to the United States (if indeed there was a migration), the U.S. authorities' and public's reception of the group, and the group's legal standing in the United States. In fact, as Oboler has noted, some scholars suggest that together with social and cultural differences, the various national groups' respective citizenship status also differentially affects local and national concerns and experiences. Thus "the political issues currently raised by the issue of immigration . . . take on a different institutional connotation for Mexican immigrants than they might for Cuban exiles and refugees."[26]

Popular culture obviously focuses a great deal on undocumented immigration from Mexico, the U.S.-Mexico geographical border, and the presence of Mexicans both at that border and across the entire United States. De Genova points out that migrant illegality itself has become a spatialized social condition "that is inseparable from the particular ways that Mexican migrants are likewise 'racialized' as 'illegal aliens'—as invasive violators of the law, incorrigible 'foreigners' subverting the integrity of 'the nation.'"[27] If dominant anti-immigrant discourses about Mexican immigration frequently assume "a specific racial character,"[28] then the border, ostensibly the site at which illegality is formed, becomes the origin of this racialization, and the stage upon which limited rights to full U.S. citizenship become expressed.[29] In addition, the border functions as a site of "exceptionality," a place where illegal bodies can fall victim to the emergency provision that empowers the state to act outside the constraints of law, permitting it to adopt extreme measures in its defense, including violence against its own citizens.[30] And according to Gilberto Rosas, the borderlands' condition of vigilantism, illegality, and exceptionalism is also "thickening," no longer remaining geographically fixed in the southwestern United States but spreading beyond it in the form of nationwide racial profiling; as he points out, "Heightened anxieties about policing the territorial border often translate into heightened anxieties concerning those who resemble 'immigrants' within the nation-state."[31] Racial profiling and racialized citizenship extend figuratively beyond the geographical borderlands, thus informally governing all those who appear potentially illegal.[32]

As a result of this racialization of undocumented status, Mexican Americans who are U.S. citizens (through birth or naturalization) or legally resident in the United States can also experience some of the stigma attributed to illegal immigrants. Their national identity is thus significantly determined by a sense of "unbelonging," an unbelonging that operates both at the border and throughout the geographical space of the country. Leo Chávez argues persuasively that U.S. Mexican citizens have been represented as "the quintessential 'illegal aliens,'" and that their social identity has been "plagued by the mark of illegality," which often renders them, in public discourse, into criminals and thus "illegitimate members of society undeserving of social benefits, including citizenship."[33] Particularly important for my discussions on Mexican American literature in chapters 2 and 3, Chávez also interprets this illegitimacy as a spatialized displacement, noting that as Mexicans are rendered "out of place," they are often thereby constructed in popular culture as a threat to national identity.

This process dates at least back to the nineteenth century: after the United States' 1848 colonization of northern Mexico, approximately 80,000–100,000 Mexican nationals were deprived of their Mexican nationality and became U.S. subjects, if not citizens.[34] Almost immediately these new U.S. subjects were racialized as nonwhite, and that, together with the particular nature of Mexican migrant patterns into the United States, established a precedent for recognizing all Mexicans in the United States as nonwhite, secondary "alien-citizens."[35] The development of immigration control laws meant that Mexicans entering into the United States could be illegal as well; in fact, the idea of illegal Mexicans as criminals has been pervasive since the 1920s. Like current discourse, the 1970s also imagined Mexican immigrants invading the United States, while the 1980s targeted native-born Americans descended from the first Spanish-speaking explorers of the Southwest, imagining them as participants in a separatist reconquest of the land.[36] In short, Mexican Americans, regardless of their legal status, place of birth, or proximity to the border, have frequently been rendered permanent outsiders because of the way in which the politics of citizenship in the United States has been so thoroughly racialized. Thus, as De Genova notes, the production of migrant "illegality" has "directly or indirectly affected all Mexicans in the U.S., regardless of nativity or citizenship" and "supplies a defining feature in their racialization as Mexicans."[37]

In terms of issues of belonging, the most apparent distinction between Mexicans and Puerto Ricans in the United States is that of legality: because Puerto Ricans are U.S. citizens and cannot therefore be undocumented migrants, the stigma of juridical illegality should be less acute. It is certainly important to note the important and real benefits of legal residency in the nation, particularly in comparison to the lived experiences of many undocumented migrants: Puerto Ricans are not subject to fears of deportation, and their border crossings are legal, although it is also worth noting that national identities are constantly refigured and destabilized through geographic, cultural, and linguistic border crossings, even when they are politically legal.[38] But many critical analyses of the island's colonial and subordinate relationship to the United States and of Puerto Rican experiences in the United States nevertheless argue that Puerto Ricans, as "territorial citizens," are still treated as second-class citizens.[39] For example, Flores and Benmajor note that while Puerto Ricans may not face open legal attacks and harassment, they are still "viewed as foreigners" and "receive the same harsh anti-immigrant treatment as other Latinos."[40] As with legally resident Mexicans, then, it is necessary to look beyond the juridical definitions of citizenship in order to ascertain the sense of unbelonging that contributes to Puerto Rican experiences in the United States.

The intersecting reasons for this unbelonging—a combination of mainstream perceptions of Puerto Ricans and material socioeconomic circumstances—that I want to emphasize are the historic and ongoing U.S.-Puerto Rican colonial relationship (one that has been read as economic, military, and symbolic),[41] the racialization of citizenship (as with Mexicans), and the portrayals of Puerto Ricans as culturally deficient un-American exceptions to the narrative of social mobility that other legally resident (im)migrant groups supposedly exemplify.[42] Puerto Rico's relationship with the United States, for example, is not in itself an "ordinary" colonial situation because of the United States' designation of the island as an Estado Libre Asociado (ELA) in 1952, which essentially allowed it to reinvent and mask the island's subordinated status. The ELA thus represented a new strategy for containing potentially anti-imperialist sentiments against the United States, creating "an illusion of political autonomy" (for islanders) and concealing the United States' economic absorption of the island.[43] In effect, the ELA produced "national subjects without a state."[44]

It becomes evident, therefore, that even on the island the rhetoric of belonging to a nation was from early on complicated and compromised: described as "orphaned" because of the island's colonial condition (and the ramifications of that colonial status on the mainland, in the form of internal colonialism), Puerto Rican national identity becomes highly paradoxical.[45] Narratives of belonging at times function in opposition to American institutions, and at other times as complementary to them.[46] On the mainland, Puerto Ricans are in effect "treated as second-class citizens"[47] because, like the patterns of Mexican migration to the United States that began in the nineteenth century, Puerto Rico's colonial status also supplied the United States with a cheap labor force in the form of contract migrant workers, particularly to the urban Northeast. This established them as socioeconomically subordinate and disadvantaged (albeit legal) subjects of the state.[48] For these sorts of reasons, critics often bring together Mexican and Puerto Rican experiences of "citizenship" (broadly defined as belonging) by noting that in spite of their differing legal rights, Mexican Americans and Puerto Ricans have not been fully acknowledged as "fellow citizens" of Americans and that "denied full citizenship and human rights by the customary practices of exclusion, they could be routinely bounced in and out of the 'national community' according to the ever-changing political and economic needs of the nation."[49]

Part of the reason for this denial of full citizenship is due to a process of racialization analogous to that experienced by Mexican Americans. Although critics generally concur that on the U.S. mainland, Puerto Ricans' mixed racial community cannot be fixed as a single racial category, even "white" Puerto Ricans are racialized as an inferior group (perhaps by openly identifying as Puerto Rican and/or by others' assumption of origin through the use of Spanish, name, and/or accent). In other words, note Grosfoguel, Negrón-Muntaner, and Georas, "regardless of phenotype, all Puerto Ricans are considered a racial group in the social imaginary of most Americans, accompanied by racist stereotypes such as laziness, violence, stupidity, and dirtiness."[50] The mass media still tends to frame Puerto Ricans as "alien savages" who "challenge the forces of law and order."[51] This racialized devaluation of Puerto Rican citizenship, needless to say, significantly contributes to Puerto Ricans' emergent sense of unbelonging in the United States. In fact, De Genova argues that Puerto Ricans' automatic U.S. citizenship confers upon them a distinct disadvantage in terms of their reception on the mainland, explaining that the fact that all Puerto Ricans "inherit the seeming advantage of being born into U.S. citizenship further accentuates the insinuation that endemic poverty and 'welfare dependency' can ultimately be attributed to Puerto Ricans' own 'failings.'" This image of welfare dependency marks Puerto Ricans as a "culturally deficient group" who lack "good immigrant values." Thus Puerto Ricans are often treated "as a public liability" whose "birthright citizenship" paradoxically seems to disqualify them from full membership in the nation.[52]

In many ways U.S. Cubans do not experience the consequences of the nation's racialized citizenship in the same way that U.S. Mexicans and Puerto Ricans do. In fact, as Laura Gómez has pointed out, while Mexican Americans' selection of "some other race" in the 2000 U.S. Census suggested an affirmation of a racial heritage that includes white, black, and Indian ancestry, as well as a rejection of white identity as a political statement, Cuban Americans have "little in common with this history."[53] Cubans identify as "white" on the same census 90 percent of the time, while the United States' opposition to the Castro regime has overdetermined its policies toward and reception of Cubans migrating into the country. The majority of Cubans did not arrive as a conquered people, but came to the United States as voluntary immigrants in the 1960s. Most of those who fled Castro were members of Cuba's most socioeconomically affluent class, entering American society during the midst of the civil rights movement and benefiting from the shift to formal equality and antidiscrimination policies that were mandated by law.[54] Furthermore, although theoretically Cubans can have undocumented status in the United States, for all intents and purposes none do. The nation's long-standing approach to Cuban immigration, beginning with Congress's Cuban Adjustment Act of 1966 and continuing into the current "wet foot, dry foot" policy, has given all Cubans seeking asylum in the United States the special status of political refugees.[55] Historically, then, Cubans have faced very few of the restrictions governing immigration, and have benefited from legislative acts that virtually guarantee permanent resettlement in the United States, whether they have overstayed their tourist visas or reached Florida's shores with no documentation at all.[56]

However, considerations of Cuban American national identity, and the sense of unbelonging and foreignness that I argue contributes substantially to the formation of that identity, cannot ignore the United

States' historical imperial interest in the island (which long predates Castro's revolution). The United States' interest, while not replicating Puerto Rico's colonial status vis-à-vis the United States, did historically create conditions (over the late nineteenth and early-to-mid-twentieth centuries) that allowed the United States to gain a position of political and economic dominance over the island, a military presence, and a formalized right (through the Platt Amendment) to intervene in Cuban political, economic, and military affairs if necessary. Pre-Castro, the United States' economic and political influence on the island cannot be overstated, making the postrevolutionary shift to economic sanctions and trade embargos even more startling.[57]

Given the United States' historic paternalism toward the island, then, it is unsurprising that (negative) influential interpellations of U.S. Latinos/as—led, for example, by texts such as Samuel P. Huntington's 2004 *Who Are We? The Challenges to America's National Identity*—still include Cuban Americans. When Huntington focuses on Mexican immigration and presence in the United States in order to argue that national identity is being eroded and citizenship devalued, he cites Cubans in connection with Mexicans, noting that the "demographic *reconquista*" of the Southwest by Mexicans is comparable to the "Cubanization" of southern Florida: Florida thus becomes another beachhead of a generalized Latino invasion.[58] When he analyzes the "Hispanization of Miami" (a process that is directly attributable to the elevated socioeconomic status of the initial first wave of exiles into the city) to prove that the United States is becoming culturally bifurcated, he finds that Cubans have become an example of "nonassimilation" as they perpetuate their home culture and social institutions in the new country.[59] In fact, "Miami Hispanics" have "little or no incentive to assimilate into American mainstream culture."[60] In this context Cuban culture—rather than body and phenotype—becomes racialized as "other" and foreign to the integrity of the nation, as well as threatening to the security of the city. Huntington argues that the Cubanization of Miami coincided with high levels of crime, and cites statistics that demonstrate the high concentration of foreign-born Latin American and Caribbean persons in Miami, and the predominance of Spanish-language use both in private home settings and in public settings. As Spanish becomes the principal language of commerce, business, politics, and media communication, Miami becomes transformed "from a normal American city into a Cuban-led Hispanic city," an "enclave city with its own cultural community and economy, in which assimilation and Americanization were unnecessary and in some measure undesired."⁶¹ And while anti-Latino rhetoric ordinarily tends to focus on the economic and welfare drain posed by underprivileged sectors of the community, for Huntington, the alarm bells also begin to sound when he considers the influential cultural, political, and economic power wielded by this more socioeconomically successful Latino group. He asks, "Is Miami the future for Los Angeles and the southwest generally? In the end the results could be similar: the creation of a large, distinct, Spanish-speaking community with economic and political resources sufficient to sustain its own Hispanic identity apart from the national identity of other Americans and also able to influence significantly American politics, government, and society."⁶² In other words, although Cubans are different from other Latinos, they still achieve, through socioeconomic clout, what Mexicans are achieving by sheer numbers.

As the discussion above should make clear, in the context of unbelonging to the nation we can and should speak about a collective "Latino/a" entity despite national-origin groups' differences, and consider in a broader way the commonalities between Latinos/as. First, the most obvious connection is the colonial background and immigrant/migrant arrival to the territorial United States that nearly all Latino groups in the United States share at some point in their history. Even critics who are careful to delineate the experiential, legal, and material differences between, for example, Mexicans and Puerto Ricans in the United States recognize important similarities between the groups. As George Sanchez puts it, "The colonial background is critical to an understanding of the incorporation of various Latino groups in the nineteenth and early twentieth centuries; the migrant experience becomes the basis for comparative understandings of all groups in the twentieth century up to the present."⁶³ De Genova similarly notes that while in some ways it is hard to locate commonality between Mexican Americans and Puerto Ricans, particularly as exemplified in the historically specific spatialized politics of Chicago's North and South Sides, it is also advantageous to understand Latino commonalities within a broader transnational perspective, one that "connects U.S. Latinidad to Latin American history and, more specifically, to the historical specificity of the U.S. nation-state's imperial projects in Latin America that have so commonly produced Latino migrations to the U.S."⁶⁴

Second, this historical transnational view of Latinos/as in the United States also allows us to consider the concept of citizenship beyond its legal definition as a lived experience (especially racialized and second-class) that is often collective.⁶⁵ For example, the focus on the "illegal" place of Mexicans in the nation becomes, to some critics, symptomatic of the fragile citizenship status and lived experiences of all Latinos/as: Renato Rosaldo states that many question the citizenship of Latinos because "by a psychological and cultural mechanism of association all Latinos are . . . declared to have a blemish that brands us with the stigma of being outside the law. We always live with that mark indicating that whether or not we belong in this country is always in question."[66] Raymond Rocco similarly contends that despite differences between national-origin groups, "the initial cultural and ideological construction of the Mexican population in the region as racialized 'foreigners' has . . . served as the lens through which later-arriving Latino/a immigrants have been conceptualized."[67]

Third, critical scholars have thus particularly recognized the ways in which notions of citizenship in the United States have been, since the nineteenth century, racialized, rendering Mexican Americans, Puerto Ricans, and sometimes even Cuban Americans as nonwhite, and certainly "other" to mainstream perceptions of U.S. national identity. This historical racialization of citizenship and belonging clearly has a significant impact both on contemporary perceptions of Latinos/as and on their material and socioeconomic experiences in the United States. Again, this process has deep historical roots. The nation's identity in the nineteenth century, for example, was forged partly through the creation of racialized perceptions that homogenized Latin America's populations (and that in turn set the context for the later emergence of the label "Hispanic" in the twentieth century).[68] Even though, as Arlene Dávila cautions, the terms "Latino" and "Hispanic" do not denote a race but an ethnic group that comprises people of different racial backgrounds, the great percentage of Latinos (she does not specify the national-origin group) who selected "some other race" in the 2000 U.S. Census "has been interpreted as a sign that Latino ethnicity has been racialized and that Latinos see themselves as a distinct race beyond black, white, and Asian."[69]

What, then, is the connection between this racialized concept of national membership and cultural experiences and perceptions of unbelonging? Cultural critics have pointed out that in addition to racial differences, cultural and linguistic differences also seem to set Latinos/as apart from dominant society.[70] For example, behind stringent anti-immigration laws that are phrased as "practical responses to the economic problems posed by the presence of migrants," Alejandra Castañeda suspects that the real concern is "the political and cultural impact migrants have in the overall dynamic of life in the U.S."[71] Nicholas De

Genova and Ana Y. Ramos-Zayas similarly talk about the ways that race has often been construed not just around the idea of what people naturally "are" but also "in terms of difference that might otherwise be glossed as 'cultural'—what people 'do' and how."[72] In this sense one can argue that racism has taken a new turn: it can be defined in general terms "as the belief in and/or practice of excluding people on the basis of their membership in a racially defined group" but is now practiced more as a "cultural racism . . . or cultural fundamentalism." Specifically, "this new cultural racism . . . emphasizes differences of cultural heritage and their incommensurability" and potentially represents a political threat and disruption to the distinct community of the nation-state.[73] This explains how it is that Latino cultural difference, whether real or perceived, has been interpreted as such a significant threat to the nation's identity: constructed as a racialized difference, it has come to denote some kind of essentialized clannish and separatist otherness. No matter the national origin of the Latino/a group, and no matter its history in the nation, if it is observed to be culturally "foreign" in some way, it becomes immediately susceptible to any of the various popular narratives of Latinidad (illegal aliens, undocumented migrants, welfare drains, reconquering land, and so on) that commonly render Latinos/as as collectively not quite belonging to, and being out of place in, the nation.[74]

This unbelonging has tended to underline much of mainstream popular culture's perception that all Latinos/as are somehow culturally "out of place," or at least not quite "in place" in the nation and its assumed normative "American" identity. Leo Chávez writes, "although Mexicans are often the focus of the Latino Threat Narrative, public discourse . . . often includes immigration from Latin America in general, as well as U.S.-born Americans of Latin American descent. . . . [T]he threat is often generalized . . . at times to all Latinos in the United States."[75] Such perceptions have become a real part of the lived conditions by which Latinos/as experience and measure their sense of belonging to the nation. Gilberto Rosas notes that dominant anti-immigrant rhetoric in the United States assumes a "specific racial character" and that this characterization can move beyond immigrant discourse: "Heightened anxieties about policing the territorial border often translate into heightened anxieties concerning those who resemble 'immigrants' within the nation-space. . . . That is especially the case for those 'figurative borders' that mark particular bodies."[76] Thus we find that although public discourse about Latino presence in the United States varies, it is most often motivated by anxieties about the problematic "placing" and presence of

Latinos/as in the United States. Clearly, the physical geography of the U.S.-Mexico border and its political and national significance are paramount to most discussions, but so are questions about the alleged destabilizing impact of Latino cultural and bodily presence in the nation. As Alejandra Elenes puts it, "Mexican and Central American immigrants' presence in the United States fuels anxiety of certain white communities about losing *ground*."[77]

Popular Discourses of National Unbelonging

The example that began this chapter—the *Gourmet* reader's response to Latin American culinary presence in the United States—is just one of many instances of xenophobic rhetoric that must be interpreted in light of these critical questions about Latino influence, presence, and belonging to the nation. For example, Huntington's infamous anti-immigration piece "The Hispanic Challenge," in the March 2004 issue of *Foreign Policy*, with its dogmatic premise about the WASP foundations of "America's" creed and culture, cites "Mexican" (interchangeable for him with "Hispanic") presence in the United States as uniquely unassimilable due, in part, to the nation's contiguous border with Mexico, which creates continued contact with the country of origin and thus in his view prevents assimilation into the mainstream. Similarly, *Time* magazine in the 1980s, 1990s, and postmillennially has frequently engaged with the changing ethnic "face" of America, pointing almost as overtly as Huntington toward the special and troubling disruption of Latino presence in the United States. Perhaps exemplary of what mass U.S. culture imagines itself to be thinking, in both its July 8, 1985, "The Changing Face of America" issue and its 1993 Special Issue, "The New Face of America," *Time* constructs and reconstructs the nation through its attention to immigrant and migrant experiences of assimilation and belonging.[78] Rhetorically, while both pieces are careful to celebrate the fact that immigration is part of America's national identity, it also becomes clear that "instilling fear of the real or imagined consequences of introducing foreign ways into American life has at times also contributed to defining the national identity of the United States."[79]

The 1985 issue, whose cover depicts a collection of crowded, mostly dark-skinned and/or Asian faces all gazing off into the distance with somber yet hopeful expressions, reassures its readers that immigrants continue to assimilate into mainstream culture. The faces on the cover are all illuminated by a distant light: presumably the illumination of the promised land. The issue then features many articles that celebrate the entrepreneurial and commercial success of mostly non-Latino/a immigrants, showing how they in general continue to fulfill the destiny of the American nation, eventually becoming part of that same national narrative. Every article addressing new immigrants begins with an old "founding" story of the nation, recounted so that every new story will fit into the old myth. The immigrants' hard work, in fact, "makes the American juices flow," and by "contributing their bloodlines, their spirit and their energy" they "preserve the nation's vitality and uniqueness." Although "many bemused Americans" ask the question "What country is this?" as they watch it continually reinvent itself, readers are assured that these foreigners—or at the very least, their children—are good future citizens of the nation.[80]

How, then, does the newsmagazine negotiate the uneasy presence of Latinos/as as part of—and apart from—the general influx of immigrants into the United States? In the magazine's article on Latinos ("Hispanics: A Melding of Cultures) Latino *physical* presence in the physical space of the United States determines and structures conversations about Latino cultural, political, and national influences, no matter their national origin. And the reverse is also true: fears about Latino cultural influences are collected in narratives about Latinos/as occupying and disrupting the physical space of the nation. The article opens with examples of how Hispanic presence in the United States reaches far beyond the geographical border with Mexico, and even beyond the southern border-states. Southern Washington State and Union City, New Jersey, lie thousands of miles from Mexico and Cuba, yet Mexicans and Cubans, respectively, dominate those spaces. Chicago, itself "far from any entry point for Hispanics into the U.S.," has nevertheless "drawn such a diverse Latin population that the Spanish language alone is no guide to what kind of neighborhood a visitor has wandered into." In a sense anticipating *Gourmet*'s presentation of Presilla's "Fiesta Latina," the authors write that you can tell where you are "from the sounds and the smell of the cooking."[81] The implication is clear: in the near future, there might be a Hispanicization of America, much like the one feared by Huntington and *Gourmet*'s angry reader, where neighborhoods in the heart of the United States appear decidedly foreign. The authors, treating Latinos/as collectively, argue that this threatening cultural influence is exacerbated by their "highly fertile population" and by the fact that "they keep coming too in such numbers that even if all illegal immigration could be stopped the Hispanic population would still grow."[82] It is no wonder, the magazine remarks, that "frightened Anglos sometimes whisper about a 'silent invasion from the south' that will transform parts of the U.S. into annexed territories."[83] With their "un-American insularity" Hispanics "colonize" larger chunks of cities than any previous waves of immigrants could.[84]

The magazine's conclusion—that "the Americanization of Hispanics will be far more rapid and thorough than any Hispanicization of Anglo culture"[85]—does little to temper its presentation of Latinos' troubling and insistent cultural difference. In fact, as evidence of the United States' ambiguous foreign/familiar relationship with its southern neighbors, the magazine runs another feature about the "third country" that has formed between Mexico and the United States, along the border. An oddly ethnographic and celebratory description of "the world's most extraordinary border," the piece predates by two years (but certainly echoes, when read thirty years later) Gloria Anzaldúa's seminal *Borderlands/La Frontera*, positively describing the hybrid "cooperative culture" that has sprung up in the borderlands that is "neither American nor Mexican" but has "latched on to the strengths of both national heritages." Along the border, we thus see "the Americanization of Mexico and the Mexicanization of America."[86]

Later, in 1993, the newsmagazine in large part presents Latinos/as as collectively illegal—describing the "dozens of hungry men" waiting to get work as mostly "Hispanic and many of them illegals"—even though by its own admission only 24 percent of immigrants are actually illegal. The focus, once again, is on the United States' loss of control over its land due to some kind of illegitimate Latino presence on it: "*The U.S. has effectively lost control of its territorial integrity, especially in the Southwest.*"[87] And a piece about Miami as "the Capital of Latin America" mirrors the 1985 issue's presentation of the United States' "third country" border and anticipates Huntington's 2004 fearful analysis of the city, describing a geographical space in the United States that both is and is not part of the nation. Despite the commercial success story of Miami, the city's cultural and economic hybridity separates it from the rest of the United States and at the same time calls into question the entire nation's foundational story of Anglo roots, reimagining its identity as Latino/a.[88]

These perceptions of Latinos/as as infiltrating geographical and national borders generate a national and cultural sense of crisis; borders, after all, work on a principle of difference whereby territory is demarcated and mediated. Indeed, territory itself is a cultural production that must be constructed in order to become a nation.[89] For example, in a June 2010 interview aired on National Public Radio, host Robin Young asked her guest, Susan Martin (a director of the Institute for the Study of International Migration at Georgetown University), to comment on why there is so much vilification of illegal immigrants and so much anger directed at laborers and those crossing the border and coming in through Mexico, when 40 percent of illegal immigrants in the United States actually enter the country legally and then overstay their visas, and might well be "the person working next to you."[90] Martin's response reasons that the overemphasis on border enforcement and illegal border crossing makes for good sound bites if you rail against it, but that there is also a basic ambivalence about illegal immigration because of the necessary work that illegal immigrants do.[91] What stands out again, however, is the intersection of place (both figurative and literal) and nation. In part a spatial representation of the nation's identity, the physical border structures conversations about all Latinos' ethno-cultural presence, positioning that presence as "other" and threatening to Americanness. The geographical and political border works as a visible sign, marking the point at which the nation begins and ends, and perceived foreignness begins, ends, and resides, becoming one of the main things against which the nation needs to define itself. Thus spatial representation determines mainstream responses to new cultural presences and the extent of their membership in the nation, and for this reason, all Latino/a presence and literary production in the United States potentially troubles and challenges mainstream national identity in ways that European and Asian immigration cannot.

The examples cited above of popular culture's writing and reading of Latino (particularly Mexican) presence represent just part of the attempt to articulate Latinos' cultural, physical, and racial unbelonging in the nation. The rhetoric, railing as it does against the ethno-cultural and spatial presence of Latinos/as in the United States, rests on the belief that the nation must, against all odds, maintain its perceived integrity and homogeneity. But the obsession with national character and nationhood is not new: since its inception, U.S. identity has evolved through differentiation, initially from Europe, and later from Latin America. At issue then, as now, was the question of how to define a national identity that appeared to be continually in flux. Then, as now, the issue was often framed geographically. It is thus worth looking, briefly, at one of the important ways in which that sense of American identity, that definitive quality of "Americanness," took shape during the eighteenth century, just around the time when the nation was declaring and constituting itself as a separate national entity. In terms of literary representations of the nation's emerging cultural codes of ethnicity, Hector St. John de Crèvecoeur's *Letters from an American Farmer*, as a colonial text that attempts to define the nature of the emerging American, represents one of the first literary examples of the rhetoric of assimilation. In that respect it can be read as one of the foundational texts that established the roots of contemporary dominant culture's continued drive toward assimilation.[92]

The narrative, a fictional account of life in colonial America that consists of twelve letters purported to be sent by a colonial settler, James, the American farmer, to a friend in London, is, particularly in its early sections, eager to demonstrate how certain fundamental American cultural values—meritocracy, work ethic, and assimilation—are bound up in a specific "moral geography," a crucial tie to the physical land itself.[93] Through Crèvecoeur's description, we see how geography and physical place become important measures of cultural and national character. Critics have duly noted Crèvecoeur's celebration of the large and fertile land; for our purposes here, however, what is remarkable is the way that land and its cultivation from wilderness to farmland become connected to definitions of political and cultural belonging, citizenship, and national identity. Crèvecoeur's rhetoric pinpoints a connection between geography and nationhood at the precise moment when the American nation was in transition and in formation, shaking off one empire and simultaneously forging itself as one. Thomas Jefferson, in fact, famously praised farmers as "the chosen people of God," and adapted physiocratic ideals—the belief that the wealth and virtue of nations reside in the cultivation of land—to the American environment, declaring that "cultivators of the earth are the most valuable citizens."[94]

Although Crèvecoeur describes an agrarian lifestyle in the years just preceding the American Revolution, his "American" qualities foreshadow those of industrialization and capitalism, cocooned within a reification of land. He writes about coming home, after being away from it: "The instant I enter my own land, the bright idea of property, of exclusive right, of independence, exalt my mind. . . . What should we American farmers be without the distinct possession of that soil?"[95] The private ownership of property and the importance of homesteading are valorized over any sense of collective or communal tribal living.[96] Most significant, once cultivated, the formerly "rude" soil "has established all our rights; in it is founded our rank, our freedom, *our power as citizens.*"[97] When Crèvecoeur's narrator, James, outlines, in Letter 3, the new colonies' "perfect government" (compared to Europe's), he describes the new mix of nations and the new race with metaphors of nature. They who are "now called Americans" were previously "useless plants, . . . withered, and . . . mowed down by want, hunger, and war," but now "by the power of transplantation, like all other plants, they have taken root and flourished!"[98] And just as he blends cultivated land with citizenship, he sets down the nation's assimilative code: "Here individuals of all nations are melted into a new race of men. . . . The American is a new man who acts upon new principles . . . he has passed to toils of a very different nature, rewarded by ample subsistence.—This is an American."[99]

This "American," newly defined around the time of the United States' national formation, was an assimilated individual with strong ties to the cultivation and taming of the land, and thus an early practitioner of the cultural nationalism of the Monroe Doctrine and manifest destiny that would become established a century later. Although here Crèvecoeur's definition of nation comes about in opposition to Europe, with no mention of Spain's colonial settlements, his attributes of national identity persist into today's mainstream culture. Without a doubt, his work implies that the Americas were (and would continue to be) invented and produced through displacement, and consequently that the United States' ideology of cultural assimilation (its response to that displacement) has geopolitical origins. Thus when U.S. Latina literature tries to "re-nationalize" the United States as part of a collective of the Spanish-speaking Americas, it writes against long-standing understandings of cultural and geopolitical assimilation, and reimagines the nation-state, in many respects, as a transnational space.[100]

Transnational Discourses of (Un)Belonging

In this context transnationalism challenges the idea of a fixed nation, questioning nationalistic paradigms and privileging diasporic or migrant exiles. It is also an inherent part of the history of U.S. geography because of the way that the nation's borders expanded in the nineteenth century to incorporate Spanish-speaking peoples, whose cultural affiliations turned as much toward Latin America as they did toward eastern and central parts of the United States. But this kind of configuration of global geography is also problematic for my analyses here. Global transnationalism does not dilute the material reality of the nation's borders, which continue to be policed and militarized, nor does it erase the historical and ongoing prejudices maintained by dominant culture in order to preserve the contours of the nation-space.[101] In fact, one of the ramifications of the United States' cultural and political identity manifests itself, as David Slater notes, in the nation's construction of its "foreign" insiders as outsiders, and the positing of difference as "inferiority and danger."[102] It is thus important to keep at bay the seductive and often fictional reimaginings of space offered by the concept of transnationalism. Although the "transnational" label usefully describes the broad, sweeping phenomenon created by global population movements and economic exchange, critics warn against unduly celebrating it as a liberatory movement. The temptation can be to conceive of the world more "in terms of a mixture of flows of capital and individuals, and less in terms of boundaries," forgetting to recognize the material barriers faced by many of the world's immigrants.[103] The sobering reality is that rather than signaling the end of nations, transnational corporations are "the messengers of Western culture and its mode of production." While in some respects transnationalism may make "the borders of a nation insignificant," rendering them "merely geographic and no longer culturally meaningful," in other respects the border's very geographic and cultural presence turns it into a politically significant barrier.[104]

Historically, the United States' relations with Latin American nations have reflected this contradictory tension. The frontier mentality or manifest destiny, for example, that ploughed not just westward but also southward toward Latin America imagined (and to an extent created) porous borders between nations. Similarly, the United States' acquisition and control of land and property both contiguous to the homeland and geographically separate from it after the 1848 Treaty of Guadalupe-Hidalgo and the 1898 Treaty of Paris effectively dissolved or shifted the political borders between the United States and Mexico, Cuba, and Puerto Rico. In some respects this expansion of U.S. territory and acquisition of property can be understood as a series of transnational moments. The United States' very interest and long involvement in Latin America, its varying policies of "soft power" and military and economic presence in the region, and even the continent's shared history as the New World separate from the Old, its "common denominator" as something "new in history, in people, new in nature and experience," all speak to a form of transnational exchange and psyche.[105] Yet at the same time, the United States' creation of the Border Patrol in 1924 and strict policing of its borders and border-states speak very much to nationalist preservation based on cultural, political, and geographic differentiations.

One of the ways in which the forthcoming chapters and the structure of this book are attentive to both the erasures and possibilities of transnationalism lies in my groupings of the literary works. For my purposes here, what is important are the implications of the nation's authoritarian placing and displacing of groups of people inside and outside its boundaries, not just in terms of nomenclature (for example, with the use of terms such as "Latino" or "Hispanic" as discussed above) but also in terms of cultural, ethnic, and political identity. If manufacturing national identity entails manufacturing an "other," and if historically and ongoing to this day U.S. Latinos/as (or Latins, or Hispanics) are sometimes part of, and sometimes apart from, the nation, what happens when that foreign/familiar element of the nation engages in its own collective act of nation-building? In the forthcoming chapters I treat the selected works of literature both collectively and separately: their very grouping together both in this introduction and in the book's vision as a whole is an acknowledgment of panethnic similarities, but as each chapter deals with authors and/or material that can and does also classify itself as part of a distinct national-origin group (Mexican American, Puerto Rican, Cuban American), I am also attentive to their distinct national origins.

All the U.S. Latina narratives I explore in the forthcoming chapters demonstrate the reality of historical and ongoing U.S. relations with Latin America, positing hemispheric community and connectivity as a new expression of U.S. national identity. But each group's reimagining of nation is also specific to the particular dimensions of its historical (and ongoing) relationship with the United States. Chapters 1 and 2 look at how selected Mexican American literary works disrupt national identity in the Southwest and Midwest by deconstructing the national and political border, and spectering the United States' physical and cultural landscape with Latin American history and memory. In chapter 1's exploration of Denise Chávez's *The Last of the Menu Girls* and *Face of an Angel* I ask what kind of geopolitical identity is established in a New Mexican southwestern setting that spans both Mexico and the United States. I argue that the narratives depict a joining of territory, recalling the ancestral legacy and heritage of the land between Mexico and the United States. Without this reterritorialization of a colonized space, the Southwest, perhaps unexpectedly, presents a geography of *dis*location rather than rootedness that manifests itself through dis-ease, unease, and anxiety. Chávez's female characters themselves suffer diseases that are only healed through the imaginary blurring and conjoining of Mexico's and the United States' natural terrains, and through the cultural assertion of Mexican American voices and memories. Both of these dismantle the political border, trouble national identity, and assert belonging. Mexican American geography in the southwestern United States, then, creates a collective rather than individualistic national history that also legitimates Latino presence in New Mexico.

While chapter 1's texts imagine the colonized landscape of the Southwest as diseased, and envisions collectivity as a necessary healing strategy, chapter 2's texts move through the thickening borderland to territory beyond the geographical borderlands, and infuse Latina belonging into the Midwest through mestiza consciousness and praxis. Ana Castillo's *Sapogonia* and Sandra Cisneros's *Caramelo*, in their attempt to privilege and recognize the interdependence between Latin America and the United States, illustrate the impact of Chicano and Latino relocation—immigration—to the U.S. heartland, and disrupt U.S. discourses about race, geography, and homeland by marking the physical and cultural landscape with indigenous presence.

Chapters 3 and 4 then turn to Puerto Rican literary production written on the mainland by mainland Puerto Rican writers who are also immersed in the island. I argue that in Judith Ortiz Cofer's and Esmeralda Santiago's works, the cultural and geographical identities of Puerto Ricans on both the island and the mainland are figured through the unbelonging that results from neocolonial commodification, but that the storytellers' voices, blending authority and authorship, also assert their belonging through collective resistance to that colonialism. In chapter 3 Ortiz Cofer's *The Line of the Sun* and *The Meaning of Consuelo* show how legacies of Spanish colonialism and U.S. imperialism on the island have created a fractured sense of national identity for Puerto Ricans on both the island and the U.S. mainland. Ortiz Cofer is interested, I claim, in how acts of transgression resist this colonized identity. The novels ask what kinds of community can be formed out of and despite that identity, what impact those communities can have on the United States' writing of Puerto Rican unbelonging, and how transgression can upset the cultural and geographical landscape of both the island and mainland.

Continuing the focus on U.S. colonial presence and history on the island, in chapter 4 I show how over the course of her three memoirs Santiago explores how legacies of political and cultural colonization on the island develop on the mainland, and connect to her personal dislocation and stigmatized second-class citizenship. In part, I argue that by the end of the last memoir she has forged a resistant authorial presence that validates her belonging in the United States. In addition, in connecting the two nations she imagines a process of transnational decolonization, rather than having Puerto Rico vanish under the auspices of the United States. Specifically Santiago troubles nationhood by renegotiating her autobiographical identity: her metamorphosis into a commercially successful author has meant undergoing a transformation of national identity and socioeconomic status, from poor Puerto Rican islander to U.S. mainlander. It is significant, then, that in the memoirs the U.S. autobiographer's body pens and creates the Puerto Rican islander's body.

Himilce Novas's novel *Princess Papaya*, explored in chapter 5, goes further than any of the preceding narratives in its radical troubling of U.S. national identity. Novas's work—up until now critically neglected—contends with the historical and cultural estrangement between Cuba and the United States, and challenges the status quo, representing a new trend in Cuban American writing whereby narrative accounts are shifting away from nostalgic remembrances of the homeland to a process of settlement and connection to the United States. Her work thus expands the novelistic universe of many Cuban American texts, moving beyond Miami and shifting from an exile consciousness to an ethnic status, so that Cuban identity in the novel becomes negotiated within the political and geographical borders of the United States. Cuba itself is figured as a site of trauma that extends into the United States and is only healed through a new collective, socialist economic system in which nontraditional family structures are privileged. Thus the novel interrogates the idea of heterosexual reproduction as a privileged pillar of national continuity (and thus identity) by radically refiguring U.S. national identity under a socialist rather than capitalist system and by validating alternative relationships of intersexuality and nonbiological kinship. This enables some of the most underrepresented citizens of the nation (in the text, Juban, Native American, and Afro-Cuban) to legitimately belong to its political, geographical, and historical/ancestral spaces. In fact, through such a new understanding of presence in the United States, the novel retheorizes the very notion of U.S. Latina belonging, positing it as an experiential, socialist, and communal practice.

Finally, in the book's postscript I explore how these issues of national identity play themselves out in current debates about immigration, in which Latino unbelonging is frequently articulated through a rhetoric of criminalization. Focusing on the issue of immigration briefly referenced in this introduction, I show how various recent legislative measures have contributed to and become part of a national popular discourse that vilifies and at times criminalizes Latinos/as. I find that the mainstream's rhetoric depends specifically on geopolitics not only because the attention to place and border enforcement actually determines illegality and citizenship but also because it establishes the cultural otherness of all Latinos/as—no matter their legal status—as a potentially criminal or threatening presence. The postscript thus offers a case study in how the literary works, in deconstructing borders and blending the United States with Latin America, themselves force a reframing of discourses of national belonging by undermining the border, thus legitimating Latino cultural, political, and literary presence in the United States.

1 / Spaces of the Southwest: Dis-ease, Disease, and Healing in Denise Chávez's *The Last of the Menu Girls* and *Face of an Angel*

One of the most striking aspects of Denise Chávez's short-story collection *The Last of the Menu Girls* and novel *Face of an Angel* is the figuration of New Mexico's southwestern terrain as a space of dislocation, unease, and dis-ease. Given the long history of Mexicans (and Mexican Americans) in the Southwest, one would perhaps expect a narrative of rootedness and belonging rather than displacement. Instead, Chávez's stories depict the geographical, political, and cultural space of the region as a complex environment that has both suppressed and maintained its ancestral legacies and histories, and whose characters, I claim, consequently experience symptoms of disease that can only be healed through the imaginary blurring and conjoining of Mexico and the United States' nation-spaces.

In presenting a troubled and troubling southwestern cultural and physical landscape, Chávez is indirectly responding to one of popular culture's most powerful and dominant narratives about Mexican Americans in the Southwest: their presence here (whether legal or not) is greatly influenced by the presence of undocumented migrants who cross the border and enter the United States at various places along the nation's borderland region. As I discussed in the introduction, many critics point out that while undocumented Mexicans are often potentially subject to racial profiling that renders them foreign to the cultural and national identity of the United States, the United States' racialized notions of citizenship also informally govern all those who appear potentially illegal, so that Mexican Americans who are U.S. citizens or legally resident in the United States can also experience some of the stigma attributed to illegal immigrants.[1] Thus Mexican

American national identity, even in the Southwest, is particularly marked by a sense of "unbelonging," an unbelonging that is understood as cultural and physical presence in place. Some critics argue that U.S. Mexican citizens have long been represented as the quintessential illegal aliens, and that Mexican "illegitimacy" in the United States can be understood as a form of spatialized displacement based on the group's early racialization as nonwhite, secondary, and "alien."[2] Furthermore, the public's identification of "illegal aliens" with persons of Mexican ancestry is so strong that at times many Mexican Americans and other Latino/a citizens, through sheer cultural practice and presence, are presumed to be undermining the United States' national character.[3] This alienation of Mexicans (and often of all Latin Americans) is also strongly dependent on particular narratives of Latin America that separate it, in historical, cultural, and political terms, from the United States.[4]

Without question, manifest destiny—the United States' dominant theme of racial superiority justifying territorial expansion in the nineteenth century—played a crucial role in the nation's construction of territorial and geographic identity, with particular consequences for the Southwest. Even as early as 1846, the conflict between Mexico and the United States, which began as a dispute over the western boundary of Texas (recently annexed by the United States), signaled the United States' interest in acquiring land as property from its Southern Hemisphere neighbors. And, of course, the watershed 1848 Treaty of Guadalupe-Hidalgo, which ended the Mexican American War, definitively ceded the northern Mexican borderlands (from Texas to California and Oregon) to the United States and resulted in Mexico losing 40 percent of its territory. As Marshall Eakin notes, "Incorporation into the United States and its legal system would have devastating consequences for 'Hispanics' (Californios, Tejanos) and indigenous peoples in what would become the U.S. Southwest."[5] In fact, some descendents of the Spanish-speaking population of the region see the subsequent "occupation" of these lands as a form of colonialism. Clearly, literature coming out of the southwestern borderlands has long reflected the concerns, tensions, and history of this particularly blended cultural, political, and geographic space; many border critics have noted that literature written from, about, and/ or within the U.S.-Mexico border region is subject to the influences of that region. Rosemary A. King, for example, argues that because it is the site where the national territories of the United States and Mexico abut, "The border 'orders' the geography of this region," influencing the ways that "writers construct narrative space" and "the ways their characters negotiate those spaces, whether landscape, domestic sphere, national territory, public school, or utopia."[6]

How, then, are Chávez's New Mexican narratives a part of this border writing, and how do they counter and write back to the assumptions of unbelonging perpetuated by popular discourse? In one respect it is not immediately obvious that she is particularly engaging with popular discourse's obsessive attention to either illegal immigration or the cultural "otherness" of Mexicans: the New Mexican towns depicted in the stories are insular, their stories narrated predominantly by Mexican Americans, and there is little mention of either undocumented workers or any hostile Anglo presence.[7] Because her writing is not polemical, it appears to act rather than react, create rather than "talk back." Of course, this very rootedness and centering of Mexican American voices is part of what legitimates their presence in the United States. But, more important, the long presence, insularity, and rootedness in the region experienced by Chávez's characters are also strongly marked by personal and political experiences of dislocation that, I would argue, are effects of the continual narratives of unbelonging that delegitimate Mexican presence in the United States. Clearly, when Chávez's narratives engage with the region's geographical terrain and physical land, they attempt to reterritorialize it and lay claim to the nation in terms of its physical space. But when the texts describe her characters' experiences of sickness, abuse, and trauma, when they recount familial and generational histories of violence, recall suppressed memories, engage in discussions of race, or depict cultural practices (particular cuisines and/or languages) that are specific to Mexican American identity, they are also troubling imperialist notions of nationhood, in which political borders and the United States' long history of intervention and colonization beyond those borders have come to shape the way Mexicans are defined as other to the nation.

The narratives demonstrate Mexican cultural and physical belonging specifically by reimagining the United States as part of a collective of Mexico, forcing a rethinking of the place of the United States as an intersection of physical land and cultural practices/experiences.[8] In other words, when, in Chávez's narratives, the geography and cultural presence of Mexico become part of the geocultural landscape of the United States, a transnational identity emerges that delegitimates the nation's practice of identifying who belongs and who is foreign. Thus the cultural assertion of Mexican American voices and memories in the stories and the novel dismantle the political border, trouble national identity, and assert belonging. Ultimately, then, Mexican American geography in the southwestern United States creates a collective national history that legitimates Mexican and Mexican American presence and belonging in New Mexico.

As narratives, *The Last of the Menu Girls* and *Face of an Angel* lend themselves particularly well to a geopolitical hermeneutics not only because of the way they feature geographical terrain but also because of Chávez's own personal connection to the desert landscape of southern New Mexico.[9] In interviews she reiterates her strong connection to the land, saying that she writes in order to memorialize Mexican American cultural presence and identity in this space. She says that from the moment of her birth in Las Cruces, "in a time of extreme heat, in August," she has "carried that heat with me, wherever I have lived. A sensitivity to heat, a release in rain, these are my earliest memories." She continues, "the sky is a part of my interior/exterior world. . . . The change of seasons, so subtle in the south, has occasioned many an observation from me, and has found its expression in my writing."[10] The world within and the world without are so closely interrelated for Chávez that they blend, and narrative production offers a transposition of that blended world from the self's place on the land, to the written page. She has commented that "I feel as if I am New Mexico," that "I am a combined world of heat and dust and little rain," and that she loves to write "about the people of this world, the compadres and comadres I have grown up with, the maids I have loved, who've taken care of me, taught me the language of love, the handymen who left their indelible mark of kindness in my heart."[11]

Although Chávez's interviews and poetry explicitly describe desert landscapes, the cultural and physical topography of her fictional prose is largely unexplored. As I discuss below, while *The Last of the Menu Girls* and *Face of an Angel* have received some critical attention, with particular emphasis on her narrative strategy (stories within stories), the empowerment of Chicana identity, and the valorization of women's labor and service, the ways in which the texts negotiate geographic and cultural space in order to legitimate Mexican American belonging and presence in the nation have not been explored.[12] In this chapter I consider what kind of geopolitical identity Chávez's southwestern texts establish, arguing that her particular metaphor for this colonized space—that of disease and sickness—challenges the nation-state's fixation on the region's political border, and consequently troubles its demarcation of Mexicans as foreigners. Situating not just the land and the border as diseased sites but also the characters as sick, Chávez critiques the United States' amnesia regarding its historical topographical incursions southward, and imagines the possibility of healing through a revisioning of the nation's space. The narratives in fact rethink the very binary of healing versus sickness, presenting sickness as both a real condition for the characters and a metaphor for the way illegal and legal Mexican bodies are perceived to be a sign of ill health for, and alienation from, the nation. "Healing" therefore means integrating those bodies into the mainstream—reterritorializing the land—by recognizing how healthy bodies are regularly differentiated from sick ones in order to maintain and identify the normative space of the United States. My reading of Chávez's work thus recognizes how the nation's mainstream rhetoricizes Mexican presence as sick and damaging to the physical and cultural health of the nation, and interprets Chávez as troubling this rhetoric.

This geopolitical reading of *The Last of the Menu Girls* and *Face of an Angel* interprets the cultural markers of the texts as signatures of the physical geography of the land, which displace normative understandings of the nation's political borders, a displacement that heals the dis-ease experienced by the characters. In other words, in her fiction, Chávez's natural desert landscape roots Chicana narrative voices into a space of the Southwest that is part of both Mexico and the United States, privileging the region's borderland identity over the United States' separation of political nations. Tey Diana Rebolledo notes that this cultural-physical signature is typical of Hispanic and Chicana women's writing of the region, a writing that frequently describes the enduring cultural historic stamp on the landscape that has been apparent in the region for generations. She writes, "The signatures of their landscapes, both interior and exterior, are a monument to their survival, sense of self, and identity. They use the power of their perceptions of the landscape to transmit this sense of identity: one that is female, Chicana, and deeply connected to land, myth, and self."[13] Any reference to the natural regional landscape is thus a politically important gesture of empowerment: a monument memorializing a long and difficult history of estrangement and home on this particular land.

Specifically, this signature represents a literary "talking back" to and taking back of the land from the Anglo writers, travelers, and inhabitants of the late nineteenth and early twentieth centuries who saw the land as virgin territory without traditions or roots. While for them the land represented a kind of primal freedom, an empty space to be created by their own hands, early Hispanic women's writing countered this imaginary with cultural descriptions. For those writers, the land meant a long tradition of families tied to the land that were, more crucially, "nourished by it."[14] Similarly, historical referents for Hispanic writers came not from the large cities in the American East, with their concepts of progress based on materialism, but from the land south of the border, and a past in which the American Southwest belonged to Mexico. The land, and the Hispanic literature produced on it, exemplified a heritage and tradition in conflict with dominant Anglo values.[15] As a consequence of these Anglo incursions, the land has suffered and continues to suffer a profound sense of dis-ease, while its inhabitants experience displacement that can only be healed through acts of reterritorialization such as Chávez's.

In this respect Chávez continues the tradition of previous Mexican American women writers: speaking of the land as hers, while at the same time recognizing and respecting the limitations of the territory and the inherent otherness of its topography. She says, "I have always felt the burningly beautiful intensity of *my* dry, *impenetrable* land."[16] Her repeated statements in interviews about the connections between her inner and outer landscape—"My exterior landscape is who I am inside," "I wanted to connect with the exterior landscape," "My internal landscape is the desert"—can themselves be read as reconquests of a terrain that has long disenfranchised Chicanos.[17] Of course, the notion that landscapes have cultural and personal meanings, and that they express our identities, talk to us, and influence our behavior, is not new.[18] Chicana writers, however, have a particular interest in configuring their works with images and themes of place, creating, as Cordelia Chávez Candelaria notes in relation to *The Last of the Menu Girls*, "thematic *zones*" that may center on "the geography of birthplace and homeland," or "the home and personal surroundings." Ultimately, "these external spaces also serve to inscribe aspects of the interior dimensions and private spaces of Chicana experience."[19] For Chávez's characters, these zones of place are classic borderland terrains, layered with multiple interconnected voices that combine interior (often feminized) spaces with exterior, traditionally masculinized ones.

In this way Chávez's narratives legitimate the legacy and presence of Mexican Americans in the Southwest, a region that, from an Anglo point of view, has consisted only of empty desert. Building on these ideas, I argue that the most salient implication of her borderlands writing lies in the way that the rhetoric of domesticity and regional geography comes to redefine national and political identities beyond the immediate region. Ultimately, the unease and dis-ease felt by Rocío (*Menu*) and Soveida (*Face*) is healed through the blurring and conjoining of Mexico and the United States' physical terrain, and through the cultural assertion of Mexican American voices and memories of that land, both of which dismantle the political border and trouble a broader national identity. From a politics of geographical displacement, then, there emerges the possibility of Mexican American geography within the United States' natural landscape: a location from which to articulate a plural subjectivity, produce a communal narrative, and speak of a collective, rather than individual, national history.

The Last of the Menu Girls

Chávez's interconnected collection of stories *The Last of the Menu Girls* recounts in chronological order the childhood and adolescent experiences of Rocío Esquibel, a young Mexican American girl growing up in a southern New Mexico town with her mother and sister.[20] Over the course of the stories, Rocío moves from a domestic to a geopolitical understanding of place, allowing her to ultimately contextualize her personal sense of dislocation within the broader, national setting of the Southwest borderlands. In some respects my reading of the role of disease in these stories adds to the work of both Douglas Anderson and Elizabeth Wright. Anderson reads the "sick body" in the stories as abject, arguing that this abjection allows Rocío to differentiate herself from the sick bodies around her and to psychologically distance herself from what she now regards as the "other." Wright, looking at the title story and "Space Is Solid," extends Anderson's argument, using theories of disability to discuss the cultural construction and meanings of the stories' bodies and to show how disability is a culturally loaded term that the characters negotiate.[21] Interestingly, both Anderson and Wright conclude that Rocío herself initially distances herself from the abject (or disabled) bodies, but ends up identifying more with abjection (or is herself read as disabled). In my analysis of the title story, "The Last of the Menu Girls," and the collection's final story, "Compadre," I build on their readings by interpreting this notion of sick or diseased bodies more broadly and metaphorically as markers of Mexican American cultural and social unbelonging from the nation-state. Thus I understand Rocío's (Chávez's) emergence as a writer at the end of the collection as an empowering experience not because she herself becomes othered or abjected but because her narrative production can trouble the nation's writing of Mexican Americans as alien residents, and potentially legitimate Mexican American cultural and political presence in the Southwest.

I read the stories' rhetoric of displacement as expressions of the Southwest's colonized cultural and political geography, whereby domestic and personal spaces become connected to national ones.[22] The title story, "The Last of the Menu Girls," where the intersection of geography and politics remains implicit, and where the borderland and its inhabitants are described as diseased, offers some creative possibility for healing, as sick bodies become integrated into the same space as healthy ones. The last story of the collection, "Compadre," heals by reterritorializing the land, discrediting the national U.S.-Mexican border, and figuring storytelling itself as the most effective way to reassert Mexican American belonging in New Mexico. Here, geography—physical terrain, regional and national spaces and places—connects explicitly to the characters' political consciousness and identity formation, and the United States' new transnational identity reimagines the entire collection's borderlands by topographically joining the United States and Mexico, privileging the region's ancestral legacy and heritage, and legitimating the creative authorial voice that comes out of the borderlands.

"THE LAST OF THE MENU GIRLS": DIS-EASE AND DISLOCATION

Out of the entire collection, the title story is most explicit about using physical illness as a metaphor for the political and sociocultural ills of the borderlands.[23] Specifically, Rocío's psychological dislocation occurs through her encounters with those who are sick, and her translation of their disease into her own dis-ease emphasizes the entire collection's rhetoric of displacement as an expression of the Southwest's colonized cultural and political geography. The story takes place in two separate locations simultaneously: one, in the hospital where Rocío, just out of high school, has taken a summer job as a menu girl, distributing daily menus to patients; and two, in her house, where she is haunted by her great-aunt Eutilia who died five years earlier in one of the rooms, but still appears present and continually dying to Rocío. The only direct mention of the U.S.-Mexico geographical border in this story occurs in a brief conversational exchange in the hospital, when a migrant worker, Juan Maria, is brought in for surgery after getting into a fight. One nurse describes him as "an illegal alien," and another talks disparagingly about "people sneaking across the border" as part of "an epidemic."[24] Here, the language of disease and infection is used to describe illegal Mexicans in the state, so that for this story in particular, and for the collection as a whole, the rhetoric of personal sickness becomes paired with political sickness and with descriptions of illegal Latino presence. Thus, although after this moment illegal Mexicans are not directly referred to, they haunt the narrative of sickness on which the story does focus, providing a political backdrop to the more personal traumas that Rocío endures in the story.

Both at home and at work, Rocío is disturbed by the way that dying bodies do not remain contained or separate from healthy ones, seeming to defy boundaries both physically and spiritually. The story is full of descriptions of the failure of flesh to hold itself together and preserve the distinction between exterior and interior. Eutilia's dying body is particularly porous, with "the blown evacuations of the dying: gas, putrefaction, and fetid lucidity. Her body poured out long held-back odors" (67). Here the body escapes its own boundaries and spills over into the outside space. In other words, the dying sick body solidifies and textures the normative space around it, haunting it permanently. Rocío's haunted space is also exacerbated by the stories her mother recounts, in particular one about a Doña Mercedes who lay dying of cancer and did not want her attendants to move or lift her. Later, after her death, they found "huge gaping holes in her back where the cancer had eaten through her flesh" (70). The porousness of Doña Mercedes's sick body leads Rocío to wonder, essentially, where her former healthy body is, and what one does with the memory of that former self. Doña Mercedes had been "an imposing lady" of Spanish ancestry "with a head full of rich dark hair" (69), and after her death, the memory of her living body seems stronger than the reality of her dying one: "Everyone remembered Doña Mercedes as tall and straight and very Spanish" (70). How, then, can these two apparently distinct bodies belong to the same person? What is the relationship between healthy and sick bodies, and to what extent do they define one another? What Rocío learns here and over the course of the story is that memory does the important work of recalling the healthy body, even within the sick one it has now turned into, in order to emphasize their proximity rather than distance. In other words, given the story's metaphorical representation of illegal migrant bodies as presumably damaging to the health of the nation, the realization that memories of healthy bodies can be written into narratives of sickness troubles that very separation of illegal (diseased) bodies from legal (healthy) ones.

The hospital job then brings together these experiences on a broader and more institutional scale. As the menu girl, Rocío enters almost every patient's room, and has to face not just her own fears in the face of sickness but also acknowledge her tendency to put up boundaries between her own healthy body and the sick ones she encounters: "We rolled up the pain, assigned it to a shelf, left it there, with a certain self-congratulatory sense of relief at our own good fortune as we looked the other way . . . and soon, we forgot we had ever felt any discomfort" (88). The story essentially tracks Rocío's shift in understanding as her psyche adapts; as she recognizes her own desire to separate herself from the abject bodies around her, she gradually accepts and reinhabits the textured space that they all—the healthy and the sick—share. The dislocation and dis-ease are neither comfortable nor easy: "My walks home [from the hospital] were measured, pensive. I hid in my room those long nights, nights full of wrestling, injured dreams" (94), but toward the end of the story she understands that her summer has been formative: "I had made the awesome leap into myself that steamy summer of illness and dread—confronting at every turn the flesh, its lingering cries" (95). The lesson for Rocío is clear: to have imagined the sick as "other" to the healthy—to in fact realize she was defining them through opposition and differentiation—prevented her from recognizing the humanity of the sick. Similarly, the story suggests that the nation's abject othering of illegal Mexican presence in the United States maintains Mexican bodies as undesirable and inhuman.

This psychological growth also allows Rocío to change the way she memorializes her great-aunt. At the start of the story she remembers Eutilia as helpless and insane—recalling her shredding her hospital gown to pieces, staring at the ceiling, and playing an imaginary piano long into the night. Eutilia is "a little girl in tatters in her metal bed" (68). But by the end Rocío imagines Eutilia as more liberated. Rather than being trapped dying on her metal bed, Eutilia sings "Cielito Lindo" and plays the piano with energy: "She pumped the gold pedals [of the piano] with fast, furious, and fervent feet. She smiled to the walls, its faces, she danced on the ceiling" (95). In the narrative space of memory that Rocío writes for herself, Eutilia's physical decay is tempered by her physical energy and spiritual creativity. However, this does not completely eliminate the memory of bodily deterioration. Instead, physical creativity and physical deterioration combine. Toward the end, part of Eutilia's song is written out in the text. The refrain of the song, "Ay, ay, ay, ay. Canta y no llores! Porque cantando se alegran, Cielito Lindo, los corazones . . ." contains the same cry of pain—"ay, ay, ay"—that the hospital patients and Eutilia herself have uttered (95). Within the text the pain of dying is textured with the joy of song, and vice versa. By the end of the story Rocío remains haunted by Eutilia's ghost, but the ghost occupies a more benevolent presence in her mind. She states, "Farther away, from behind and around my head, I heard the irregular but joyful strains of 'Cielito Lindo,' played on a phantom piano by a disembodied but now peaceful voice that sang with great quivering emotion" (97). Over the course of the story, then, Rocío comes to accept that sickness is part of the national terrain, and that her spaces (domestic, public, and private) are haunted by memories and ghosts of diseased and dying bodies. In fact, she is even able to reconcile with that haunting, translating it from a threatening presence into a benevolent and creative one. Given that the language of illness in the story also represents the region's historical and contemporary political ills, this reconciliation also recognizes that the dislocating ills of the southwestern borderlands can be reintegrated through a legitimated creative voice.

"Compadre": Dislocating the Political

The title story thus foregrounds the memory of past creativity as healing, rather than figuring Rocío herself as a storyteller and writer. In "Compadre," however, Chávez more fully legitimates Rocío's cultural and political presence in the Southwest. This legitimacy in turn gives authority to the production of narrative within this landscape, and, in an act of decolonization, undermines the effects of the United States' historical and cultural acquisition of this land. "Compadre" directly creates connections between its cultural, geographic, and political topographies, supporting Elizabeth Jacobs's comment that "descriptions of the town indicate its 'borderland' location as a place where national and international, rural and urban economies coexist in complex and contradictory ways."[25] Most important, that coexistence also beckons to the blending of Mexican and U.S. landscapes, and a new collective national identity that emerges out of it.

The story's descriptions of southern New Mexico's natural landscape and the state borders, all set against the looming backdrop of the U.S.-Mexico border, point Rocío to her new direction as a writer. "Compadre," told in seven sections, focuses on an old migrant worker, Regino, the neighborhood handyman who has been Rocío's mother's compadre for as long as she can remember. The story describes Regino at work in their yard, Rocío and her mother's visit to Regino's house, Regino's brief abandonment of his wife and daughters, his installation of a fountain in the yard, and finally, Regino's own narrative about home and place. At the very end, we learn that Rocío now lives in the northern part of the state and is a writer. The story ends as her mother encourages her to write about the places she knows best—her street, her house—and the reader realizes that the whole collection is precisely that: the centering and rooting of southwestern culture and geography that, through narrative, reterritorializes the land. And as a writer, Rocío herself becomes an explicit border crosser at the end, translating experiences into narratives and connecting them to the broader landscape beyond the immediate one.

One of the most obvious ways in which this story renegotiates geographic terrain is with its descriptions of the town's boundaries and the landscape's ideological, economic, and political significance. Her description of the "North" is particularly important: "North was a point beyond knowing; it led to a difference in climate, large cities, other cultures. North led to the beginnings of icy cold rivers, those streams and lakes whose water fed the crops of southern farms: cotton, red chile and green, beans and melons, alfalfa and onions" (167). The North—that is, the northern part of New Mexico—is described as an unknown space, by all implications a different country that is only distantly connected to the South. Rocío's description of the state's spatial features is also traced with her own personal experiences: she notes that the "Northern Road" also leads to her father, who left his family and now lives farther north. The North's "world of arts," "bastion of government," and "aging, fading movie stars" in "their summer ranches" is where "the arias of art and politics intertwined" (167). The North is a world of transplants from other parts of New Mexico or other parts of the United States, while the South is a place of natives, an enduring homeland for both U.S. citizens and migrant workers. From Rocío's viewpoint, the North's popularity with transient visitors and tourists makes the South an all-the-more permanent home.

This binary, however, is complicated by Regino's status in their southern border-town. He originally comes from Mexico, and thus in some respects his presence is a continual reminder of the larger national and political border between the two nation-states. However, the regional boundaries within New Mexico itself that demarcate different cultural lifestyles are actually more important to Rocío and the other characters than the demarcation of any national border. Thus Chávez remaps the geography of the state: perhaps contrary to expectations, the focus is less on the international U.S.-Mexico border and more on other boundaries. Regino's Mexican nationality, for example, is a reminder of the area's proximity and connection to Mexico rather than their political separation. Rocío notes that Regino was "born in Mexico, but as long as I'd known him, he'd lived in town" (162). The story suggests that while the U.S.-Mexico border is in some respects real because of its political status (the collection as a whole acknowledges, from time to time, the xenophobia that migrants face after crossing), it is also irrelevant in terms of the natural history of the landscape. That is, the border line that divides New Mexico from (old) Mexico does not erase the continuity of the topography, nor the connection that both old and New Mexicans feel toward the Southwest.

The real foreigner in New Mexico is thus not the Mexican national but the tourist from the East Coast of the United States, who is "new to the desert, unused to the land, not yet understanding or seeing past the scrub bush and the random and disquieting disorder," who complains about the messy, weed-filled lots and exclaims, "You would never find this back east! . . . This is what I don't like about New Mexico" (168). Although the assumption is that the landscape does eventually grow on you ("not yet understanding or seeing"), Chávez's move here is clear: because the U.S. tourist in New Mexico is the real intruder, while Regino, the Mexican migrant worker, belongs here, the United States must reassess its national borders and identity. While in the title story Chávez began to heal the Southwest's unease by filling interior spaces with ancestral ghosts, here such healing takes place by reshaping the geographical terrain of the region, and redrawing the national and political borders around New Mexico.

Out of this geographical displacement there emerges a tradition of collectivity and interdependence, illustrated in part by Regino's role as compadre to Nieves, Rocío's mother. In the fourth section of the story Nieves explains the nature of the compadrazco relationship. Nieves wants Regino to build her a fountain in the yard, and when Rocío objects to Regino's slovenly work, Nieves reminds her of the central obligation in the relationship: she is "bound by the code" (186) and will provide work for him whenever she can. Nieves, as the madrina (godmother) of one of Regino's daughters, Atocha, is "bound by the higher laws of compadrazco, having to do with the spiritual well-being and development of one of God's creatures. Compadrazco puts me in a direct line to Heaven" (186). The relationship draws in familial lines and boundaries where there are none, frequently simulating and replacing bloodlines that have vanished.[26] Nieves remarks that without a madrina or padrino, "you could be left relationless, and what could be worse than that?" (186). While she acknowledges that there is warmth in a biological family, compadrazco goes even further, allowing "the best of a family's qualities to shine through" because "to be a compadrazco is to be unrelated and yet related, and yet willing to allow the relationless relation absolute freedom—within limits" (186–187). Regino's relationship to Rocío's family is defined through this epitome of ambiguity: it is absence and presence at the same time, simultaneously limited and limitless. In other words, it operates within porous boundaries, and this is precisely what makes it valued, as a relationship, beyond others: it is a "union truer than family, higher than marriage" (187).

The compadrazco relationship offers a new paradigm for integrating migrant workers into New Mexico, particularly because of the contrast drawn between Salvador (Rocío's father) and Regino. Salvador left home—"his south"—long ago "for the crowded freedom and anonymity of the north" (167), and his connection to the family is far weaker than Regino's. While southern New Mexico is Salvador's homeland, he wants more space and freedom, and "like many people before him, he couldn't tolerate the heat, the blinding sun of his hometown. His was an easier world, untransformed by the slow, hot, impatient, and restless nights of incredible stillness" (167). Significantly, Regino's bond to southern New Mexico long outlasts Salvador's: he remains there, an old man, even after his wife and daughters move away to Montana. Because the story continually places Regino on the land, and has him working it thoroughly, it establishes his deep connection to it. He has, in effect, a compadrazco relationship to the land, a relationship that privileges the connections created through acts of work and that understands the ambiguity of those connections. His house lies in the midst of a lot that is "now tamed" of its wildness, but that is nevertheless "framed . . . by the wild, uncultivated land" that surrounds it (168). The house is situated on the edge of Chiva Town, a mostly Latino neighborhood where recent developments do not entirely eliminate the memory of the old landscape, "where goats and pigs once roamed freely along with fowl and other domesticated animals among the brush and desert grass" (168). The desert is always there, at the edge of the neighborhood and at the edge of the narrative, defining the landscape and the subject's ambiguous relationship to it.

Earlier stories in the collection make occasional references to the desert landscape, but in "Compadre" the desert landscape works as an influential environment that mediates the characters' emotions and movements. Near the start of the story, Rocío watches Regino digging in the yard and describes the trenches he has built that lead from one tree to the next, to save on water: "They served as an artery of life to this phantasmic otherwordly Garden of Eden fallen on hard times," adding "a ravaged bombed look to what little yard of grass there was" (156). To the family the land outside serves merely as a backdrop to the dramas unfolding within the house, as Rocío, her sister, and her mother argue with one another. But Regino's patient attempts to salvage the parched, difficult land are also a reminder of the way that this setting is part of an important ancestral legacy and ongoing historical presence, one that requires constant attention and work. Its ugly "bombed" look, an implicit reference to the misuse of New Mexico's land as the site of the first nuclear weapons test in 1945, represents a disease-ridden wasteland that must nevertheless be integrated and healed. At one point Regino bends over and pulls out a "large specimen of plant life" from the ground, which looks "prehistoric, invincible, the ancestress of countless weeds, accursed mother of our present shame" (157), suggesting that their inattention to the land and its migrants is deep-rooted and shameful. And water, of course, is precious: recognized as nourishing and sustaining. After Rocío hands Regino a lukewarm cup of water, he drinks it gratefully and thirstily, "as if it were a golden elixir" (164), showing a respect for the water that legitimates his respect for, and belonging to, the land.

But ultimately that connection to the land—ancestral, cultural, and physical—does not guarantee him ownership of it. By the end, Regino has been displaced from his own house on the other side of town and is living alone in a government-subsidized house. He continues to work the land at Nieves's house, but as her handyman he is still bound by the class divisions that separate and stratify him from the place. Earlier on in the story, Rocío notes that Eleiterio, Regino's son, does not talk to her, because "it was not his *place* as our handyman's son to speak to me" (165, my emphasis). Regino belongs to this place more than Salvador, and more than Rocío, who moves away, but at the same time he is continually displaced from it. The story thus raises difficult questions about the role of U.S. national borders on this southwestern terrain. How, for example, do we reconcile Regino's ancestral connection to the land he works with the rhetoric of illegitimate presence that some characters, such as Salvador, associate with him?[27] Should we be troubled by Regino's apparent detachment from or blindness to his own disempowerment? And what is the nature of his disempowerment if indeed he is not stirred to change it? But the story's privileging of collective visions of national identity in fact renders these questions redundant. In the sixth section of the story we finally hear from Regino himself as the narrative turns to his interior monologue. We learn that he has refused to move to Montana with his family because this town in New Mexico is his home, providing him "order" and "peace" (204). Although he lives in a subsidized duplex that he doesn't own, he finds solace in the landscape: "Peace is sitting out there watching the trees move and feeling the wind" (205). He recalls the conversation he had with his wife, Braulia, when she said she was leaving him. While she is impatient to "see things, to live" and to have a "new life, a real life," for Regino, the whole "world" is present in this town (205). Like the weeds he is trying to dig up, his presence here is persistent and "deep-rooted" (203) because of his continuity in the location, and in Regino's worldview, this, not ownership, provides sufficient legitimation. And because the story has reshaped the state's boundaries, rendering the political and national ones less immediate than the cultural and regional ones, Regino belongs to this land because of his enduring presence on it.

To the extent that Regino's connection to the land legitimates his presence on it, that legitimacy is further strengthened by Rocío's dissemination of his story.[28] With her explicit coming-out as a writer at the end of "Compadre," Rocío's emergent storytelling voice also discovers a healing way to talk about the relationship between personal borders, geographical borders, and the inarticulate national and political border. Although Regino does not own the land he works on, and Rocío, by the time of writing, no longer lives on that land, her narrative both validates his connection to it and transports her back to southern New Mexico, creating for both of them a cultural and geopolitical attachment to that landscape in particular. Rocío differentiates herself early on in the story from her father: in contrast to him, she knows that she will never be able to permanently leave the land. She has wondered, "Did my father ever miss his hometown, the people he once loved? For to me, the southern nights were nights of waiting, nights worth waiting for, nights that heralded bright dawns in which dreams were heard and seen in the first glimmer of the daytime's moon" (167). The magical, intimate pull of southern New Mexico not only pervades her narrative but also redefines the entire border-state region.

Of course, many writers create and re-create their homeland spaces through narrative, and in doing so make a political statement, but Chávez's writing reterritorializes the desert with a strong historical, ancestral, and cultural Chicana presence in order to renew the connection between land and national identity. In particular, her narratives point to a paradox of presence that is peculiar to this landscape, a landscape that memorializes its own connection to Mexico and the United States, and thus both displaces and reclaims the boundaries of national identity. When Nieves, at the end of "Compadre," recommends to Rocío that she just write one thing, something like *Gone with the Wind*—"Just write about this little street of ours. It's only one block long, but there's so many stories. . . . Write about . . . our house . . . and that will take the rest of your life" (214–215)—there is humor in the moment, as the mother instructs the daughter to simply produce another great American classic. But the humor is cut through with Chávez's political intent, too. Nieves adds that in order to write this great work, Rocío need not "go anywhere," not even "down the street" and "not even out of this house" (215) because there are plenty of stories within the domestic and female space of the house itself. These stories—of the neighborhood, the small town, the borderlands—are American stories too. Rocío does not directly reply, but her response—which is to turn to Regino, address him for the first and only time as "compadre," and offer him "Más tamales?" (215)—tells us of her intent to write. Regino, a marginalized migrant worker from Mexico, will not just be the protagonist of her story but is also integrated into the moment when the decision to write occurs. Chávez's collection cuts against the grain by imbuing the desert landscape of New Mexico with personal, political, and national narratives, and by disrupting and redrawing the borders between the United States and Mexico she also writes herself forcefully into the landscape of American literature, and in the process re-presents an inseparable U.S./Mexican space as part of U.S. national and cultural identity.

Face of an Angel

Face of an Angel, Chávez's first novel, is most clearly a novel about gender and politics. But like *The Last of the Menu Girls*, it is also inherently about place: the story's negotiation of geographical landscapes, in fact, determines and orders its gender politics. It tells the story of Soveida Dosamantes, a southern New Mexico waitress from Agua Oscura (a fictional town in southern New Mexico) who, over the course of the book, examines her matriarchal ancestral lineage, tells the stories of those who came before her in order to work through the generations of abuse that they have suffered, and eventually finds fulfillment and healing through education and service.[29] In the novel several generations of abuse toward the women of Agua Oscura, particularly the Dosamantes family, have left a legacy of dis-ease and emotional dis-ease that is ongoing into the present. As in *The Last of the Menu Girls*, displacement is healed through a reterritorialization of the borderlands; in *Face of an Angel*, furthermore, this healing and sense of belonging also come about by integrating memories of abject abuse and

trauma into the present space, and by making the land—its geographical and cultural signatures—a sacred site of collectivity and community.
Healing thus involves not only resituating the self in place through work,
and conjoining familial and personal history with geographic terrain, but
also, ultimately, articulating the legitimacy of a blended U.S.-Mexican
national identity and discrediting political boundaries.[30]

As in *The Last of the Menu Girls*, descriptions of geographical landscape are muted until near the end, when Soveida begins to understand
her cultural identity in relation to the broader geopolitical and historical signatures around her. While physical geography does not feature
explicitly in most of the novel, the rhetoric used to articulate the painful
memory of abuse is one of spatial displacement, pointing to the powerful pull of the southwestern landscape and thus emphasizing its influence throughout the novel. Initially, as in the earlier stories that Rocío
tells, Soveida describes her uneasy relationship to place by focusing
on domestic, interior spaces that are filled with ghosts from the past,
creating a strong and specific cultural assertion of Mexican American
history and memory. Over the course of the novel Soveida attempts to
rebalance herself in order to feel more whole—to heal herself—but she
is only able to do so after recognizing how her own displacement is part
of a larger pattern of abuse. Personal and collective abuse itself—psychological, physical, and sexual—is figured as a dislocating experience, and
thus Soveida, unable to speak directly of her own experiences of abuse,
adopts a rhetoric of displacement in order to articulate its effects.[31] She
begins her story, for example, with an image of unbelonging and displacement: "I was always Soveida. The Soveida who sat in other rooms."[32]
She later notes that "when you grow up in the Southwest, your state
is your country. There exists no other country outside that which you
know. Likewise, neighborhood is a country. As your family is a country.
As your house is a country. As you are a country" (171). It follows, then,
that any sense of displacement from her body and her house parallels a
regional and national displacement, while any replacement represents a
reintegration into the domestic and national space. The sense that the
entire world exists within the smallest of spaces echoes Nieves's advice
to Rocío, but here Soveida also remaps the borders of the nation-state,
figuring them as political borders that operate on a local, domestic level.
In this way domestic and national spaces seem to determine one another,
and interrelated narratives of domestic abuse and abuse of the land can
shed significant light on each other.

COMMUNITY DISPLACEMENT: ABUSE AND LAND

Abuse in *Face of an Angel* is both rampant and dislocating. The narrative clearly establishes both that abuse is manifested in a communal pain that is inseparable from individual suffering and that it has, for generations, been displacing women from their domestic spaces. Toward the end of the novel, Chávez makes it clear that the women's domestic disenfranchisement is a symptom of a larger wrongdoing—that of Chicano disenfranchisement from the land—but even before this, Soveida's narrative implicitly draws attention to the desert landscape that the family has inhabited for generations as the crucial setting for this abuse. Introducing the notion of generational abuse, Soveida points out that "the longer I live, the more I see that it is the same life, the same story, the same characters. All of them with the same face" (4). Until the silenced abuse is recounted, however, the healing that comes about through recognizing the collective (rather than isolated) nature of illness cannot begin. In particular, the women in the novel all share a history of violence and disease that manifests itself directly through their bodies' experiences, but that is not articulated until Soveida tells their shared stories. She thus explains that she suffers from endometriosis, yeast infections, and "other myriad symptoms and sicknesses of a woman's body during her childbearing years" (364), and strongly implies that these are caused by women's collective illnesses. Her body absorbs other women's illnesses when she sleeps with her first husband, Ivan, from whom she always feels that she has "caught something secondhand, from someone else . . . when I made love to him, I felt as if I was making love to all the people he'd made love to in his life" (364). The past and present history of Ivan's infidelities surface and haunt her during sex, until she knows his girlfriends by her own body's symptoms: "infections, fevers, tiredness, allergies" (366). However careful she is, her "bile and rage" spill out when he is with her (365). Through her adult body's experience of sexual infidelity, then, Soveida experiences a memory-knowledge of generations of physical and emotional abuse, and turns their individual experiences into communal ones by recounting them.

Soveida's cousin Mara Loera also endures a raging body that has inherited a legacy of displacement, and suffers the pain of physical disease. Furthermore, as the daughter of Dolores's deceased sister and thus a matrilineal rather than patrilineal relation, Mara is aware of her fragile connection to the family. She tells Soveida, "You're a Dosamantes. At least you have a history. I'm a Loera. And as far as everyone is concerned,

Loeras have never amounted to much, like my mother, Lina" (51–52). Without a written history Mara has no legitimate place: as an orphan she is shunted off to live with Mama Lupita (not her real grandmother); is allegedly sexually abused by Soveida's father, Luardo; and finally, as a teenager, runs away from home. After one brief visit back to Agua Oscura, pregnant and married, she disappears bodily from the text. But even after she has left the chronological account she continues to haunt the text as an adult, usually as a disembodied voice at the other end of a phone line in conversations with Soveida. Her stories of abuse, however, resist telling: while she is still a child, for example, her direct and indirect accusations against Luardo are heard by Soveida, but never resolved. And as an adult, her testimonial is fragmented and full of gaps. This failure of testimonial—the inability to produce any sort of productive or whole narrative—is clearly connected, in the narrative, to Mara's displacement and subsequent symptoms of homesickness and disease.

Mara is the only character that we know of who visits the "original" homeland—Mexico—and seeks a connection to it by trying to find her father's village. She never knew him, but explains, "I just wanted to see the place he came from, that's all. To walk the streets, to look inside the houses when it got dark, to eat the food, to wash myself clean early in the morning from water heated on a stove, and to cry with the beauty of the stars at night" (340–341). Crossing the national border, however, does not erase the traumatic somatic memories that she carries with her. Her mother, Lina, bled to death following complications during labor, and never complained of her pain "because she was ashamed . . . that's the way the Loera women are . . . they abuse their bodies in the guise of shame" (340), and as an adult Mara continually abuses her body as part of that same legacy inflicted on the Loera women. Her self-abuse manifests itself in health problems, as she admits, "I'm an alcoholic who has ulcers, drinking to the future and trying to settle the past. But it comes up like the bile I try to keep down . . . some kind of acid. . . . Sometimes I'm afraid I'm going to regurgitate my whole life on the floor" (341). In Mexico her dis-ease becomes a disease: rather than finding answers in the lost homeland, she gets diarrhea in Mexico City, and ends up sick in a toilet stall in the subway, excreting all over another woman's white purse (341). Her past is not just indigestible but also firmly rooted within her no matter where she goes, in part because she cannot connect her sick body to her displacement.

Repeatedly, the novel figures displacement and disenfranchisement— not just domestic but also territorial and geographical—as effects of abuse. Refusing to speak directly about the emotional abuses they suffer, the Dosamantes women exacerbate and perpetuate the abuse, and as Soveida notes, their whispers "pull the rug out from under you, leaving you forever *off-balance*, like Mamá's whispers about Mara" (125, my emphasis). Furthermore, the "evil" (90) in the house has always been "formless" and nameless (49), thriving on the secrecy and whispers that hold the girls of the household in this uneasy imbalance. Dolores, Soveida's mother, recalls her own mother Trancha's domestic violence and cruel words set against the desert landscape: "The high, sharp Pss! of Trancha's voice snapped the desert air, stung and burned like sand in a dust storm" (123). As the setting for Trancha's words, this particular physical landscape becomes the inextricable context for abuse. One, it seems, cannot be separated from the other, and the pairing of desert and violence suggests that they continually trace and texture one another throughout the narrative. The implication is that this desert town that has been, for generations, the site of domestic violence—a violence that is simultaneously silent and spoken, remembered and suppressed—is itself a diseased or disused terrain.

Clearly the land of her ancestors cannot steady Soveida in the face of historical and contemporary evidences of abuse. And in the house in which she was born and raised, she remains continually "elsewhere" because the abuse and its ghostly legacy render her continually displaced. Chávez's rhetoric of abuse is again topographical, as she describes her characters as permanently displaced ("forever off-balance" 125). Like Regino in "Compadre," who is both at home and displaced from the southern New Mexican landscape he inhabits, Soveida experiences a paradox of presence: while the geographical landscape is inherently her home, she is haunted by generations of women who, like her, have been continually separated from history, either relegated to the margins of the family's historical narrative or erased from it entirely. The absence of women in the official historical family record, then, represents this troubling dis-ease in place, shown most visually in the Dosamantes family tree on the frontispiece of the book. There, the names of the women who haunt Soveida's spaces and her writing do not appear, implying that their voices have remained inarticulate because of the long cultural tradition of silence that sustains the patriarchal hierarchy of their family and society. To recover not just the women's voices but, by extension, the colonized Mexican territory that, the text later explains, has created a broader ethnic and gendered patriarchal disenfranchisement (the abuse of Mexican American women at the hands of their men, who themselves experience abuse at the hands of Anglos), Soveida must over the course of the narrative heal herself by writing the illegitimate and legitimate women back into the family record, and producing a communal story out of their experiences.[33]

It is evident from the beginning of the novel that such a communal narrative account would temper some of the violences of history inflicted on both the domestic and geographical spaces of the Southwest, and thus trouble the historical and political landscape. The novel's layered multiple voices and narrative strategies build up a collective new history that draws strong connections between the telling of memories and stories and the desert topography itself. In the San Pedro cemetery, where Dolores's many siblings and ancestors (Trancha's great-grandparents) are buried, wombs produce ghosts, as Trancha gives birth to one stillborn baby after another. But in the cemetery there are also enough "wildflowers" to make it "bearable," and as a child, Dolores spends hours tending to each of her brothers' and sisters' plots. Some have thorns, others have crabgrass or sand, worms, and ants. Her favorite brother Eulid's grave is "the lushest, blooming with early spring flowers and summer ice plant" despite its thorns (38). Here, Chávez suggests that the communal narratives that must be told in order for any healing to occur are mediated through, and are part of, the land of New Mexico itself. Oralia, for example, who performs her domestic labors "with a sense of novelty, even if it was for the thousandth time and she knew every nuance and permutation of the job at hand" (141), also has a sacred relationship to the land. She concocts medicinal teas from herbs that she grows herself in her thriving garden, and attends to the soil carefully. When not cooking she is "busy cleaning the pebbles out of a pot of beans, weeding her garden patiently every day, or sweeping the ground in front of Mamá's house until the earth shone like skin, work she found joyful and never monotonous" (141). Her work in the yard is not only transformative, however. She tells Soveida that long ago her own mother gave her seeds to plant, and that the ones she tends to now are "the seeds of those seeds, 'las hijas de las hijas,'" her "only children" (413). Like Regino, her connection to the land is thus based not on ownership (because she does not legally own any of the Dosamantes property), but on the products of her continuous labor on that land. In this way, then, she reorients notions of belonging by valorizing the terrain itself, and by placing her own historic signature on it.

POLITICAL DISPLACEMENT: INTERROGATING CHICANO AND U.S. IDENTITY

Oralia's connection to the land thus demonstrates how domestic practices such as gardening and cooking can strengthen cultural belonging and legitimate Latina identity and presence in the Southwest. However, this only begins the process of healing the Dosamantes women's familial and personal experiences of abuse. In order to firmly relocate herself on southwestern land, Soveida needs to develop a new geopolitical identity in which she negotiates the region's collective memory in relation to U.S. national identity. Thus over the course of the narrative we see Chávez begin to strongly challenge mainstream notions of American nationhood by reorienting racial belonging and identity in the United States, and politicizing the personal and communal traumas that Soveida has endured. When as a child Soveida complains about having to learn to make tamales, asking, "Who cares about making tamales? . . . We're Americans" (139), Oralia responds, "You may be an American in your little finger, but the rest of your hand is brown, like mine. And that means you're an Indian like me, although Mama Lupita might not agree with me. She's got her Indian blood as well, and she knows it, only she won't admit it" (139). Oralia's answer is perhaps as reductive as Soveida's: both assume Americanness to be Anglo-American and white. But Oralia's vision imagines a collective vision as well, where white America (as the minority) and indigenous America (as the majority) must coexist for the whole to operate. They are, in other words, both necessary parts of a shared whole. Oralia refigures Soveida's Mexican American presence in southern New Mexico by recalling her body's long memory in that land, and insisting on the significance of her Indianness in the here and now. In other words, Oralia rewrites Soveida's national identity by connecting it to the Southwest's history and geography, and by clarifying the nature of her "American" presence in New Mexico with a reminder of indigenous ancestry. Despite Lupita's desire to silence and marginalize the family's Indian ancestry, Oralia centers it. In this vision, then, Soveida's indigenous heritage becomes important and visible, and legitimates her presence in the Southwest above and beyond any Anglo-American's place in it. Soveida's "brownness" is not a vilified addendum or apostrophe to the United States' articulation of national identity, but takes center stage with its own purpose, shape, and history.

The Chicano movement, which Soveida becomes connected to through her first husband, Ivan, further broadens and contextualizes the "brownness" of her history on the land. Before this, Soveida only knows that she is, as she puts it, "a Mexican-American and that was it." She adds, "I knew vaguely that my family's roots were in Mexico, but what did Chicano mean?" (130). Learning and hearing about César Chávez and the workers' struggle, the damage of pesticides, and the field laborer's backbreaking work broadens Soveida's world, teaching her "about the people I was supposed to be connected to and yet barely knew" (131). Soveida's developing class-and-race conscious political identity, and its connection to the Southwest's historical geography, unfolds most explicitly in the papers she writes for her community college sociology class on Chicano culture and tradition. In this setting the text is able to interrogate Chicano identity and at the same time draw attention to the fact that historically, Chicano social and geographic displacement has made it difficult to find a common ground from which to pose some of these questions. In the text, then, academia provides a space for thinking about how Chicano/a identity should be defined, how we should speak of and about it, and how it should be disseminated. But while academia offers up a useful rhetoric for this exploration, it also fails to acknowledge any residual and continuing marginalization of class and gender within the community itself.

In her intellectual growth Soveida thus has to understand how to form a politics that will be adequate to her situation as a working Chicana. Although she knows about "life on the border" firsthand, she does not know her "Chicana self" because she has been, as she puts it, "so up to my neck in food" that she has not "had the eyes to see what was happening around [her]" (283–284). In fact, as soon as she meets her new professor, J. V. Velásquez, she is forced to ask questions about the nature of her experience and knowledge. She immediately brushes up against the barriers that divide objective and personal responses, and begins to challenge the privileging of the former over the latter. When she arrives late to the first class from her job at El Farol and senses disapproval from J.V., she thinks to herself, "Dr. Velásquez, you want to know about Chicano culture? Well, here I am, smelling of hard work" (287). For the duration of the semester, J.V. consistently dismisses the personal nature of her scholarship, which is borne out of the affective memories of Lupita and Oralia's home-spaces and the revalorization of her own waitressing job. Nevertheless, Soveida's practice of writing gives her the agency to articulate her own ethnic identity. Her personalization of the political offends

J.V., but the flip side of her intellectual development—the politicization of the personal—eventually allows her to fully understand her cultural presence in the region.

When, for her first writing assignment, Soveida conducts and transcribes an interview with Oralia, Chávez's narrative strategy is clear: the device of the interview/essay form perfectly illustrates the need to write down and record a woman's experience that has historically been deemed marginal, unimportant, and illegitimate, and to trouble both traditional Chicano culture and, beyond that, Anglo-American practices of exclusion. In her introduction to the transcribed interviews Soveida states, "This interview is a composite of several 'cornerings' that took place between Miss Milcantos and myself, usually late at night, when she was tired after a long day's work. She would stop briefly, to rest, to talk to me as I recorded her, and to humor me, as she said, because it made me so happy" (307). Oralia's story does have a place; it belongs in the Blue House's kitchen as an oral narrative, told in snatches between tasks. Soveida adds, "Using a tape recorder, I tried to convince her that her life mattered and that her story needed to be told" (307).

However, the need to widen Oralia's audience and to centralize her presence brings it into an academic framework. As one might expect, J.V.'s scholarly training objects to Soveida's focus on "purely emotional, non-analytical details of a life spent in small gestures" and her lack of objectivity (311). Although he recognizes that Oralia is "a resource of valuable material" (311), academia cannot legitimate the telling of an experience as a subjective or emotional story; the divide here is presented as traditionally gendered, with an objective male rendition of material opposed to a personalized female narrative account. Ironically, it is Oralia who has advised Soveida to listen to women, saying that otherwise, "how will you ever expect to understand the human heart?" (137). Obviously the community agrees that these experiences should be told and heard; the real question, therefore, is how they should be told. Soveida's "emotional" and detailed focus that looks at "a life spent in small gestures" is in fact an acknowledgment that this story—and the responsibility for telling it—is not hers alone, but a collective one.

Soveida's term paper thus offers her a place from which to begin to understand her own personal history in a broader light, and to read her family life as symptomatic of a larger disease of the land and its history. It is an explicitly political expression of her own disenfranchisement, which contributes in part to helping contextualize the legacy of abuse that haunts her and allows her to insert and write herself into the history. In it she admits, "I grew up . . . a woman in a long line of battered women. Abuse was rampant, and it was mental, emotional, physical, spiritual, and sexual" (318). She brings to the surface the geographical, political, and historical dislocations that have, up until now, existed only as traces in the book. Trauma and abuse, that is, have been narrated on a psychological, personal, and sexual level, but not on a political and historical one.

In some respects the term paper works as another voice in the narrative, perhaps most explicitly Chávez's authorial voice. The narrative strategy—to articulate the unspeakable by conveying it in a term paper—shows how the formal adopted discourse of academia can express the trauma of both personal and national trauma, and disclose their interrelatedness. The boundaries of the domestic spaces (houses and homes) of the earlier parts of the novel expand when Soveida asks at the outset of her paper, "What homeland have our men?" (315), and establishes that they are born into a borderland existence that breeds confusion and placelessness. The men are "born to women divided between worlds, México to the south, the United States to the north" and thus are "born in bondage" (315). She refers to the violent conquest that robs them of their legacy, and the inherent birthright of subjugation and suppression that comes to men "conceived in anger and frustration and born to mothers who knew no real home, no real peace" (315).

Although Soveida's main argument is that such a legacy of anger and homelessness has resulted in men's violence toward women (an emotional and physical violence), the significant issue here is her representation of abusive behavior as a consequence of political and geographic dispossession due to Anglo-American insertions into the borderlands. The entire novel's explicit focus on abuse and violence, and its rootedness in New Mexico as the location of that abuse, thus needs to be read through Soveida's interpretation: one that views the abuse through generations of political homelessness. Thus the term paper highlights the novel's implicit intent: to talk about political displacement, and the personal and psychological effects of that displacement on families. At this point in the novel, then, readers are asked to rethink the worlds of the book so that the various houses and dwellings occupied by Soveida and by other characters become part of a national landscape.[34] Crucially, Soveida also explains the roots of disenfranchisement, and the nature of the community's relationship to its land. The men, she says, were born to fathers who "were the lowest of laborers" and who "were animals who were expected to toil in the fields of others" (315).

This history of disenfranchisement from the land one labors on not only echoes Regino's role in "Compadre" but also adds a specter of shameful irony to the portraits of Chata and Oralia in this novel. As figures that continually turn their surroundings into beautiful home-spaces but simultaneously remain on the margins of those homes, never legally being able to lay any claims of ownership to them because of their class positions, they critically trouble the landscape. Despite their rootedness they do not quite belong, suggesting that the national border exerts its long historical legacy in all directions, across place and into the present time. This national and class-based disenfranchisement, at the root of the collective psyche and lying behind every moment of violence, is multifaceted: it separates people from their native land, it mistreats immigrants who cross the border, and it is responsible for generations of economic hardship and poverty.

Soveida continues to explore the history of Mexican American cultural disenfranchisement, first by examining the psychological effects of being admonished, educated, and punished in a language other than Spanish, "that was not their own, that did not sound of home" (316), and second by describing the way that her family's cuisine was othered in its own land. She says, "Our fathers and mothers brought to those schools a meal unfamiliar to others: tortillas and beans, no sandwiches of white bread eaten in the sunlight, but dark food, tasting of earth, hard work, and clay pots, boiled over wood stoves in that one big room where many children scampered and then later slept four or more to a bed" (316). In both cases there is a historical precedent for displacement as the dominant culture marginalizes the sounds, tastes, and textures of the land's cultural codes. However, because of the novel's emphasis on the sanctity of hard work, and the laborer's intimate and ancestral connection to the land, the very description of "foreign," unfamiliar food in fact centralizes and valorizes it. We know, based on Mara's and Oralia's stories earlier on, that the flavor and experience of food come about through one's emotional relationship not just to the food but also to one's memories and community. We are also told that food that tastes of hard work is delicious: earlier, in a chapter about El Farol's employees temporarily losing their meal rights, Soveida comments, "It was nice to finish a long shift and then eat a plate of red enchiladas in the back of the kitchen at one of the little tables set there for the staff. The food always tasted so good after you'd worked hard serving others" (298). This kind of historical politicization of cultural practices thus revalorizes domestic labor and makes it part of the text's broader reterritorialization of the land.

RECLAIMING SOUTHWESTERN TERRAINS:
MEXICO AND NEW MEXICO

One of the main ways in which the text challenges U.S. national identity is by recording positive memories of Mexico in the later parts of the narrative, and by foregrounding the physical topography of the New Mexican borderlands. Early in the novel, however, negative images of both Mexico and New Mexico are prevalent, emphasizing the unhealthy historical legacy that they exert in the region. Mexico itself appears in the first few pages of the novel, which describe the Dosamantes patriarch Manuel's migration across the border. This is the only national border crossing in the text, and although it is recounted without anxiety—"He came to the U.S. through Nuevo Laredo, and worked for a while in Texas. His destination was California but he never made it" (5)—it sets into motion a series of events that will position Mexico as the ghostly and abject "other" of the text. Initially, Manuel works in West Texas on a ranch, until the owner's unattractive daughter, Tobarda, seeks him out. By now, the land has already exerted an effect on him: "that magic, soul-sinking pull of West Texas had affected him. He longed to stay awhile, maybe a long time, in that place that had almost brought him peace" (5). To escape Tobarda, however, he has to escape Texas, too. He sleeps with Tobarda and then walks away, wishing he could love her. In leaving Tobarda he also leaves behind all his photographs of Mexico, and, according to the text, all his memories of his homeland. Thus, as in *The Last of the Menu Girls*, the important border is not so much the national one that divides the United States and Mexico as the psychological and emotional one that differentiates between different areas of the borderland: Texas and New Mexico. Tobarda and Texas are remembered as dry and parched and unforgiving, and Manuel runs and runs "toward the heat and the desert, toward the mesquite and the scrub brush" (7). When he stops running, he finds himself in Agua Oscura ("dark water"), and responds to the severity of this land "as a hearty, hungry woman does to lovemaking" (7). He enjoys the dramatic change of the land when it responds to his toil—"Water was this land's lover, and this love affair, this push and pull of nature with man, a man with his spirit, was what drew him to Agua Oscura. It allowed him to feel, at last, at home" (7)—and understands the extent to which the fertility of the land is due to his own labor and connection to it.

Because of Manuel, Soveida's secondhand memory of Mexico becomes associated with the haunting memory of Tobarda, who acts like an avenging ghost on the text: "Tobarda was a parched memory. . . . What became of Tobarda and his photographs, he didn't know. After he lost his photographs, he lost contact with the world of his birth: Guanajuato, that celebrated place where the clay in the earth preserved its buried corpses. Yes, he was far away from those human mummies that were later dug up and displayed for the tourists: leering men, defiled women, and pathetic children, with leathery, caked limbs, dusty, sparse hair, flaccid breasts and crumbling penises that reminded him of who he was, where he was always going" (7). The sense of morbidity that haunts Manuel's descendents, and the "ash" (4) that seems to coat Soveida's tongue as she struggles to make sense of the family's narratives, originates in Mexico, a place here defined through dust and death, in contrast to Agua Oscura's fertile hopefulness. In New Mexico Manuel shifts his perspective, knowing that "he would never again see those [Mexican] mountains, those valleys" and that "the view was now of another land, a land where his children would grow and flourish" (8). But Tobarda still haunts his dreams, so that even in the daytime he associates her with a particular "scent of decay" that can transport him back to Guanajuato, to Texas, or to "the grave" (8). The legacy that Mexico has imparted on the family is thus that of ghosts, graves, and burial sites, although it remains a largely inarticulate legacy until Soveida acknowledges it as part of the U.S. geopolitical landscape.

Mexico is also associated with Mexican migrant workers: references to them illustrate the way that national "otherness" (Mexicanness) is manifested in and perpetuated through the borderlands' structural classism. This systemic classism clearly relegates migrant workers to a position of socioeconomic dependency in the region. They are "mojados from el otro lado . . . people who needed jobs, jobs [Dolores] let them do for her, at little pay" (11). Mexico is best experienced from a distance: too close, and it becomes abject, certainly undesirable. Connie, Larry's mother, for example, sends him to the north, away from New Mexico so that he will meet and marry someone Anglo, because for her there are "two main races: Anglo and Mexican," and she is a "Mexican Mexican, a once-middle, now-upper class American who was proud of her Mexican roots, just make sure they're clean and don't shove them in my face" (146). Her internalized racism is later more fully explored in Soveida's narrative account of Albert Chanowski, a lecherous old man who is one of Soveida's regular customers at El Farol. His chapter gives us a negative view of both Agua Oscura and Mexicans from an Anglo point of view. In it he recollects the Mexican women he once knew in Mexico City and

Acapulco, animalizing them as wild hairy creatures that nevertheless fascinate and attract him. About Agua Oscura he thinks, "He didn't care for this place, not really, anyway. And yet the West had a way of growing on you. He could have felt comfortable here, if it weren't for all the Mexicans speaking Spanish in the street. This was the good old U.S.A., but you'd never know it. Not that many pressures here, and yet something about it, the poverty, the mess—and all those Mexicans. . . . He couldn't make his home here. Settle down. Die here. In the dust?" (239). Like the tourist in "Compadre" who complained about the topographical mess of New Mexico, Albert finds the geographical landscape frighteningly dusty and morbid, and the cultural landscape threateningly foreign to the rest of the United States, so foreign, in fact, that it seems set apart from the "good old U.S.A." The text, of course, centralizes the region's Mexican culture, rendering the Anglo perspective to the margins and troubling "Americanness" as a definitive or singular national identity. Albert's voice, however, although brief, is disruptive, giving us a taste of something larger and broader—racial, sexual, and class-based prejudices—that we are to understand always lies at the edges of the text.[35]

Clearly, in order to articulate a decolonized geopolitical identity that will legitimate and strengthen Mexican American identity in the borderland region, both Mexican and New Mexican lands need to be recovered. Mexico begins to be reclaimed in Soveida's college term paper, where she remembers it as a substantial and positive place. She specifically acknowledges its status as an ancestral and political homeland but also pays attention to its geographical landscape, noting that the men in her family have come from "the sierras and mesas of our homeland, México" (316). She also centers the nation of Mexico as the birthplace of cultural and racial mestizaje, and as the root and origin of the "world of borders" that still belongs to them and still "flows in [their] blood" (316). The emphasis on the geography of origin—the mesas and sierras—connects the people to the land and, like the stories in *The Last of the Menu Girls*, remaps and shifts the borders until New Mexico is explicitly traced with the cultural and geopolitical presence of old Mexico. It is this level of understanding—that the "world of borders" is porous and layered with textures that connect Soveida's U.S. landscape with that of her great-grandfather's homeland—that allows her to reclaim the desert landscape of Agua Oscura.

In Agua Oscura, toward the end of the book, Soveida falls in love with Tirzio, J.V.'s married older brother, and becomes pregnant with his baby. Although the relationship cannot last, it plays an important role in the process of healing and recovering the New Mexican terrain. Importantly, everything about Tirzio immediately represents wetness, shifting all her prior relationships with men into drought-ridden landscapes that were barely noticeable at the time. The first time she and Tirzio make love, they are near a river, and it begins to storm. They get drenched in the rain, and get into his van. When she looks into his eyes, she sees "clear eyes, no fear. I could swim out to sea" (353). Inside his humid van in the rain, his kisses are "salty," and the perspiration and rainwater on their skins mix. The images of water in the desert integrate and heal the history of ghosts that hark all the way back to the dry and abandoned Tobarda in the Texan desert, and the dry forgotten landscape of Mexico. In other words, with Tirzio, Soveida is able to cleanse the personal experiences of abuse that she has suffered, and express them, for the first time, as a healing of the thirsty natural land around her. She is also able to imagine, like a mirage, a world beyond yet simultaneously within this desert, understanding that she can "swim out to sea" even in the dry desert, and thus connect to the place in unexpected and new ways.

The descriptions of the desert in this brief final section of the book are the most lush and the most detailed, as if Soveida seems to recognize that making the connection between the local and the national, and the interior and the exterior landscapes is crucial to articulating a collective new national identity that blends Mexico and the United States. Although Soveida is Tirzio's "other" woman, the mistress who ostensibly always remains absent from the official family record, and although their baby will be illegitimate, their relationship is clearly celebrated and legitimated by the quenching and healing nature of their union. Their love-making is "as natural as the sudden storm," and afterward she says, "I felt cleansed, whole again, no small wonder in that vast desert of so little rain" (354). While with Ivan she felt malaise and sickness, and with Veryl (her second husband) only dryness, with Tirzio she becomes pregnant: itself no small feat because of the endometriosis that has plagued her for years. She is, finally, at ease rather than diseased.

The relationship with Tirzio does not survive because he has a family that he cannot leave. But he provides fruition in her body and in her garden, helping her plant a small yard by her trailer, recovering and nurturing the previously unacknowledged desert landscape: "The buffalo grass was patchy, but after I'd watered it faithfully for some time it seemed to be finally taking hold. I wanted a desert garden and had recently planted a desert willow, several Mexican elders, and a variety of ocotilla, cholla, agave, and yucca plants, as well as a few nopals along the back of the trailer" (454). The natural landscape clearly reflects its personal and collective cultural history: it is a harsh place that requires labor and love, whose prickly fruit must be recognized and rewarded for what it is. Soveida does not mourn the loss of Tirzio as she mourned Ivan and Veryl because Tirzio seems to become part of the landscape itself. After she tells him about the baby and they decide to end their affair, he is silent: "Tirzio avoided my eyes, returning his gaze to the majesty of the Lagrimas Mountains. He took my hand slowly and held it firmly. Then, with a deep sigh, he bent his head. We both looked at each other, and then toward the mountains. Gathering strength from stone, Tirzio quietly began to cry" (456). The mountains, again a feature of the landscape that Soveida has barely acknowledged until now, become foregrounded as she establishes a sense of peace within herself.

The final lengthy description of the physical landscape appears after Tirzio leaves, as Soveida sits outside alone, listening to the song of the cicadas, the thunder rumbling in the distance, and the crackling lightning behind the mountains. She says, "I could smell rain. I would sit outside and await its approach. Surely it would come and nourish the yellow and blue desert flowers in the sand, the white yucca flowers by the side of the winding road, the ocotillo's red-tipped tendrils waving to the seemingly empty sky, the nopal's sweet, blood-red fruit" (457). The "surely" denotes faith, while the tangible and sensory expression of desert flowers in the wilderness represents her explicit connection to the earth. By the end of the novel, the external geographic landscape has been watered and nourished, and the internal landscape of the Blue House has also been cleansed free of ghosts. In the last chapter of the book, "The Blue House," Mamá Lupita has moved into the Brown House with Dolores, and given the old Blue House to Soveida. After Chata and Soveida clean out the Blue House, which Chata calls "a good house" (463), Soveida paints it bright colors, making it "full of life and light" (465). From this space, Soveida can raise her baby and continue to create a narrative born out of a fertile history, spectered by women who through it assert their legitimate presence on the geographical and literary landscape of their New Mexican homes. Such legitimation, of course, represents a new geopolitical identity for Latinas that deconstructs the U.S.-Mexico border and decolonizes the nation-space of the Southwest, rendering it in many ways inseparable from Mexico.

2 / Mestizaje in the Midwest: Remapping National Identity in the American Heartland in Ana Castillo's *Sapogonia* and Sandra Cisneros's *Caramelo*

As the introduction demonstrated, U.S. anxiety about nationhood and citizenship has long been expressed through a rhetoric of unbelonging whereby the spatial, political, and cultural separation of the United States from Latin America has often rendered Latinos/as within the United States into outsiders, no matter their place of birth or historical continuity on the land. In this chapter the central exploratory question of the book—how Latina writers have challenged this rhetoric of unbelonging—is directed more closely at the concept of the "thickening borderlands" discussed in the introduction. The legitimation of Mexican Americans that we saw in chapter 1 clearly emerges out of a new geopolitical identity that reimagines the United States' geographical and cultural identity as part of a collective with Mexico, decolonizing the nation-space and the political border of the Southwest, and allowing it to be recognized as a transnational space, a former—and ongoing—part of Mexico. In this chapter the midwestern settings of Ana Castillo's *Sapogonia* and Sandra Cisneros's *Caramelo* need to be understood not only in relation to the southwestern settings of Denise Chávez's texts, and not only as relatively new destinations for Latinos/as in the United States, but also as complex representations of Latino belonging in a "thickened" physical and cultural borderland that has extended northward, into the heartland of the United States.[1]

The "thickening borderlands" discussed by Gilberto Rosas refers to various particularities of the borderland condition that are no longer necessarily fixed in the southwestern United States.[2] Rosas's interest lies in the ways that the state's power, demonstrated through militarized policing practices along the geographical U.S.-Mexico border, functions under a condition of "exceptionality" in that physical location, constituting an exemption from the normal constraints of the law that permits the state to practice violence upon immigrant bodies (or those that appear to be immigrants) in the borderland area.[3] Such "policeability" not only militarizes the border but also elaborates notions of undocumented "illegality," and renders race, in the borderlands, into an ideologically charged social and political relation instead of an attribute or simply a "color."[4] For Rosas, an interesting (and alarming) consequence of such exceptionality is not only the number of violations that occur against U.S. citizens on the border but also the fact that when the border is "thickened," such acts of vigilantism and policing become legitimated throughout the space of the nation.

However, Rosas does contend that "suggestive of the thickening of the borderland condition, potent new political imaginaries have likewise emerged in conjunction with this intensified exceptionality."[5] In the introduction I briefly discussed some contemporary examples of this extended vigilantism (such as the Texas Virtual Border Watch Program); here, I am interested in how Castillo's and Cisneros's novels challenge the nation's identity by depicting this midwestern landscape of the border (this "thickened borderland") as a newly imagined site of political empowerment. Without the more obvious geopolitical markers that we saw in Chávez—the contiguous border with Mexico and the ancestral topography—this chapter asks how the texts trouble the United States' political borders, its understanding of citizenship, and its definition of certain bodies as legal or illegal. How does the U.S. heartland become reimagined as part of Latin America, embedding the two nation-spaces within one another? And, finally, what kind of "potent new political imaginary" has emerged in this space? I argue that while the novels (particularly Castillo's) show the marked extension of policing and racial governance in the Midwest, they also challenge this geopolitical extension of a policed space by infusing and empowering the thickened borderland with practices of mestizaje, thus troubling and radicalizing normative definitions of nationhood.

Both the introduction and chapter 1 explored how the literature undermines the United States' sense of nationhood based on geographical borders; clearly the southwestern narratives imagine the healing of colonized topographical spaces through the conjoining of Mexico and the United States. In this chapter Ana Castillo's *Sapogonia* and Sandra

Cisneros's *Caramelo* also remap Latin America as part of the United States, but use mestizaje as the predominant geopolitical strategy, displacing and deconstructing the political borders of the United States, relocating them throughout the nation, and thus engaging in a new nation-building activity. Broadly speaking, mestizaje, as Ilan Stavans notes, defines a "pluralistic Latino identity," and is the "physical, social, religious, political, and cultural miscegenation of foreign and indigenous elements."[6] Historically, however, the term refers to the new ethnicity that emerged during the colonial period in Mexico when Spaniards and natives crossbred. And Gloria Anzaldúa, as I discuss below, defines the by now well-known "mestiza consciousness" as one that is comfortable with contradictions, can reject the notion of a single origin, and recognizes the border area as a porous fluid space.[7] Bringing together these elements—the miscegenation, the creation of a new ethnicity, and the deconstruction of borders—I ask, what is the effect of a mestiza consciousness and praxis outside of the Southwest? What does such a presence mean in the Midwest, and what are the implications of thus reimagining and rewriting Mexican American presence in the United States? I argue that mestizaje, in *Sapogonia* and *Caramelo*, creates a new blended "borderland" nation that has been extended far beyond its geographic location, and that is based on connections with, rather than separation from, the United States' southern neighbors. As part of this newly extended borderland nation, the narratives foreground indigenous history in Latin America, in turn rewriting the politics of race in the United States. The Midwest, then, is reimagined not just as part of Latin America but also legitimated as an indigenous and mestizo land that is home to an indigenous and mestizo nation.

In an important way Anzaldúa's own interpretation of mestizaje sees it as a geopolitical practice that demonstrates the same politics of location as the writers I discuss in this chapter. While her narrative in *Borderlands/La Frontera* focuses closely on the geographical and historical landscape of the Southwest from which the praxis of mestizaje has most frequently emerged, it also thickens and extends into a consideration of Chicano/a lived experiences and national unbelonging throughout the United States. She adapts her formulation of mestizaje from José Vasconcelos's imagined "cosmic race," but it was originally intended as a nation-building project in Mexico's early twentieth-century postrevolutionary context, one that hoped to incorporate the diversity of Mexico's peoples—in particular, the indigenous populations—into a new nation-state.[8] It is therefore appropriate to read Anzaldúa's mestizaje, both in the southwestern geographical borderlands and in their extended "thickened" state across the United States, as a distinctive act of nation building. This nation building forges a strong relationship between a people (mestizos) and a land (the U.S. Southwest) and both troubles and renews the United States' cultural, racial, and territorial understandings of national identity.

Anzaldúa's concern with physical landscape is obviously central to her project. Maria Herrera-Sobek, one of the critical theorists eulogizing Anzaldúa's work in the PMLA after the latter's death in 2004, notes that *Borderlands* is imbued with a sense of physical place, and "evidences a will to reconfigure this loss of place, space, and history and reterritorialize the Chicano population in the American Southwest."[9] As if swayed by its subject matter, Herrera-Sobek's own theoretical piece also reads like a lyrical ode to the past and the place, continuing, in a sense, Anzaldúa's political gesture of taking back the land through writing. She notes that the land is Anzaldúa's "muse"—"Chicanos are the land, and vice-versa."[10] Generally speaking, the last chapter of *Borderlands* is the most frequently anthologized section of Anzaldúa's work, and has come to be recognized as a voice of authority on the theory of borderlands and mestizaje. However, the previous chapters that describe the Tejana's displacement from land, culture, language, and storytelling play a significant role in preparing for and enabling that climactic final chapter in which she articulates the emergent borderland consciousness. In chapter 2, for example, Anzaldúa's address of the sensitive issue of the status of homosexuals in the Chicano community attempts to relocate the Chicana subject firmly in place, through writing. And chapter 5's discussion of language—her description of the "linguistic terrorism" incurred by hostile Anglo-Americans toward Chicanos—works similarly as a political response to Euroamerican displacement of Chicanos from their land.

In the first chapter of *Borderlands*, "The Homeland, Aztlán," Anzaldúa combines Mexican and U.S. history (precolonial, colonial, 1800s, and contemporary) with personal accounts and memories of living in the border area, refiguring place by rewriting the U.S.-Mexico border as "una herida abierta where the Third World grates against the first and bleeds," forming a scab and creating a third country, a border culture.[11] The chapter opens up with an untitled poem that destabilizes the border itself, setting up a contradiction: the geographical border is a material reality and also an arbitrary man-made wound. The poem, which precedes the discussion of borderlands, ends by emphasizing the triumph of nature over political and national boundaries, stating that "the skin of the earth is seamless. / The sea cannot be fenced, / el mar does not stop at borders" (25). Anzaldúa calls upon the African goddess Yemaya to legitimate the forces of nature and restore the land to what it should be; it is Yemaya who "blew that wire fence down" (25). In this way, Anzaldúa gives voice to suppressed cultural presences that oppose "the white man" (25). She also anticipates the remainder of the text's strong identification with indigenous heritages by ending the poem with a nationalistic call to the future that sounds in some respects like a call to arms: "This land was Mexican once, / was Indian always / and is. / And will be again" (25). Here Indian connection to the land dominates over the constructed political nation-spaces of both the United States and Mexico. This nationalistic call, however, is hesitant, as the pause or gap between "And" and "will" implies a moment of waiting and holding back.[12]

If we then turn to the book's final chapter, keeping in mind not just the formation and characteristics of a mestiza consciousness that it describes but also that call for a return to the land that underlines most of *Borderlands*, we see immediately that the last section of chapter 7, "El Retorno," performs that return. Anzaldúa writes that she has "come back" to the Rio Grande area, and describes its landscape in order to explain not just her love for the place but also her despair at its socioeconomic decline: "I still feel the old despair when I look at the unpainted, dilapidated, scrap lumber houses consisting mostly of corrugated aluminum. Some of the poorest people in the United States live in the Lower Rio Grande Valley, an arid and semi-arid land of irrigated farming, intense sunlight and heat, citrus groves next to chaparral and cactus" (111). Despite her traumatic memories of the place, she loves this "tragic valley" that has survived "possession and ill-use by five countries" (112) and that is now even poorer due to the borderlands depression of 1982. By the end of the chapter she legitimates Mexican belonging on the land with a visual memory, in which she imagines generations of Mexican American women making a communal and peaceful home on it by productively working the land again. She sees her own family, both as a memory of the past and as a vision of the future, bending to the ground to work it, baring tiny green shoots to the elements, and sustaining them: "We water them . . . we harvest them" (113). The soil constantly changes forms, becoming impregnated and productive, almost, in an Anzaldúan sense, shamanistic and transformative. Thus she creates an aesthetic of land and geography that respects and enables the earth's ability to produce and sustain its workers. Most powerfully, she repeats the verse of the poem from chapter 1, but with a significant difference: "This land was Mexican once / was Indian always / and is. *And will be again*" (113, my emphasis). This time, there is no gap—no hesitation—in the legitimation of Indian presence on the land. The call for arms in chapter 1 has been enabled not only by the mestiza consciousness of chapter 7 but also by the cumulative effect of facing and healing the rage of the intercepting chapters. Ultimately, Anzaldúa's call for arms is a gesture of belonging: Chicanos and mestizos must own the land that they work, and Euro-Americans must acknowledge and legitimate the long presence of Indians on it, effectively reconsidering the history and memory by which the nation has written its identity.

Although Anzaldúa's writing focuses on her specific connection to the Southwest, her politics of relocation is relevant to us here when she considers the extension of Chicano life throughout the United States. In chapter 5, in her discussion of language as place, she notes that language is frequently "a homeland closer than the Southwest—for many Chicanos today live in the Midwest and the East" (77), and identifies the emerging conflicts that occur when that nuance, this apparent "tolerance for ambiguity," seeps through the physical borderlands and into North American ideological understandings of racial identity. She refigures Vasconcelos's mestizaje by highlighting the suppressed indigenous populations that he hoped to assimilate, showing how the mestiza consciousness adapts to the specifics of this location. In Castillo's *Sapogonia* and Cisneros's *Caramelo* we see how this extended midwestern mestizaje operates in its new location: disrupting and rewriting the narratives that determine the nation's ethnic identity, and dislocating its myths of origin, race, geography, and homeland. Through this relocated mestiza consciousness, *Sapogonia* draws attention to the presence of indigenous cultures in Latin America, bringing them into the Midwest.[13] *Caramelo* similarly troubles the space of the Midwest by acknowledging Indianness as part of both Mexican and U.S. mestiza praxis and presence. The implications of this mestiza consciousness and its suppressed Indian nucleus upon the heartland cannot be overstated: both novels suggest that the language of mestizaje, of the borderlands, is or can now become the language of the entire United States and of U.S. literature. In effect, then, the nation's new geopolitical identity is written as one in which mestizaje validates cultural "otherness" and mestizo nationhood becomes embedded within the space of U.S. citizenship. In this space Mexico and Latin America are refigured beyond the geographical southwestern borderlands, into the thickened borderlands of the United States where Latino belonging is validated.[14]

Borders, Bodies, and Art: Confronting Indianness in *Sapogonia*

Castillo's creation of a fictional nation—Sapogonia—in her second novel itself works as a significant geopolitical strategy that disrupts normative understandings of national identity.[15] In the prologue to the novel she describes Sapogonia as a "distinct place in the Americas where all mestizos reside, regardless of nationality, individual racial composition, or legal residential status—or, perhaps, because of all of these."[16] Although Sapogonia is a nation (of mestizos), the usual categories that would define nationhood (such as birthplace, residence, and race) are undermined by its mestizo population, or by mestizaje itself. And although it is a geographical homeland for mestizos, it is "not identified by modern boundaries" (2), and seems to resist the demarcation of nation-spaces through political borders. As a fabricated nation, then, Sapogonia occupies a fictional space, and can exist anywhere and everywhere regardless of physical location. In this landscape of the imagination mestizaje comes to define a migrating nation-space that is not tied to location or place. It is, in effect, a nation without political or geographical borders: a nation constituted only by its population of mestizos and its migrant status.

Despite this apparently transnational state of nationhood, Sapogonia is also a Central or South American nation that endures the legacy of a long colonial history and ongoing civil wars. Its history of slavery, genocide, immigration, and civil uprisings has affected the political and geographic landscape, and while it seems not to be identified by modern boundaries, its political borders tighten during the country's civil wars, emphasizing the shifting subjective reality of material borders. Most significant, the text suggests that these wars, together with Sapogonia's socioeconomic and political dependence on the United States, and the latter's imperial presence in the hemisphere— "international achievement now weighs almost exclusively on recognition by the United States of America" (2)—have contributed to the mestizo population's northward migration beyond its national borders. Furthermore, despite a dominant national population of mestizos in Sapogonia, where "racial composition" does not matter, it seems that racial appearance does matter. Castillo refers in general terms to the Sapogón's attempts to pass as North American (2), and in more specific terms when she examines her main character Max's acts of passing once he is in the United States, suggesting that Sapogonians themselves have internalized North America's anxiety about indigenous ancestry.

She makes an explicit point about Sapogonian physiognomy, noting that while through mimicry and "by affectation he [the Sapogón] may acquire the mannerisms and the idioms of the North American with the intent of assimilation," his "genetic make-up immediately sets him apart," and specifically, his "indigenous blood" and Spanish ancestry make him "shorter in stature with dark features not characteristic of the Aryan or Anglo" (2). This indigenous ancestry is closely paired with the geographic space of the Americas and strongly overrides any European or Latin-European ancestry: the Sapogón can only "fake" a Mediterranean background as long as he remains silent about his Sapogonian nationality (2).

In its prologue alone, then, the narrative clearly begins to question the ethical dimensions of intra-American politics, history, and race relations, setting up Sapogonia as a ready exporter of migrants to the United States. Whether they are political refugees from their country's civil war (as are some of the more marginal characters in the novel), economic refugees, or simply leaving for the adventure of life in the United States (Max), they all migrate northward, and they are all racially indigenous.[17] Throughout the novel, set predominantly in Chicago, Castillo shows how those indigenous racial bodies, through their crossing over into the United States and their very presence in the midst of the United States, thicken and empower the borderland. In representing the continent's undesirable history and troubling political and national U.S. identity, they reimagine that entire history so that it becomes a part of the midwestern United States' geopolitical consciousness.[18] My reading of *Sapogonia* as a challenge to national identity complements several recent critical interpretations of the novel that discuss the novel's presentation of mestizaje: Roland Walter suggests that through the potential for change inherent in mestizaje, various cultural practices can be transformed; Kelli Johnson, who reads *Sapogonia* comparatively with Castillo's other work, argues that the mestiza experience represents a home-space of political involvement for women; and Esther Sánchez-Pardo González, reading all of Castillo's novels together with Cherrie Moraga's work, notes the ways that mestizaje is a useful model for survival on the borderlands.[19] However, the novel's critical reception remains relatively narrow, and although critics recognize the potential for change inherent in its presentation of mestiza consciousness, mestizaje's important role in the construction and reconstruction of nation has not, until now, been discussed.

BORDERS

As part of its challenge to U.S. understandings of nationhood, indigenous mestizaje in the novel interrogates the nation's geographical borders. Clearly, a crucial part of the nation's narrative of identity happens at the border, as I demonstrated in the introduction. *Sapogonia*'s geopolitical strategy, however, interprets the border as an inherently anxious site because of the way it seems to create (as well as disallow) American citizenship. Although the border itself does not define one's national identity (which is presumably fixed in place before one arrives at a border), for the illegal aliens in the book who cross successfully, it becomes the site at which an assumed U.S. citizenship and nationhood are enacted, and thus where they come into being. At the border, therefore, the act of crossing becomes the moment at which one's body is determined to be legal or illegal, and desirable or undesirable. In a sense, then, the geographical border in the novel can be said to create national and political identities, ones that are in flux and subject to the arbitrary whims of the moment, but that are nevertheless perceived as having either illegal presence in the nation (a kind of criminal unbelonging) or legal presence (legitimate belonging). The novel in turn addresses this performative moment of national identity-formation by showing how mestizos, at the moment of crossing into the United States, can take on U.S. citizenship at that border site and thus redefine that citizenship as and through a mestizo and indigenous presence.

Integral to this "passing"—in fact, the definitive element of passing, the very thing that makes this a moment of passing—is the simultaneous presence of the illegal alien's otherness, a foreignness that haunts the alien's adopted mantle of U.S. citizenship and thus the very nation-state itself. The novel is full of examples of successful and unsuccessful crossings both at the nation's geographical borders and its political borders throughout the nation-state. And with every crossing of a Sapogón into the United States, the contours that shape the nation shift, reorganizing the geographical and political landscape so that it is forced to absorb, or at least acknowledge, mestizos. Namely, mestizaje begins to reorganize the map. The sense that borders are everywhere thus becomes part of the novel's geopolitical strategy, as it creates a constant shifting of national identities, bringing Latin Americanness into the United States. However, the explicit nature of that mestizaje within the borders of the United States, or on the edges of it, varies throughout the text. The novel's material and geographical border, for example, illustrates not just the establishment of identity that occurs there as people enter (or fail to enter) the United States but also its position as a peephole into Latin America's otherness and material poverty, and its own anxious porousness.

Latin and Central American immigrants on the southern side of the U.S. border are seen as undesirable, making the border a site of anxious contestation and violence. As Max remarks, when you bring up "our amigos" south of the border, the public imagines "gritty, snot-nosed children; women in dust-covered skirts squatting before a griddle over hot stones, patting the crude dough between their dark palms for the meal of tortillas; and their men, loathsome bandit types, with beady black eyes and those wretched bodies, fought like those of desert mules—and they wrinkle their noses as if someone has just passed air" (117). The "amigos'" proximity and abject poverty are disruptive, as is their marked racial otherness ("dark palms," "beady black eyes"), cultural primitiveness, criminal tendencies ("bandit types") and "wretched bodies." As mestizo bodies so close to the border, they seem always-already about to cross that border, making it always permeable, and tapping into the fear illustrated in examples from popular culture in the introduction. Obviously, the exaggerated stereotypes here contribute to the nation's construction of its foreign, frightening "other" against which it defines itself: a self-definition that depends on building up such anxieties about the permeability of borders between nations.

Max, the novel's Sapogonian protagonist who over the course of the novel lives in the United States as an illegal resident alien, a refugee, a legal resident alien, and finally a citizen, notes that the focus on one's "nationality or place of origin" (84) begins at the U.S.-Mexico border. However, the text also demonstrates how national borders materialize wherever immigration officers show up, so that any geographical point in the country—airports, bus stations, or interstate highways in the Midwest—becomes exemplary of the thickened borderland with its potential for exceptional policeability, vigilantism, and violence. In one episode, for example, after Max is deported from Los Angeles to Tijuana and then attempts to cross the border back into the United States, we see just how illegitimate foreign bodies and presences are in the United States. In Tijuana, Max poses as Mexican American (concealing his Sapogonian identity) and befriends a North American man and asks him for a ride across the border into the United States. Here, if he were to choose to self-identify as a Sapogón (even a light-skinned one), he would risk openly displaying his mestizaje and his indigenous background. Clearly, he hopes that appearing Mexican American, while still undesirable, at least confers U.S. citizenship upon his mestizo body. However, under interrogation at the border, the inebriated driver describes Max as "some greaser that caught a ride with me," and in this way turns him in. Even at this level of inebriation, the driver remains attuned to Max's foreignness and unbelonging above all else: interpellating Max's (false) Mexican American identity as illegitimate within the borders of the United States. And Max's attempt (and failure) to pass as Mexican American is doubly significant: the driver writes Mexican rather than U.S. nationality upon Max's body (he is a "greaser"). Under the layered disguises of appropriated Mexican American and Mexican identities, then, Max's actual Sapogón nationality becomes even more invisible.[20]

As in Chávez's work, borders thus appear and disappear in part depending on one's political status in the land at a particular moment. In the United States, even as a light-skinned illegal alien far away from the physical border, Max is often "in hiding" (133). The first time he experiences the border as a threat, for example, is in Chicago. En route to Los Angeles, he arrives by mistake at the Chicago bus station. There he witnesses immigration officials interrogating some women (Pastora and her friend Perla) who "in their ethnic garb and dark hair" arouse suspicion (76). Although this time Max passes inconspicuously, dressed in denim pants, a sheepskin coat, and pale-skinned, his heart pounds with real fear as he watches them (75). He himself has only one moment of direct interaction with the officials—he drops his bus ticket and one of them retrieves and returns it, calling, "Hey you . . . Hey buddy" (76)— which only heightens the precariousness of his presence in this place: his momentary ability to erase a border occurs precisely at the point where others have involuntarily brushed up against it.

The text's most explicit moments of mestizo geopolitics emphasize the United States' refusal to recognize the conditions that often bring Latin Americans into the United States in the first place. We are reminded often of the socioeconomic hardships in Sapogonia, where the "burdened worker" has to move to the north, despite its discrimination and prejudice, because "as unsavory as the reception might have been there, it was more promising than living in his own country" (61). The novel highlights the United States' reluctance to acknowledge any ethical obligations toward Latin America, showing, for example, how it refuses to offer political asylum to Sapogonian refugees. When Pastora helps some Sapogonian refugees move into the Chicago area, driving them from Michigan to Illinois, and the Federal Bureau of Investigation (FBI) catches up with her in Indiana, they cannot be persuaded that the

Sapogonians should be given political asylum. Yet this very moment—
one where Sapogonians are refused legal presence in the United States—
is also one of marked mestizaje on the land, in the Midwest in particular. Even as the U.S. officials ignore the stories of their Latin American
neighbors, those stories—and their history and memory—penetrate into
the heartland. As the car carrying illegal immigrants makes its way to
Michigan it figuratively draws borderlines around the anxious occu-
pants of the vehicle, and remaps the Midwest as a border area. In this
way the political borders with Mexico and Latin America are redrawn
within and around the Chicago area, turning it into an explicit borderland and bringing its local and national identity into conversation with
the Southern Hemisphere.

Even legally resident Sapogonians mark the nation's cultural landscape with their otherness. Dora, for example, a more minor Sapogonian character, is married to an American citizen (Eduardo), but has
refused to apply for U.S. citizenship because "she wanted her presence in
the U.S. to remain a symbol of the political status of her country" (209).
That is, her presence in the United States speaks overtly to an absence
elsewhere: like all noncitizens, her body, language, and demeanor, and,
most important, her political status, recall an elsewhere, another location, and a speaking living memory of geographical otherness. In the
text it is precisely such an explicit and open acknowledgment of mestiza
nationhood—illustrated by default by all undocumented migrants from
Central and Latin America—that most challenges the nation's geopolitical identity.

BODIES

Whatever their status in the United States—legal alien, illegal alien,
citizen—all of the novel's Sapogonian characters are engaged, to an
extent, in acts of geopolitical mestizaje. Their very bodies exert a disruptive and troubling power: as Rafael Pérez-Torres explains, "a disjuncture
or rupture in ideology occurs through the dislocation experienced by
mestizo/a bodies" creating a "dislocation of identity."[21] This dislocation
of identity, one that calls up borders and other nations, turns the mestizo body into a "discursive site"[22] right in the midst of the very place
that tries continually to categorize and define it, suggesting, in effect, a
new ideological consideration of the boundaries of national identity, and
opening up the possibility of interconnectedness to other nation-spaces
within that identity. The central mestizo characters in the narrative all
show how some "Latinos/as" within the United States become fabricated

as an acceptable, to some extent typecast, part of the nation's identity. In fact, one could argue that all of them practice Latinidad as a form of instrumental ethnicity, using it to advance their social standing and/or careers.[23] Even in Chicago, a place where the narrator notes caustically, "one would never say one was simply Chicagoan, much less, American, but hyphenated and belonging to a particular ethnic origin" (307) and where there is no apparent need to pass, passing nevertheless occurs. Here, Maritza's, Alan's, and Max's bodies all function as sites of discursive anxiety because their Hispanic identity that is so welcomed—even applauded—has been specifically manufactured as European rather than indigenous. Even in a city that embraces multiculturalism and promotes itself as liberal and politically correct, their mestizaje must mark the landscape ambiguously.

Maritza Marín-Levy, a socialite who makes herself "visible at every opportunity" and is "extremely active in every Latino issue in the city that was guaranteed to make the news" (284), was adopted at birth by a Jewish couple. While it is not clear what her national origin is—her mother was either Cuban or Puerto Rican—she certainly cashes in on the sudden popularity of the Hispanic label. Her friend Miguel accuses her of ethnic opportunism: "When I first met you, Maritza, supposedly you were born in Cuba. That was during the days of the Venceremos Brigade, the popular left. It was cool to be associated with Castro. . . . Later, you became Puerto Rican," and he adds, "Of course, you're Latina now, Maritza! It's cool to be Hispanic, whatever that means!" (287, 288). Maritza, who is at the time dating the Latino mayoral candidate, Alan García, is, according to Miguel, "Proud to be Hispanic from her head of red hair to her red painted toenails" (288). Maritza moves between different Latina nationalities with apparent ease, rendering their cultural specificities invisible, and aggrandizing—and banking on—the viability of the marketable umbrella term "Hispanic." The sexy Maritza appears to be a caricature of the manufactured and malleable Latina, a Latina that the nation can find a place for within its borders. In fact, without a specific national origin, only a generalized Hispanidad made and commodified in the United States can give Maritza an ethnic identity that makes her foreignness palatable and manageable.

Beneath her instrumental identity, however, lies one that would be more detrimental, if it were to surface: Pastora points out, "If you really look at [Maritza] you can see the strains of African blood," but because of her Jewish surname, people "assume those are Semitic features" (320). Depending on how the beholder beholds, then, Maritza's physiognomy shifts and changes along a spectrum of ethnic otherness. Africanness has been subsumed and hidden beneath the more easily articulated Jewishness, as Maritza's name defines what her body will signify to others. With this revelation Castillo shows how African ancestry takes on a dissembling character: it remains present in its very status as a hidden thing, forcing a remembrance (of indigenous and African presence) rather than a forgetting. This kind of remapping of the nation-space also occurs with Alan García, who looks white but is not: "If you *study* his features, they could be Indian" (319, my emphasis). Although in the novel the consensus on García is that he "acts like a politician" (320), that is, passing as white, a particular kind of gaze marks his Latino body as specifically indigenous.

Max also attempts a similar strategy of indigenous erasure: his light-skinned physiognomy enables his body to pass, or at the very least, to resist absolute categorization. While he certainly does not belong to the white mainstream, he can carry off a Latin-European or Mediterranean background, and doing so brings him some fame and fortune in his career as a sculptor (142). But throughout the text his body also represents an anxious site of repressed memory and ancestry, as his indigenous heritage remains somehow apparent. His physiognomy is geographically ambiguous: ethnically "other," possibly Jewish. He is never mistaken for North African, "but always for European; if not Spanish, then Greek or Italian. Sometimes someone inquired discreetly if he did not have Semitic blood, the hook in the nose, the dark hair and beard" (26). Max's friend Girafa concurs, saying, "You look like a Jew, man" (43). Jewish ethnicity again offers a more palatable way to speak of foreignness, and represents the outermost limit of otherness, but it remains only a possible rather than certain ethnic marker.[24] In other words, the very fact that Max's body continually provokes questions and resists any absolute racial categorization points to its mestizaje. That mestizaje in turn points to the United States' own history of imperialism and highlights the role of that history in determining the creation of both borders and nationhood, forcing a reconceptualization of the nation that renders it part of Latin America.

The novel's characterization of Pastora most clearly illustrates the ways that Latino identity and indigenous culture can be absorbed into the national script. In one respect, she is as instrumental in her wielding of ethnic identity as the others. Her explicit display of indigenous ancestry in her singing performances on stage is precisely that: a display that showcases indigeneity. Indianness seems to become a spectacle: she wears Indian attire (122) or the traditional costume of Mayan women to look like a "quetzal, an aberration from the Central American highlands" (144). In contrast to the Spanish castanetist who opens one of her shows, Pastora is hugely popular. Here, the public's desire for a display of Indianness (and its rejection of European Spanish culture) reflects North America's fascination with its suppressed history, even as it resists connecting that history to its own national identity. Nevertheless, despite her commodification of indigenous cultures, Pastora's mestizaje marks the landscape in very unambiguous terms. As a "part Indian" herself (288), she often wears native garb outside of her performances on stage, thus inscribing her body with signatures of her indigenous history and ancestry. Her body, then, is not only clearly indigenous but also connected to her homeland, Sapogonia. She has also "inherited the earth-related features, coloring and instincts of indigenous ancestors" (352). This inherent connection between the land and her body emphasizes that her body, as she openly carries it, stamps her geographical history everywhere she goes, and in that respect, its very presence in the United States signals a disruptive challenge to the nation's borders.

Physically, too, she validates Indian beauty. She is not, Max notes, a European beauty ("she was not the enigmatic beauty of Da Vinci" [354]), but instead represents "the harsh enigma of nature's ferocity over man, the thrashing of a tornado, the scorching lava of the erupting volcano, the hurricane that swept away entire villages into the sea" (354). She is, in other words, a violent and natural upheaval, a disruption and disturbance of natural landscape and place. Max also imagines her as Coatlicue, the powerful serpent goddess: "Awesome Coatlicue, whose severed head was replaced with two streams of blood that became serpents' heads; the same blood that gave life demands it through war, the eternal struggle of all civilizations" (354), writing the disruption to the landscape as a specifically indigenous one. This indigenous disruption importantly reterritorializes the landscape through mestizo contradictions, as it evokes the ambiguous coexistence of deathly and life-giving forces.

COMMUNITY

Most important, though, Pastora's "instrumental" use of ethnicity is not for her own individual pursuit of fame, but to vocalize and address the serious concerns of poor Latinos/as in the city. Her "protest music" (120) is inspired by issues of social injustice and motivated by ideals of goodwill, collectivity, and community-oriented consciousness-raising. Thus the novel presents a consciousness of community responsibility that interrupts U.S. articulations of national identity. In addition, Pastora's powerful performances on stage allow her art "to be 'present'; that is, enacted, it is both a physical thing and the power that infuses it," creating a transformative experience for her listeners that changes the shape of their present place with the ghosts of elsewhere.[25] In other words, like the presence of an illegal alien, her singing highlights but also integrates otherness into an otherwise familiar setting. As a kind of modern Coatlicue, Pastora's performances, with their message of ambiguity and contradiction, and indigenous history, memory, and body, potentially threaten the nation's political understanding of its borders and identity.

Her most significant geopolitical troubling of space comes with her messages that attempt to connect global and local causes. This collective vision disrupts the model of individualism and capitalism under which most societal relations in the United States seem subsumed. The narrative makes it clear that the liberal politicians of Chicago's local government are interested in promoting only selective Latino causes. It is not surprising that Max's popularity endures while the public starts to lose interest in Pastora's urgent messages about the socioeconomic challenges that U.S. Latinos/as face in the local community. Soon enough, Pastora notices that "dominant society was closing again. The youth was interested in individual achievement, financial success. No one wanted to hear about their neighbors' starvation, rape and pillage in American cities. No one joined hands and together raised them up like chains of fists" (186). The public, though, interprets Max's sculptures—carved from the wood of his homeland, Sapogonia—as symbols of a distant, exoticized, and, most important, separate nation. Meanwhile, Pastora demonstrates the uncomfortable interconnectedness of Latin America and U.S. Latinos/as, forcing her audience to recognize—at least momentarily—the grim material reality of this second nation within the United States.

At a major press conference with the Latino mayor (García), Pastora, as the official Midwest delegate of the new Colloquium of U.S. Latinas, makes a presentation on the particular needs of working-class Latinas (310). Specifically, her goal is to raise awareness of the need for child care for working Latinas. Soon after she begins her speech, a member of the audience interrupts her, asking, "Do you work in the Hispanic community here in Chicago?" (310). To this, Pastora has a lengthy, impassioned response:

> To which community are you referring, sir? Are you referring to
> the Mexican community of the West Side or to the Puerto Rican

community of West Town? Do you mean the new Central American community in Logan Square or that of the Cuban residents on
Milwaukee Avenue? Do you mean, perhaps, to use "community"
in a broader sense and refer to all the countries of South America,
Mexico, Central America, and the Caribbean—in which case we
should not say Hispanic, because there are those territories, including Brazil, which constitutes one-fifth of South America and was
not settled by the Spaniards and therefore is not Hispanic. Or by
Hispanic, do you simply refer to the Spanish-speaking? Forty percent of the Guatemalan population doesn't speak Spanish and neither did my Yaqui mother when she came to live here. (311)

While within the story this speech is not wholly effective (she is quickly
dismissed), her explanation of the extensive national heterogeneity of
Latinos/as, and her remapping of Chicago as connected, through its
communities, to a multitude of geographical locations beyond local
and national borders, all challenge the rhetoric that attempts to classify
"Hispanics" into a single homogenous ethnic group. She imagines first
the various faces of the local community, and then expands outward
into a more transnational geography. She thus redraws the boundaries
of U.S. Latino/a identity, re-presenting Hispanics at the local, national,
and international level. And at the end of her speech she foregrounds a
non-European indigenous population of Central and Latin America and
the United States. As such, in articulating the complex socioeconomic
issues that face the community, highlighting their interconnectedness
to other nation-spaces and groups, and giving voice—or presence—to
indigenous groups, Pastora's speech represents an important moment of
resistance to the United States' closed imaginary of national history and
geography. Through its rewriting of borders, bodies, and local and international politics, mestizaje, as an ethnicity that is not tied to a particular
location, begins to belong to this midwestern borderland.

Dislocating Nations: Race, Geography, and Storytelling in *Caramelo*

In *Caramelo* multiple storytelling strategies and voices create a collective mestizaje that blends the United States' national identity with Mexico. Even the chronology at the end of the novel, which explains that the
2000 census "reveals [that] Latino and Asian immigrants, their children
and grandchildren, are remaking small towns and big cities across the

American heartland," dismantles normative understandings of the relationship between ethnicity and geography in historically white regions of the United States.[26] This emphasizes just how much the novel's midwestern setting is crucial to Cisneros's geopolitical strategy. The story—an epic-length account of four generations of the Reyes family and their migrations back and forth across the U.S.-Mexico border—recounts Mexico's history of mestizo national identity and Indian suppression, acknowledges the material and real impact of the U.S.-Mexico border, and explores the fictions that the United States and Mexico write about one another.

Given Cisneros's almost mainstream popularity, and the novel's lengthy and dense subject matter, it is not surprising that *Caramelo*, in particular its evident transnational content, has garnered much critical attention.[27] Here I build in part on Heather Alumbaugh's analysis of the novel, which looks at how Lala's particular migratory narrative ability emerges out of Cisneros's use of space.[28] I look more broadly at the use of space and place as aspects of the nation's identity, although part of that national identity formation of course includes narrative production, which I discuss toward the end of the chapter. Specifically, though, my reading expands the work done by Jordana Finnegan, who argues that *Caramelo* contests autonomous individualism in western "white space" by writing Chicana/o community into dominant versions of history. Finnegan's excellent although brief analysis of the novel's destabilization of the geographic nation suggests that Chicana/o culture in the novel is constituted by movement between national borders, and concludes that the stability of the nation becomes problematized and challenged.[29] It is this troubling of the national narrative that I expand upon and explore in more detail in this chapter, arguing that the novel shows how, out of the dismantled fictions of individual nations, mestizaje can build a new collective international identity based on the hemisphere's connected history and geography. I suggest that in the process of doing so, the novel ultimately discredits geopolitical borders and legitimates the membership and presence of cultural and political "others" in the nation.[30]

Caramelo tells the story of the Reyes family from the point of view of Celaya Reyes, the only daughter in a family of six sons, who is born in Chicago and travels to Mexico City every summer of her young life. The novel has three main sections. In Part One, "Recuerdo de Acapulco," Celaya describes the family's visits to Mexico as a child, the drives down from Chicago to Mexico City to stay with her grandmother Soledad—the

"Awful Grandmother"—and in particular, a memorable trip to Acapulco that she references several times. In Part Two, "When I Was Dirt," Celaya relates her grandmother Soledad's story (often in the first person from her grandmother's point of view), tracing Soledad's life from her birth and life in Mexico at the turn of the twentieth century, to Celaya's own birth in the United States. This section includes many footnotes that give the reader information about Mexican cultural, historical, and political events, and is also complicated by the fact that at the time of its retelling, Celaya's grandmother is a ghost, hovering, as the text presents it, in a border area between life and death. Finally, in Part Three, "The Eagle and the Serpent, or My Mother and My Father," Celaya is an adolescent. This final section recounts the grandmother's move to Chicago after her husband's death, the entire family's move to San Antonio, the grandmother's sickness and death, and Celaya's own renegotiations of ethnic identity as a young Chicana in the United States.[31]

In *Caramelo*, then, Cisneros addresses the nuances of Mexican American presence in the midwestern United States and Mexico, asking, essentially, how Mexican American ethnic identity can be written into the United States' broader national consciousness, and showing how it becomes part of that consciousness by destabilizing the borders of the United States. Even at an extratextual level, the novel's examination of geographical identity in the Americas represents a strong and at times unsettling incursion into the United States' literary and academic world of publishing. As reviewers and critics have noted, Cisneros problematizes the word "American," creating a "deliciously subversive reminder that 'American' applies to plenty of territory beyond the borders of the United States,"[32] and thus disrupting normative geopolitical ideologies. Furthermore, as "one of those novels that blithely leaps across the border between literary and popular fiction," the text problematizes generic categories of writing.[33] In fact, the novel's very movement between different types of fiction and its comic, lighthearted presentation of serious events give it a troubling presence, as it challenges the status quo and disrupts and opposes authority. These gestures of rebellion—challenging geographic borders, rewriting national identities, crossing generic boundaries, and opposing authority—are practices of mestizaje that work as important new political imaginaries, empowering the thickened borderland of the midwestern United States. In this way, the text undoes and critiques identity myths based on racial, national, and geographic purity, dismantling them to create new stories that reimagine the Midwest as a space in which mestizaje belongs.

RACE

As in *Sapogonia*, part of *Caramelo*'s geopolitical disruption occurs when it writes Indianness back into the nation-space, in this case that of both Mexico and the United States. By acknowledging, even celebrating, indigenous ancestry, Cisneros's novel becomes part of a broader mestiza consciousness that privileges its belonging to the nation. The narrative voice first highlights the problematic legacy of anti-Indian sentiment in both nations and shows how the United States and Mexico absorb and maintain one another's racial ideology on both sides of the border. In Mexico, for example, Celaya's great-grandmother Regina believes that she has "purified" her family blood and "become Spanish" by marrying Eleuterio Reyes, even though her family "was as dark as cajeta and as humble as a tortilla of nixtamal" (116). Racism against Indians is written into Mexico's public national script almost formally: in the early twentieth century Mexico celebrates the centennial anniversary of national independence by presenting itself as "civilized" (European), clearing the streets of Indians "so as not to spoil the view," and recruiting "the little girls of the well-to-do . . . to toss rose petals into the Centennial parade before a phalanx of Indians dressed as 'Indians'" (125).[34] Celaya's Awful Grandmother describes Indians as "trash" (86), shuddering in horror at the bus station, a hellish "inferno of Indians" that "smells worse than a pigsty" (79). She ignores her own indigenous lineage and berates Celaya for her Indian features. This derision of Indianness is continually transplanted into the U.S. Midwest, where Celaya grows up. Ultimately, in terms of racial identity, the move from Mexico to the United States forges Mexican nationhood from afar, beyond the political borders of the nation-state, and nuances ideological conversations about race and identity in the United States itself.

The narrative's centering of Indianness is illustrated partly through its account of the family's visit to Acapulco, where Celaya learns that Candelaria, the young Indian daughter of the Awful Grandmother's washerwoman, is Inocencio's illegitimate daughter and thus Celaya's own half-sister. Celaya's adult narrative voice, in remembering her half-sister, valorizes her Indianness for its beautiful physiognomy and its importance as an inherent part of Mexico's natural landscape and national political identity. As a child she becomes infatuated with Candelaria's "peanut butter skin" that is "deep as burnt milk candy" (34), reminiscent of the Awful Grandmother's beautiful caramelo-colored rebozo (shawl) that calls out to be touched (58). She describes Candelaria as an important part of Mexico's natural landscape, its sea and its land: "wearing her shell necklace and jumping with each wave, as brown as anybody born here, bobbing in the water. Sunlight spangling the skin of water and the drops she splashes . . . sparkling like a shiny water bird" (77). Celaya's sister thus comes to represent the population of indigenous Mexicans who belong in this natural Mexican landscape, even though the nation's political and social systems of stratification have long alienated them. The moment where Celaya understands Candelaria's connection to her—she suddenly recognizes her own father's features in Candelaria's face—is politically significant, as Celaya's narrative allows the Indian Candelaria to cross national and class boundaries. Although Candelaria is publicly humiliated and never legitimately recognized as part of the Reyes clan, Celaya's foregrounding of her acknowledges her implicit presence in narratives about Mexican history and geography. Furthermore, because of this familial connection, valorizations of Candelaria's indigenous origin also write Mexican mestizaje and Indianness onto the United States.

But despite Celaya's valorization of Candelaria in Mexico, her own indigenous features, which serve as somatic markers of her family's often unacknowledged Indian heritage, function as reminders of otherness located right inside domestic, familial, and public national spaces. According to collective U.S. and Mexican cultural definitions of female beauty—which her family upholds—her Indian looks "other" her physically: as the grandmother states, "Celaya takes after her mother's family. . . . The Reynas are all built like a mountain range. It's their Indian blood. Pure Yaqui" (241). Gender and race interrelate, as the critique of not being feminine enough is also a critique of being too Indian. Celaya notes mournfully, "I got Father's face with its Moorish profile, a nose too big for my face, or a face too small for my nose, I'm not sure which. But I'm all Reyna from the neck down. A body like a tamal, straight up and down" (258). But the novel's narrative voice, presumably an older and wiser Celaya/Cisneros, also carefully refigures Indianness more positively by emphasizing the sheer permanence of indigenous physiognomy in the Americas. Regina's facial features, for example, are described as follows: "The same face you see in the Mayan glyphs and everywhere in the Mexican Museum of Anthropology. Snarled lips and jaguar eyes. Often this face is seen even now driving an M&M-colored taxicab or handing you a corn-on-the-cob on a stick. This face, ancient, historic, eternal, so common it doesn't startle anyone but foreigners and artists" (113). Indianness is thus legitimated not only through its transcendental historic presence but also through its quotidian and habitual presence—its belonging—in contemporary urban landscapes. Indian female bodies are also rewritten as historically and powerfully desirable. Regina, who as a child is considered "homely" because of her Indian features, is in Celaya's retelling irresistibly and legendarily striking, "like la Indian Bonita, that Indian girl, wife of the gardener, whose beauty brought Maximilian to his knees as if he was a gardener too and not the emperor of Mexico" (117).

One of the most important aspects of privileging indigenous ancestry in this way occurs when the text dismantles Eurocentric origin myths of Spanish purity that are so central to nineteenth-century Mexican national identity, and consequently, to the racial ideology of twentieth-century Mexican and U.S. nation-spaces. When Celaya recounts her great-grandfather Eleuterio Reyes's arrival in Mexico from Spain in the late nineteenth century, she suggests that it was only that particular historical moment in Mexico that allowed his "Spanish" blood to appear pure. The family's Spanish blood is in fact "mixed with so much Sephardic and Moorish ancestry" that "all it would have earned them in an earlier Mexico was a fiery death at the Plaza del Volador" (163). The fiction of racial purity, in other words, is enabled by geographic migration and accidents of history. Celaya's father, Inocencio (whose face is like hers), is similarly marked by ancestral migrations and movement rather than rootedness and purity: "his face from Seville, Fez, Marrakech, a thousand and one cities" (245). His face is thus from everywhere and anywhere, representing endless border crossings and mestizaje, showing the impurity of Spanish origin myths in Mexico, and empowering a new political imaginary in this space, where the dichotomy of Spanish/Indian national identities becomes troubled.

NATION AND GEOGRAPHY

The narrative's geopolitical rhetoric, which centers Indianness in Mexico by valorizing its physical beauty and recognizing its place in history, also shows how the United States has inherited a similar legacy of interconnected geographical and national identities. As Celaya recounts the story of the family's indigenous ancestry on both sides of the border, she layers Mexico onto the United States, showing how ideological constructions of race in the United States are significantly determined by Mexico's historical and contemporary writing of indigenous and mestizo bodies within its own borders. Remapping marginalized indigenous ethnicity back onto the geography and history of Mexico and the United States allows Celaya to acknowledge the interconnectivity between the nations, and to renegotiate her identity as a Mexican American midwest-erner. By the end of the novel, at her parents' anniversary party in Chi-cago, Celaya has developed a powerful mestiza consciousness, through which she experiences everyone and everything as connected. She says, "We are all, like it or not, one and the same" (427). The party essentially becomes a site of borderlands, with "everyone, but everyone, moving in a lazy counterclockwise circle. The living and the dead" (424). Here, place loses all boundaries, and the past, the present, the dead, and the living all merge into one. The implications of this envisioned collective space, however, go beyond shifting the boundaries of Celaya's personal identity. They also explicitly address the question of how and from where political and national identities can be narrated. An important part of Cisneros's geopolitical strategy thus lies not only in her creation of a blended, con-nected borderland space (United States/Mexico) but also in her explora-tion of the narratives of identity that such a nation might produce.

In the text both Mexico and the United States are reimagined as con-structed spaces that only become real when read as extensions of one another. While the southwestern texts in chapter 1 specifically negoti-ated southwestern territory as Mexican, here the cultural and political nation-spaces of Mexico and the entire United States become remapped as merged and merging borderland spaces. Mexico, for example, is refig-ured as fictional through Celaya's unreliable memories of her father's homeland. Although Celaya has her own firsthand experiences of Mex-ico, in transcribing those memories into narrative she encounters the limits of the country's knowability. In fact, despite her frequent trips to Mexico as a young girl, when she tries to write down her impressions of Mexico they seem unreliable. Consequently, she creates testimonials about Mexico from the standpoint of a migrant mestiza who is always everywhere and nowhere, placeless, and un-rooted.[35] Although she tries to root her displaced and diasporic voice in Mexico, her knowledge of Mexico remains limited and contradictory: at times she experiences it as a foreigner or tourist, regarding it with a distant eye; at other times, it is her home. In Acapulco, for example, her family behave like tourists, don-ning straw hats with "ACAPULCO" stitched in orange yarn, bearing "two palm trees on either side, or a maguey stitched in green on one side and on the other, a Mexican man asleep under a sombrero" (74). Here, running about on the beach wearing straw hats, Celaya and her family construct and narrate Mexico as an exotic tourist destination, borrow-ing from one of the United States' dominant discourses on Mexico. Such exoticization obviously makes Mexico briefly knowable and manageable and allows Celaya to indulge in nostalgia for a Mexico that in turn gives her control over its narratability.

But such narrative control comes at a cost. Celaya's writing of Mexico produces stereotyped images perpetuated both by the dominant culture in the United States and the Mexican tourist industry's own commodification of its natural landscape. Furthermore, Cisneros's disclaimer at the start of the novel, which admits to the fabrication of memories and thus stories, blurs any supposed authority that might be borne by someone with firsthand experiences of Mexico. In it Cisneros admits, "these stories are nothing but story, bits of string, odds and ends found here and there. . . . I have invented what I do not know. To write is to ask questions. It doesn't matter if the answers are true or puro cuento. After all and everything only the story is remembered and the truth fades away like the pale blue ink on a cheap embroidery pattern." If firsthand experiences of Mexico do not necessarily turn into narratable memories, and popular images of Mexico objectify the land, then what remains of Mexico is, at worst, a hollow simulacra, or, at best, a story for consumer culture to appropriate. The boundaries between fabrication and authenticity are porous, and thus U.S. popular culture's writing of Mexico is arguably as legitimate as any other imagining of the nation.

Even through this apparent construction, however, the text also privileges and politicizes Mexico's geography, declaring it to be a nation-space that is not exactly fictional, but is certainly in flux. When Celaya recalls her own (possibly unreliable) experiences of Mexico, she is able to valorize and legitimate the cultural and emotional power that the nation holds over its returning diaspora. She describes the drive into Mexico City as follows: "The center of the universe! The valley like a big bowl of hot beef soup before you taste it. And a laughter in your chest when the car descends" (25). Here she celebrates the Mexico of her childhood and past, and re-creates the vibrancy and excitement of an arrival that is always simultaneously a return. She also decenters the United States in the consciousness of the narrator and the reader: for that moment, Mexico moves from the edge to the center while the United States shrinks to the margins of the text. The description emphasizes the landscape's powerful pull on the family's collective body as they approach the city: "The rising in the chest, in the heart, finally. The road suddenly dipping and surprising us as always. There it is!" (25). In recollection, the experience perfectly blends the anticipation and renewal of return that occur on each visit: there is suddenness, surprise, and then a sure and familiar recognition of their destination.

Eventually, when Celaya's grandmother leaves Mexico and Celaya's last direct link to it disappears, "Mexico" becomes possible only through the writing of memory, from afar. When Celaya returns to Mexico as a teenager to help her grandmother pack and move to the United States, Mexico has already shifted and changed. She arrives wanting to relive and then bid farewell to her childhood Mexican memories, but finds that the public spaces in Mexico City that she longed for earlier have become sinister and threatening because of her own changing body. When an old man exposes himself to her, everything becomes frightening: "Suddenly I feel funny, a sadness and tenderness all mixed together" (261). This particular memory seems to wipe out all her other memories: "I forget about the balloons, the milk gelatins, the cookie vendors.... I forget about everything on the way to the Grandmother's house except what I wish I could forget, that man's ugly pipi with the fly on it" (262). And, of course, because these sections (and the entire novel) are written after the events and from the United States, their entire perspective is one of loss, homesickness, and even exile. It seems that Mexico can only be known—and constructed—through its fictional state on the page, in abstentia, from afar, and through a lens of dislocation, written from the United States.

But in the novel the United States also loses much solid grounding, as it is frequently deconstructed, fictionalized, or imagined as marginal to Mexico. Describing it as "the other side, el otro lado," the novel continually dismantles the possibility that the United States could provide a foundational space for narrative production or belonging. Chicago in particular is rendered ambiguously. For the grandmother, who is recently arrived there, the promise of Chicago as a new home-space collapses once she realizes that "to visit Chicago is one thing, to live there another" (290). Obviously, "this was not the Chicago of her vacations, where one is always escorted to the lake shore, to the gold coast, driven along the winding lanes of traffic on Lake Shore Drive in the shadow of beautiful apartment buildings" (290). Staying at her youngest son's house, in her granddaughter Amor's "borrowed room" (288), she is homesick for Mexico, and alarmed to find that she is stuck "in the middle of nowhere it seemed, halfway between here and where?" (287). How, then, can Mexico—and the United States itself—be narrated? Ultimately, *Caramelo* offers up a blended or borderland space—one that is inherently defined through mestizaje—as a new site from which to rewrite the relationship between place and national identity, and legitimate Mexican belonging and presence throughout the United States.

For example, for Chicago Mexican Americans the city is deeply familiar, as evidenced through the ethnographic footnotes that describe the changing pulse of the city, from the demise of the Maxwell Street flea market to Jim's Original Hot Dogs, which is now "a memorial to Maxwell Street's funky past" (9). The text locates Chicago as a place of roots and long history and memory for Mexicans both because of and despite the circular migrations back and forth across the U.S.-Mexico border. Celaya's grandfather says to her, "Did you know I used to live in Chicago once? A long time ago, before you were ever born" (56). Here, Chicago and Mexico City connect: while neither operates as a foundational center for regional or national identity, both offer a shifting borderland area in which a mestiza identity can locate herself. The text carefully shows the long history and presence of Mexicanness within this midwestern city: situating Chicago as both home and abroad, displacing the boundaries that determine one's presence in a place, and suggesting that this midwestern borderland belongs to the mestiza narrator. This thickened borderland region thus becomes an imagined site of political empowerment rather than an area of "unbelonging."

In some respects, then, the United States and Mexico function simultaneously as "el otro lado" for Celaya, implying that any sense of authenticity or origin tied to place is purely fictional and constructed.[36] Clearly, the narrative's project of nation building can be read as purely deconstructive, as each nation's rhetoric about its neighbor undoes the foundations of both nations. But through this undoing comes a collective identity: while they cannot sustain individual national identities, the United States and Mexico can begin to imagine a hemispheric, transnational identity. Each nation's meaning rests on the existence of the other, and this blending of Mexico and the United States has significant consequences for the text's negotiation of the geographical and political border between them. The border in fact determines not just the contours of the two nations, but their proximity to one another and their presence within one another. At times, Mexico appears distant because it is located beyond a rigid and anxious border. Celaya's father describes the divide as "the savage border" (379), and Celaya notes that during their car trip from Chicago to Mexico City, they cross Illinois, Missouri, Oklahoma, and Texas all singing songs, but that "crossing the border, nobody feels like singing" (16).[37] The narrative voice acknowledges the difficulty of representing this border. In real life, it is not as clearly delineated as on the map, yet it is nevertheless material and absolute: "Not like on the Triple A atlas from orange to pink, but at a stoplight in a rippled heat and a dizzy gasoline stink, the United States ends all at once, a tangled shove of red lights from cars and trucks waiting their turn to get past the bridge. Miles and miles" (16).

Here the geopolitical border seems material: one nation ends suddenly and becomes clearly differentiated from its neighbor. Celaya then describes what it means, in fact, for a nation to end in this way: "As soon as we cross the bridge everything switches to another language. Toc, says the light switch in this country, at home it says click. Honk, say the cars at home, here they say tan-tan-tan" (17). For the rest of the car trip down to Mexico City, different billboards, snacks, and songs on the radio all define the cultural and material experiences that separate the United States and Mexico. The border thus creates a particular definition of nation that is identified through differentiation: the quotidian details—and differences—between the United States and Mexico make each place what it is. Similarly, when the family crosses back into the United States from Mexico with the grandmother, that same narrative of nation—one of differentiation—is repeated. The grandmother, with her impending departure from Mexico, has "suddenly turned nationalist" (276) and has planned to be momentously patriotic at the moment she crosses the border into the United States, perhaps to recite a poem or hum the national anthem. But instead, she becomes distracted when the border agents take away her Manila mangos—which she insists are superior to any found in the States—and complains all the way to San Antonio. At the moment of crossing, then, Mexico is not evoked through patriotic narrative discourse, but defined through cultural absence. At that moment the mangos represent the homeland as familiar, superior, and vanished.

But the novel also makes it clear that these shifts from Mexican to American and from Mexico to the United States depend on an arbitrary line that alternately dissolves and reappears, and that stretches well into the characters' lives in Chicago. Mexican national identity, of course, does not end at the border, and neither does Mexico. In many respects, then, Mexico is almost inseparable from the United States. In all three parts of the novel, but especially in the last section, it becomes evident that the lines between Mexico and the United States are blurred, and that the two nations exist within one another. Anzaldúa's words—"Admit that Mexico is your double, that she exists in the shadow of this country, that we are irrevocably tied to her"[38]—can be seen as a backdrop to the novel, as Cisneros asks North American readers to acknowledge the extended presence of Mexico within the United States, the haunted and traumatic relationship between the two nations, and the psychological and political consequences of that intimate trace of one nation within the other.[39] The nations' interconnectivity is material as well as imaginative: in one interview Cisneros refers to the "back and forth" movement between "the Midwest and Mexico" and notes that many Latino communities in Chicago "consider Mexico as a commuter suburb."[40]

As if to illustrate this, throughout the novel the characters seem to drive easily not just from San Antonio to Mexico but also between Chicago and Mexico City, so that Mexico becomes the kind of commuter suburb of Chicago that Cisneros has talked about. Mexico comes right into the United States, and similarly the United States comes right into Mexico, each leaving a residue of itself in the other. The border between the two countries, so rigidly mapped on the atlas and so materially real, is also porous and diluted, seamlessly connecting the cities that the family drives through: "Chicago, Route 66 . . . all the way to Saint Louis, Missouri, which Father calls by its Spanish name, San Luis. San Luis to Tulsa, Oklahoma. Tulsa, Oklahoma, to Dallas. Dallas to San Antonio to Laredo on 81 till we are on the other side. Monterrey. Saltillo. Matehuala. San Luis Potosí. Querétaro. Mexico City" (5). Here, the moment of crossing—"Laredo on 81 till we are on the other side"—is almost imperceptible: the narrative voice acknowledges the "other side" but appears to shift to it smoothly. Because the two spaces of nation exist within one another, each one functions as a trace, or ghost, in the other, becoming an inextricable part of its national character. When in Mexico, Celaya remembers the United States; she cannot help but bring it with her. Similarly, while in the United States, Mexico surfaces and troubles the northern nation-state.

However, Mexico's haunting presence in the United States, in particular its mestizaje, is often inarticulate and undialectical. For example, when Inocencio first moves to the United States in the 1930s, and works in a seafood restaurant shucking oysters, his mestizo body blurs national identities and becomes marked ambiguously by others. The customers wonder if he is French or Spanish but "don't say 'Mexican,' because they don't want to insult Inocencio, even though Inocencio doesn't know 'Mexican' is an insult" (210). Here, Inocencio's degree of empowerment remains ambiguous. Is he empowered because he does not recognize the silent insult beneath what is actually spoken? More significant, however, is the way that "Mexican" is interpellated. It is unspeakable, and thus only known or spoken through its absence. Its moment of identification occurs through the presence of a different word. That is, the words

"French" and "Spanish" come to signify "Mexican." While it seems that "Mexican" is erased and made invisible or even absent through the presence of other articulated nationalities, it in fact exerts a linguistic—and therefore cultural—presence that troubles the nation-state precisely because of its concealed status. The nation's inability to comfortably articulate or define Mexico, or Mexican, and its various attempts to replace, erase, or sully the word, only reiterate the insistent belonging of Mexico and its mestizo bodies within the United States.

MESTIZA STORYTELLING

One of the most significant ways of bringing a politically empowering mestizaje into the American heartland is through the production and publication of narratives and stories that recount that mestizaje. At the authorial level, of course, Cisneros has done just that. Her earlier works (*The House on Mango Street, Woman Hollering Creek*) were the first ones by a Chicana writing about Chicana issues to receive a lucrative contract from a mainstream publisher, and their success has made Cisneros into something of a Latina literary star who is also recognized by mainstream America.[41] The story of *Caramelo*'s publication is also a successful one: it was the first Chicano/a novel to appear in Spanish (in translation) without first having to become a best seller in English, and it received extensive popular and critical acclaim. Cisneros is also explicit about her intent, through her work, to change the U.S. mainstream's understanding of Mexican American history.[42] The implications of this shift in understanding are important. Although, as Rebolledo notes, minority communities in the United States have not experienced the same level of political and social oppression that exists in Latin America (where testimonial narratives emerged in response to political terror), they nevertheless do experience oppression that needs to be validated through story, the kind of story that Pastora, in *Sapogonia*, was trying to tell. Rebolledo writes, "Because Chicana writers also function within cultures that have silenced and erased them . . . this notion of testifying and remembering in order to achieve 'presence' is seen throughout their writing."[43] In this sense, Cisneros's novel is a borderlands testimonial: a witnessing to stories narrated from and by characters who move between various psychological and geographic borders and live in liminal spaces.

Within the narrative, too, Celaya, like many multiethnic and immigrant subjects, uses her writing to create a resistant space of nation. She realizes at the end of the novel's epilogue that her recollections, "these things, that song, that time, that place," are "all bound together in a country I am homesick for, that doesn't exist anymore. That never existed. A country I invented. Like all emigrants caught between here and there" (434). Here, what begins as an expression of loss for a nation-home becomes quickly unraveled into fiction; nation becomes reconceptualized as a borderland space "between here and there." Thus she develops a mestiza consciousness: her writerly presence becomes bound up with her physical, intellectual, and political presence. As part of this mestiza undoing of centers, Celaya also moves between various positions of storytelling, and plays with her authorial identity and presence: she is all at once an autobiographer, biographer, ethnographer, historian, and fiction writer. By producing various genres of writing, Celaya forges an emergent mestiza consciousness, defines herself as a migrant and borderland storyteller, and creates a mestiza storytelling praxis. This borderlands identity allows her to tell her own and others' testimonials, give voice to and inscribe their histories and fictions, and unearth residual memories that lie beneath the usually unspoken family narratives. As such, she redefines the possibilities of storytelling itself. In providing testimony for others, she experiments and moves between different subject positions—autobiographer, ethnographer, biographer, historian, fictional storyteller—and refuses to locate herself or her body as a permanent or fixed site of knowledge.

Instead, as both a listener (of her grandmother's tales) and storyteller, Celaya's writing of history and memory through a mestiza consciousness destabilizes the authority of both Mexico and the United States to create differentiated and separate citizens within their nation-states. In undoing any definitive truth of testimonial, Cisneros thus suggests that the way for these stories to belong to the nation is for Chicana writers to write their silenced and unknown histories in the language and psyche of the borderlands. It is important, therefore, that the grandmother's ghost tells Celaya her story. At a fictional level this dissolves the boundaries between life and death: it is only after death, with "so much left unsaid" (91), that Soledad's story can be shared. The ghost-storyteller, occupying a borderland space, argues back and forth with Celaya for control of the story and disagrees about the status of fiction and lie within the stories (97–98). The narrative in Part Two is also frequently interrupted by narrative asides to the readers about the truth-or-lie status of storytelling in general, and this story in particular: "This next part of the story," we are warned, "I know sounds as if I am making it up, but the facts are so unbelievable they can only be truth" (143). The testimony itself, then, comes out of a fraught battle for control of the narrative, and consequently the

"Mexico" that emerges here is clearly a construct of personal fictions and histories. And if Mexico is explicitly fictionalized, that means that the writing of nation is made up of multiple voices telling stories: nation, in other words, becomes refigured as the collective experience of shared storytelling.

But borderland testimonials also emerge through collective silences, making the scope of their new political imaginary even more potent. In Part Two, Eleuterio Reyes, Celaya's great-grandfather, has a cataleptic attack and is rendered speechless (as the grandmother will be later on in old age). As characters slowly lose oral language in the text, they find alternate ways to communicate. Eleuterio still plays the piano, "trying his best to rise from the ashes of his near-death" (149), and only the young Soledad who cares for him understands him, "because she was as mute as he was, perhaps more so because she had no piano. . . . All she had was the caramelo rebozo, whose fringe she plaited and unplaited, which was a kind of language" (151). Soledad, who will later become the Awful Grandmother, comes from a family of shawl makers, where mothers and daughters through the generations weave shawls, each woman teaching the next and "adding a flourish that became her signature, then passing it on" (93). But because her mother died during her infancy, Soledad was never taught how to make rebozos, and is left "without the language of knots and rosettes, of silk and artisela, of cotton and ink-dyed secrets." Specifically, "there was no mother to take her hands and pass them over a dry snakeskin so her fingers would remember the patterns of diamonds" (94).

The rebozo, as a fabric that directly connects past and present, itself represents a borderland text that contains and transmits stories, but Soledad has been denied both the collective memory and continuity of her family's historical narratives, and the chance to put her own "signature" on those tales. However, when Soledad narrates her stories to Celaya, who in turn shapes them into her own literary account, the resulting written text retains an echo of its oral origins, and Soledad's testimonials, created by multiple signatures, begin to circulate. Like the patterned narrative created in the folds of a traditional shawl, oral storytelling also occurs through gaps and hesitations, reluctant or absent witnesses, and interruptions. With its blurred genres, contested stories, and tales of silence, Celaya's borderland narrative challenges and resists the authority of both written and spoken words, disrupting the national and literary identity of the United States' mainstream culture and refiguring it through the ethnic markers of collective mestizaje.

At the very end of *Caramelo*, Cisneros presents a select but specific historical chronology of Mexico and the United States that shows the various ways that "Mexico" and "Mexican" have been interpellated by popular culture (law, politics, the media) within the United States. The chronology reads as a cultural and popular account of the troubled history of the U.S.-Mexico political border (beginning with Cortés's conquest of Mexico) that shows the border to be historically and geographically fluid, and overdetermined by xenophobic U.S. foreign policies. In the chronology Mexico and the United States are inextricably joined, with their borders spreading throughout the nation-space. In this way *Caramelo*, like *Sapogonia*, redefines political and geographic nation-spaces, and explores Mexican American literary and cultural belonging in the United States. It imagines a mestizo identity within the United States; plays with the limitations, possibilities, and potential stories that reside in the body's memory of place; and asks dominant culture to acknowledge Mexico's haunting and continuous presence in the United States, to share in its history and memory, and to recognize the inhabitants of the midwestern borderlands as legitimate members of the U.S. nation.

Clearly, as I have shown, the texts in chapters 1 and 2 displace and deconstruct the political borders of the nation, rewriting the spaces of the southwestern and midwestern United States as part of Latin America, especially Mexico. Beginning this study with the geopolitical strategies of Mexican American writers is an obvious choice, given, as my introduction illustrated, the almost special status that Mexicans have in U.S. popular discourse, whereby "Mexican" has become an easily and casually applied misnomer for any Latino, apparently illegal, certainly foreign presence on this side of the geographical border. Of course, this misnomer directs dominant culture's attention toward the U.S.-Mexico border as a vivid site of separation between the two nations, as an entry point for all Latinos/as, and as an important place of national identification. Where, then, does this leave Puerto Ricans? In the popular imagination, it seems that Puerto Ricans are differentiated from Mexicans by their status as U.S. citizens: because their presence on the mainland is legal, they are not subject to fears of deportation, and any border crossings are seen as movements of internal migration. Nevertheless, the narratives in chapters 3 and 4 show how Puerto Ricans in the United States and on the island itself have an ambivalent political presence, occupying at best a position of marginalized second-class citizenship. What is less acknowledged, and what the texts in the following two chapters highlight, is the sense of unbelonging that emerges from this secondary citizenship status. The island's historic and ongoing colonial relationship with the United States, the mainland's racialization of citizenship, and the U.S. mainstream's portrayal of Puerto Ricans as culturally deficient all raise questions, in the novels, about Puerto Rican national identification and cultural practices both on the island and on the mainland.

3 / Colonization and Transgression in Puerto Rican Spaces: Judith Ortiz Cofer's *The Line of the Sun* and *The Meaning of Consuelo*

Unlike Mexico, Puerto Rico lacks the contiguous geographical border with and proximity to the United States, as well as the stigma of illegality, that make Mexico—and Mexicans—appear to be the most apparent threat to mainstream notions of national identity. An analysis and discussion of displacement in U.S.-Puerto Rican literature, then, cannot ignore these material differences. It is certainly the case that there are important and real benefits to legal residency in the nation, particularly in comparison to the lived experiences of many undocumented migrants: Puerto Ricans, clearly, cannot be illegal border crossers and are not subject to fears of deportation. It is worth noting, however, that national identities, even in a juridically legal context, become constantly refigured and destabilized through geographic, cultural, and linguistic border crossings. Furthermore, as I established in the introduction, critical understandings of U.S.–Puerto Rican relationships have generally concluded that despite legal presence on the U.S. mainland, Puerto Ricans often occupy a position of marginalized second-class citizenship for a number of reasons. Generally speaking, critics suggest that the island's colonial relationship to the United States, Puerto Rican experiences of racialized citizenship on the mainland, and mainland perceptions of Puerto Ricans as culturally deficient exceptions to the narrative of successful immigrant assimilation into the United States have all created a problematic sense of cultural "otherness" and subordination.[1] Flores and Benmajor, for example, argue that while Puerto Ricans may not face attacks or harassment on the basis of their legal status, they are still viewed as foreigners and "receive the same harsh anti-immigrant treatment as other Latinos."[2]

The literature in this chapter explores the implications of U.S. colonial presence on both the island and the mainland, and also conveys and addresses the sense of illicit and cultural unbelonging faced by Puerto Ricans in both spaces. In Judith Ortiz Cofer's *The Line of the Sun* and *The Meaning of Consuelo* we see how the U.S. mainstream's rhetoric of Puerto Rican cultural unbelonging, rooted in a long history of colonization, is problematized as the novels reimagine and reframe U.S. presence in Puerto Rico. Specifically, the island's geographical, political, and cultural identity is not only subsumed under U.S. colonialism but also becomes, through the characters' resistant and transgressive acts, part of a larger transnational collective of the Americas. While this does not erase the power dynamic created by the United States' presence on the island, it does challenge cultural and national boundaries, in turn challenging the distinct second-class or foreign status of Puerto Ricans in both nations. In other words, if Puerto Ricans' marginalized status on both the island and (in particular) the mainland depends on seeing Puerto Rico as separate from the United States, then one implication of a new transnational space would be to trouble that marginalization. In the chapter that follows this one, which examines Esmeralda Santiago's three memoirs, we see how the works' reframing of nation-spaces challenges the additional stigma of perceived Puerto Rican cultural and social deficiency on the mainland.

The roots of this cultural unbelonging lie in the island's long historical connection to the United States, and, like the dynamic of U.S.-Mexican history, depend to an extent on the two nations' geopolitical relationship. In the early twentieth century, after Puerto Rico segued from Spanish political control to U.S. economic (and eventually political) hegemony, the United States' interest in the island became formalized, culminating with the Jones-Shafroth Act of 1917, which gave Puerto Ricans citizenship, and the 1952 conferral of "Commonwealth" status on the island. Known as the Estado Libre Asociado (Associated Free State), Puerto Rico remains a Commonwealth (a politically organized community or state that is connected by treaty to another political system), and an unincorporated territory of the United States. Rendered as such, the island suffers from an "awkward and anomalous" political status and, in terms of some fundamental aspects of legislative life (such as citizenship, commerce, health, welfare, and military defense) remains under the control of its northern neighbor.[3] It has been described as "simultaneously a poor U.S. state and a very developed Latin American nation," suggesting that Puerto Ricans inhabit a sort of binational space both on the island and the mainland, and are part of the United States but culturally and linguistically also part of Latin America.[4] As Ilan Stavans explains, although as U.S. citizens Puerto Ricans have many of the same rights and privileges as stateside citizens, because the United States exercises territorial jurisdiction over this still-unincorporated territory, "many island Puerto Ricans perceive their status as second-class."[5]

Critics have also documented the ways in which Puerto Rico's early economic dependency on U.S. markets established a commercial and then cultural relationship between the two countries.[6] In particular, critics focus on the ways in which this neocolonial relationship connects to patterns of migration, both internally in Puerto Rico from rural to urban locales and externally to the U.S. mainland. At the root of external migration lies internal migration: a legacy of displacement that becomes expressed, in Ortiz Cofer's novels, through examples of collective and personal exile both within and without the island itself. Gilbert Muller has noted, for example, that the constant movement back and forth from Puerto Rico to the mainland, due largely to island unemployment, is also "perhaps an emblem of the fragmentation of Puerto Rican identity as it collides with American realities."[7] Yudice and Flores add that U.S. actions in Latin America—military incursions as well as economic sanctions—have "always generated Latin American migrations,"[8] and cite the "colonial dimension" of the relationship between the United States and all Puerto Ricans that makes the histories, memories, and geographies of these nations intertwine.[9] Puerto Rico's special status cannot be overstated. Flores points out that long after decolonization in other parts of the world, "This island nation is still a colony by all indicators of international relations, its economic and political life fully orchestrated by its mighty neighbor to the north, the putative leader of world democracy and sovereignty."[10] Without a doubt, then, Ortiz Cofer's literary depiction of life on and off the island must grapple with the fragmentation of Puerto Rican identity created by these continual migratory patterns.

It is appropriate, then, that Judith Ortiz Cofer's and Esmeralda Santiago's works explore not just the neocolonial relationship of the two nations but also the material and psychological effects of it, the patterns of migration within the island and toward the mainland, and the legacy of dislocation and unbelonging from place that determines Puerto Rican and U.S.–Puerto Rican consciousness. In this chapter I explore the dynamics of cultural and geographical "place" in Ortiz Cofer's novels through a framework of transgression (as theorized below by both Michel Foucault and Juan Flores), understanding transgression as a resistant act of crossing both figurative and literal borders that changes the geographical and/or cultural space of the nation. I contend that the novels explore strategies of transgression in order to trouble and disrupt the U.S.–Puerto Rican colonial dynamic: transgression marks and then discredits the cultural boundary between normative behavior and "othered" behavior, that is, between U.S. and Puerto Rican cultural practices and presence. In a neocolonial environment, however, transgression has particularly radical implications because the presence of an underlying "original" culture (in this case, Puerto Rican) can be almost entirely subsumed. Thus acts of transgression that show how colonial presence has imposed a "normative" standard can discredit and resist the boundary that neocolonialism maintains (in order to distinguish itself from the subaltern "other" of the island) and then suggest alternative cultural behaviors.

In the novels, though, Ortiz Cofer's transgressive characters are outliers who are isolated by their marginal status. In addition, the novels show Puerto Rico as a space co-opted first by Spain, then by the United States. *The Line of the Sun* in fact foregrounds the island's history of Spanish colonialism as much as, if not more than, any ongoing U.S. presence. Its narrative framework even highlights the long legacy of colonization by writing the island and its citizens from the perspective of a mainland Americanized Puerto Rican, as if to suggest the difficulty of subaltern speech. Meanwhile, *The Meaning of Consuelo* presents the island's nation-space as inextricably commercialized by the United States. What, then, is the efficacy of the characters' resistant acts? How effectively can they validate the subaltern's presence within the colonized space? I argue here that resistance occurs when isolated transgressive acts become collective through communal storytelling. Both of the central protagonists in *The Line of the Sun* and *The Meaning of Consuelo* practice storytelling as transgression: specifically they are inspired by those around them to tell a story that speaks to collective and national experiences. In this way national identity on both sides of the "border" becomes troubled, as transgressive acts permit cultural otherness within the nation-space.[11]

By showing how transgressive acts lead to communal stories, the novels significantly break down the neocolonial boundary that the United States needs in order to maintain the island as "other." In *The Line of the Sun* the possibility for community emerges through the protagonist Marisol's conscious negotiation of herself as a storyteller—in particular, as a postcolonial migrant storyteller who must cross boundaries of genre in order to speak of the island without recolonizing it. Her tale of resistance against the legacies of Spanish colonialism on the island (in the first half) seeps into the United States (in the second half), shifting its national consciousness and suggesting that the two nations' stories and histories of colonialism and migration are inseparable. In *The Meaning of Consuelo*, which illustrates not only the legacy of Spanish conquest but also ongoing U.S. presence on the island more explicitly than the first novel, Consuelo's accounts of transgression similarly trouble U.S. narratives of colonial superiority.

Transgression, the violation of a law or command that involves crossing over a limit, is of course inextricably connected to understandings of place and national identity, as normative cultural and physical borders determine and demarcate social and moral behavior. In his "Preface to Transgression" Foucault writes, "transgression is an action which involves the limit, that narrow zone of a line where it displays the flash of its passage, but perhaps also its entire trajectory, even its origin; it is likely that transgression has its entire space in the line it crosses."[12] In other words, transgression is most interested in the status of the border itself. Thus, when the characters transgress, they highlight the boundaries that they cross and make them more, rather than less, visible, destabilizing the cultural and national identity on which such limits depend. Building on Foucault, Juan Flores adds that transgression does not erase the limit by crossing it, but instead foregrounds and mediates contrasts. Transgression, that is, illuminates the spaces on either side of the limit, threatening not just the boundary but also the terrain around it.[13] Acts of transgression can therefore potentially disrupt and fracture the entire nation's normative ideologies by collapsing time and making history (the "origin") and the future ("its entire trajectory") visible in one place, again resisting cultural and national norms by writing history into the present.

Flores's exploration of the large exodus of Puerto Ricans to the mainland—what he calls "the most pronounced break in Puerto Rican collective memory"[14]—uses Foucault's analogy of the relationship between transgression and the limit, where, Foucault argues, the two are not actually in an oppositional relationship: "Transgression . . . is not related to the limit as black to white, the prohibited to the lawful, the outside to the inside—but rather it is like a flash of lightning in the night which . . . gives a dense and black intensity to the night it denies, which lights up the night from the inside, from top to bottom, and yet owes to the dark the stark clarity of its manifestation, its harrowing and posed singularity."[15] In other words, both the border and the act of crossing it enable one another, which means that transgressors are in fact essential to maintaining the border that separates them from society. The act of crossing draws attention to the border, even when, as in the case of Puerto Rico, that border does not formally exist as a political boundary. Crossing also defines the border, which itself demarcates the nation-space: thus crossing defines the nation. The implications of Foucault's analogy are important for our purposes: the moment of crossing has a brief but crucial impact on the nation's identity because it determines national and political space and, consequently, its ideological and moral norms. Foucault notes that the flash of light—the moment of transgression—illuminates the darkness around it, revealing what usually remains absent or obscured. The act of violation and crossing, therefore, draws our eye to the limit and beyond it, implicitly critiquing the norm that is being disrupted.

Thus, as I showed in chapter 2, political, national, and cultural boundaries come into sharp focus when they are crossed, but here also depend on the normative neocolonial landscape around them to determine and define their disobedient and unlawful characteristics. In this respect, the novels' narrative voices (Marisol's and Consuelo's) are transgressive and compliant, rebellious and acquiescent. They disrupt the United States' and Puerto Rico's cultural and national identities, but are also still dependent on the United States' colonial framework for underwriting the space that is to be transgressed. In other words, Ortiz Cofer's texts disrupt U.S. national identity by showing the ambiguity of Puerto Rican presence on and off the island, as it simultaneously maintains, determines, and threatens that national space.

The Line of the Sun

The first half of *The Line of the Sun* is set in the Puerto Rican town of Salud, and the second half in an urban immigrant neighborhood in New York City. The story spans the early 1940s to the 1960s, and recounts the adventures of the hero Guzmán as a young boy in Salud, his exile to the United States, and his return to Puerto Rico. In the second half of the novel Guzmán's niece Marisol relates stories of her own life in the United States, including but not limited to Guzmán's visit with her family. Eventually she becomes his "secret biographer" (282), recounting first his story and then her own experiences as a bicultural teenager growing up in New York. In many respects the novel is deeply resistant to U.S.

dominant narratives, challenging the regulatory paradigms of identity that society upholds, and writing a new and collective space of home from which the subject—Marisol—can offer her stories. But at the same time, the novel admits the limitations of this space: Marisol's eventual home is in the suburbs of New York, in a solitary landscape that cannot accommodate or provide a home for her less assimilated, darker, and more "Indian" Puerto Rican mother. By the end of the novel, then, we realize that one of the main storytellers—Ramona, the mother—does not belong to the space out of which collective narrative can be produced. In this way, the place has rejected the presence of a "foreign" and disruptive Puerto Rican in New York (Ramona) in favor of the story of a Puerto Rican, Guzmán, set back on the island. Even as we see Puerto Ricans smuggling communal stories of resistance across the United States' cultural and national boundaries, the novel shows how those boundaries also practice exclusion, writing second-class or marginalized citizenship upon Puerto Ricans.

Narrative Voice and Storytelling

One of the novel's most important strategies of resistance is its conscious splitting of the story in half.[16] This narrative structure reflects the complexity of writing out of a colonized framework: the story of Puerto Rico is clearly separated from the story of the United States but, at the same time, is underwritten or traced by it, through and through. The narrative's two halves—the "Guzmán" section narrated in the third person, and the "Marisol" section narrated in the first person—imply that neither Guzmán nor Marisol is able to write his or her own story directly. And although the Salud section appears to be spoken by an omniscient third-person narrator, it gradually becomes clear that Guzmán's story is imagined and narrated by Marisol from afar. When the action then moves to New York in the second half of the novel, and the narrative voice switches to first person, the connection between the two protagonists becomes sharper. Their connection is developed through the porous division between the two halves of the novel: it becomes evident that the boundary between them is blurred and that each side of the limit (each half of the narrative) is infused with legacies from the other side. The novel thus not only revisits Puerto Rico as a site of memory but also brings that site of memory right into the U.S. mainland, creating a collective U.S.–Puerto Rican space. Thus, in showing how a young New York Puerto Rican girl scripts the narrative of her island-uncle onto her own personal and national history, the novel fills the U.S. mainland with Puerto Rican memories of migration and displacement.[17]

But the relationship between Marisol and Guzmán is also problematic because it seems to mirror the ambiguous power dynamic between colonizer (a U.S. Puerto Rican) and colonized (an island Puerto Rican). Even though Marisol is herself a postcolonial migrant, her adolescent immigrant voice, in its observation and narration of her uncle, disempowers him.[18] Her ambiguous narrative straddling echoes, on a political and national level, Flores's description of the experience of occupying an "in-between" space, an experience that is "deeply familiar to Puerto Ricans in the United States" but that also "harbors the possibility of an intricate politics of freedom and resistance." He adds that by understanding in-betweenness in this way, "as a kind of phenomenology or philosophy of experiential space, the 'break' appears as both a limit and a breaking of the limit."[19] The novel's bifurcated narrative shows this simultaneous display and breaking of limits, performing transgressions that enable a recovery of history—both familial and political histories—and create a site from which to provide those testimonies of history.

But Marisol's story of Guzmán, built from a collection of family tales, inevitably possesses her subject, reminding us that the recovery of another's historical testimony depends to an extent on colonizing it. In her desire to know and write Guzmán she moves from storyteller to colonizer, creating a ruptured, even stolen, story, whose central character seems unaware that his story is being told.[20] Toward the end of the novel, when Guzmán leaves New York and returns to Puerto Rico, Marisol feels possessive about his story, and says, "In my mind I had made his story mine. I had kept track of him through my mother's stories, Mama Cielo's letters, and all those late-night conversations I had stolen from my parents when they thought I was sleeping in my room."[21] She admits, "I had filled the gaps with my imagination until Guzmán had shown up at our door; then I had become his secret biographer, drawing excitement from all he represented to me" (282). The secretive nature of her biographical work shifts the novel's historical recovery into a form of territorialization: the unconscious, private, or unarticulated testimonials that produce a biography of Guzmán also result in an ethnographic and somewhat folkloric presentation and exploration of Puerto Rico.[22]

By the end of the novel, Guzmán is physically and emotionally drained and shrunken, and while this is in part due to injuries he has sustained during events in the story, it is also a comment on the impact of Marisol's transgressions. As she draws Guzmán's story out of him, she herself becomes stronger. She describes him as "almost my size, a skinny adolescent with a wizened monkey face" (228). After he leaves New Jersey she can begin to write his story: "All this, of course, we did not learn from letters. It had to be later inferred from *Guzmán's Adventures*, the ongoing narrative as told by my mother, enhanced and colored until Guzmán became in our imaginations the brown giant of Island legend. There would be several versions of Guzmán's story, each one suited to his audience. And there would be gaps that would never be filled in, holes into which he would fall in silence" (176–177). Guzmán's decline and the silence surrounding parts of his life are reminders that even as the novel is flooded with his influence, even as he remains pervasive for Marisol whether or not he is physically there ("late, late into the night my uncle's voice lifted me in and out of consciousness" [200]), he is also unknowable, resisting narrative representation.

As Marisol tries to integrate Guzmán—in particular, his racialized "wild" Indianness, the "brown giant"—into the family record, and to record Puerto Rico in the United States, she also recognizes how his ambiguous status as a Puerto Rican in the United States reflects her own marginalized citizenship. The first time she lays eyes on him, he is "familiar in an oddly disturbing way, as if I were looking into a mirror in a darkened room" (189), evoking perhaps the unacknowledged aspects of her own identity and the racialized status of her own belonging to the U.S. mainland.[23] But she also describes him as othered: "Bare-chested, his thick black hair grown over his ears, my uncle looked like a wild man. It was the look in his eye too that startled me when he looked straight at me, not seeing me" (216).[24]

Over the course of her narrative Marisol seems to cement her citizenship and sense of belonging to the mainland, becoming more assimilated into U.S. mainstream society and moving away from the Puerto Rican community of the city into the suburbs. Her storytelling—and her move toward suburbia—begins when El Building, the Puerto Rican enclave in New Jersey where the family lives, burns down. As she helps her mother with tasks that need to be done after the fire she finds herself interpreting "the world for my mother" (273). This work of interpretation and translation is deeply related to storytelling; as a "secret biographer" she mediates not only between cultures and generations but also between her creative manipulation of truth and imagination. At this point, she begins to forge a more explicit and conscious U.S. Puerto Rican identity, explaining, "I learned something during those days: though I would always carry my Island heritage on my back like a snail, I belonged in the world of phones, offices, concrete buildings, and the English language" (273). On the mainland she is least displaced when translating and traversing between the two cultures, and when her emergent voice prepares to tell a story of Puerto Rico from afar.

After the fire Marisol and her father move into a suburban neighborhood, away from El Building and the Puerto Rican enclave in which she and her mother have resided. Ramona has always feared the suburbs, "with their vulnerable single-family homes sitting like eggs on their little plots of green lawn" (172). In contrast, Marisol welcomes the "cold façade of the houses" (172), although she knows that her mother will "feel like a stranger" in their new suburban house (284). Marisol's homemaking is her mother's unmaking, just as Marisol's storytelling diminishes her uncle's strength, and both gestures confirm Ramona's and Guzmán's unbelonging on the mainland because of their unpalatable—dark, Indian—presence in it. But ultimately, it is in the assimilated space of suburbia, rather than in El Building's close-knit communal space, that Marisol hears her mother's stories. For most of Marisol's narrative in the second half of the book, it is not clear whether she tells the story alone, or as part of a community. It is also never entirely clear how she has acquired the stories that she relates. At one point in the novel she says, "I heard Guzmán's story, or I dreamed it" (191). But the first line of the novel states, "*They say* Guzmán had been a difficult pregnancy for Mama Cielo" (1, my emphasis), suggesting that the story is gathered from hearsay, wisdom, or gossip rather than from firsthand testimonials. Near the end of the novel we learn that although the story is written in a solitary space (Marisol's attic bedroom in suburban New Jersey), it began as a collective enterprise. Up until now, her mother, Ramona, has for the most part occupied only the edges of the narrative, but now she sits and talks to Marisol, becoming the direct storyteller: "She took a deep breath and began her story" (285).[25]

Obviously what Marisol knows of Guzmán is gathered from varied and mixed sources: stories from her mother (Guzmán's sister) and her maternal grandmother, Mama Cielo; letters; and fabrications of her own making. Thus Marisol's narrative voice in the Guzmán section is neither omniscient nor objective. Instead, it is unreliable, problematic, at tension with her material and her storytelling subjects, and anxious about her assimilated yet foreign status in the United States and her consequent relation to Puerto Rico. It signals both a displacement and a haunting: every word in the Guzmán section is ghosted by the narrator's ambiguous status as a migrant Puerto Rican storyteller, symbolizing the United

States' presence in Puerto Rico and, later on, Puerto Rico's pervasive ghosting of the mainland. Reflecting the resistance and disempowerment of Puerto Rico's relationship to its northern neighbor, Marisol simultaneously tells the story and suggests that she cannot tell it. Thus she embodies the dynamic of a U.S.–Puerto Rican voice: one that articulates the ambiguity of Puerto Rican national and cultural identity.

RELIGIOUS PROHIBITIONS AND SEXUAL DEVIANCY

The stories that Marisol composes in her suburban bedroom recount the histories of a group of outliers in Salud who resist the founding and ongoing legacies of Spanish colonialism that still structure and determine the town's value-system. Marisol provides a thorough context for Salud's outcast figures, describing the town's religious and cultural history and the community's tightly regulated societal norms that emerged from these legacies. But behind her narrative of Salud's shunned outsiders, Marisol also tries to understand the ambiguity of her own membership status in the United States. The unconventional inhabitants of Salud—Guzmán, Rosa, and others—fascinate Marisol, as their transgressions against residual Spanish cultural norms seem to reflect her own attempts, through storytelling, to trouble her marginalized status on the mainland. And by identifying the deviant and transgressive sexual behavior of the town's marginal figures, she connects the violence of Spanish colonialism with U.S. colonialism in Puerto Rico and suggests that the residual legacies of these violences impact her New York life in the 1960s—for example, rendering her family, particularly her mother, into racially ambiguous outsiders (219–220).

In particular, the townspeople of Salud regulate sexual desire because of the legacy of their founding story: historically, Salud was founded on "a miracle" (45) that created an origin myth for the community. According to the legend, four centuries ago a pious woodcutter was charged and pierced by a crazy bull. The woodcutter, taking this as a divine message, called on the Blessed Mother for assistance. She appeared to him, spoke one word—Salud—and his wound was healed "without a trace" (45). The bull became as tame as a lamb, and the woodcutter became the spiritual founder of the town of Salud. As news of the miracle spread, people came from all parts to visit the Shrine to Our Lady of Salud, or moved there to be near "this salubrious place" (45). The town's founding story thus describes the Spaniards' attempts to tame and heal the defective spirit of wild nature, and similarly most of the Guzmán section recounts how Salud's inhabitants attempt similar "cures" on their transgressive figures. There is more to Salud's originary narrative, however. As the town's reputation grew, the bishop in San Juan, "a pragmatic Spaniard who had been sent to the Island by the Crown to lead his missionary priests in the conversion of the Taino Indians" (46), was asked to oversee the building of a church. Because "converting Indians was a slow and dreary business, with some of the priests reporting the loss of entire flocks of newly baptized savages to disease" (46), the bishop welcomed the diversion, especially since "as long as there were Indians left, labor was cheap, even free" (46). Behind Salud's founding story, then, lies a suppressed memory of violence, and a story of miraculous healing that is also one of colonization and enforced conversion. In the novel, therefore, images of domestic violence recall historical violence and perpetuate the norms and limitations established by the first colonizers. For example, when Guzmán's mother, Mamá Cielo, is pregnant with him she is prone to acts of "prenatal violence" (1) and later on, according to the narrative voice (Marisol's/Ramona's), she beats her children regularly, perpetuating a "familiar pattern of violence and guilt" (6).

In the Salud story, the church obscures the secret violences beneath the town's official history by permitting some apparent liberties. One of the novel's most significant depictions of religiously preserved boundaries is the description of the town carnival, the setting for Guzmán's first sexual experience with Rosa, the town's beautiful young healer/bruja. Here, codes of conduct are actually determined by a carefully orchestrated display of religiously mandated transgressions. During the nine days of religious services in honor of the town's patroness, Our Lady of Salud, the carnival strings up Christmas lights between the houses and the church, and sets up its games "right in the street in front of the church," turning the street into "a fantasy land of music and color" (61). The central question here, of course, is whether transgression is permitted: whether the festival is liberating or controlled by the authority of the church. The carnival itself seems to occupy a space of limitlessness, upheaval, and apparent freedom, with chaos and disorder that overturn the norm. In fact, the carnival folk wear costumes partly so that "should they run afoul of the law" (63), they can remain unidentifiable, permitting lawlessness.

However, in this almost orgiastic space, where normal social strictures and rules are apparently erased, acts of liberation are still regulated by the Catholic Church. It is a permitted and controlled space for excess, where "for nine nights Salud transformed itself from a drab, dusty hamlet into a colorful carnival, seducing the faithful like a hag in the fairy tale who turns into a beautiful woman just long enough to trick a prince into making love to her" (61). Any acts of transgression that take place here, while joyful, also simultaneously highlight the limits that they cross, and the normative terrain around them. The descriptions of the geographic proximity of church and carnival suggest that the sacred serves as a backdrop that the profane, in its flashy display, illuminates, and that "the church, a massive white structure sitting on its hill like a reproving matron, dim and dowdy" (66), remains panoptic and power-ful. Conversely, though, the two come to define one another, and in that sense depend on one another for meaning. That is, the sacred seems only able to operate in opposition to profanity and revelry, and vice versa. Thus meaning has no place from which to operate except through con-tinual absence. How, then, can the belonging that Marisol seeks from these ancestral memories be articulated and established? Such cultural belonging has to find a location through storytelling and through the storyteller's fictionalizing memory. Real subversion occurs when carni-val comes to exist outside of the space in which it was intended to occur: Guzmán's relationship with Rosa, for example, becomes particularly subversive when it continues outside of the carnival's parameters. In turn, the broadest subversion of place and national boundaries occurs when Marisol writes and integrates her tale of Puerto Rican carnival and transgression into the United States.[26]

Against this backdrop of Salud's colonized history and religious stric-tures Marisol describes how the transgressors of the town, with their sexual awareness, activity, and desires, explicitly threaten its normative values. Guzmán and his brother Carmelo both suffer the violent effects of Salud's Catholic discourses, where savages and gays, through their alleged promiscuity, disrupt familial and patriarchal sexuality. Mamá Cielo herself describes Guzmán's growing masculinity in racial terms— "Guzmán's skin was getting darker"—and his older brother Carmelo's homosexuality through misplaced feminized ideals: "When he held his book up to his face to read at night, she could see the perfect roundness of his nails, clean and smooth as those of a kept woman or a lazy man" (8). Carmelo's friendship with the young priest Padre Cesar (who makes the men of the town "feel ill at ease" [17]) is intellectual and bookish, offer-ing a temporarily liberating space that cannot ultimately transgress the boundaries that it defies. Eventually, to escape Salud's vicious tongues, Carmelo enlists in the army, goes to fight in Korea, and is killed there. Throughout the narrative Carmelo's life is overdetermined and mediated by the narrator's foreknowledge of his death, so that almost every time he is mentioned, it is with a hindsight reference to the fact that he was killed in Korea, "blown into a thousand pieces" (4) over its "foreign soil" (80). His death, therefore, becomes symbolic of Puerto Ricans' traumatic exile that began with Spanish colonialism and extends into the twentieth century, haunting the family well into Marisol's life and narrative in New York. Guzmán, meanwhile, is a "demon child" (3) who does not seem to feel pain (2), an otherworldly "nasty savage" (5), and a "troublesome spirit" (14), whose adolescence frightens his family and the community even more.[27] As neither Carmelo's tabooed desires nor Guzmán's permissive longings can be contained or integrated into Salud, both men are essentially exiled from it, and in their exile from Puerto Rico, they lose the motherland that has turned upon them: "Carmelo—handsome and sensitive, forced to leave his home because of the evil minds that could only see that he was different from other young men—killed in another man's war. . . . And Guzmán, blown about like a leaf by the winds of his passions. She would lose him too" (85). The mass migration that Puerto Rico experienced in the twentieth century, and the unspoken resulting traumatic effect of this exodus, is thus played out in the family's personal migrant history.[28]

Obviously, the threatening presence of Guzmán's and Carmelo's transgressive desires is itself a symptom of the larger legacy of Spanish colonial history that the residents cannot properly acknowledge. It is therefore important that Marisol acknowledge such histories through her narrative. Because the sacred only becomes meaningful in opposition to the profane, and in fact depends on the profane to itself become visible (Spaniard versus Indian, Christianity versus heathenism, carnival versus church), Marisol also shows how Salud's townspeople actually need the local outcast figures—Guzmán, Carmelo, Rosa, and, to a lesser degree, Franco El Loco and Amparo—in order to legitimate their own established boundaries. As the townswomen prepare to hunt down Rosa, beginning "the last witch hunt in Salud" (75), Doña Tina and her Holy Rosary Society, "the watchful guardians of the moral status of the town" who stringently enforce their "rules of conduct" (76), are able, through their regulations, to participate in what fascinates and repels them from a safe distance. The women's admonishments and control provide them with a role beyond the narrowly traditional triad of virgin/whore/mother: that of cruel voyeurs and regulators of desires who viciously exile Rosa from Salud.

Through Rosa's transgressions the unknown becomes more clearly defined: the island's legacy of psychological otherness, spiritual strangeness, and historical ghostliness, as well as the cultural and political influence of the United States, all surface. She seems to defy comprehension and compartmentalization, being referred to as La Cabra, but slipping between various roles: a whore "masquerading as a spiritist healer" (79), a "practical businesswoman" (88), and even a "spiritual mother" to the young Guzmán (27). Her house, a three-mile hike away from the town "through an overgrown coffee plantation where the Taino Indians were said to have their burial grounds" (20), exudes the spirits and ghosts that seethe beneath the surface of the island. The walk to her house involves violating the town's limits: the red river nearby, for example, is always "difficult to cross" (21) even when it is just a shallow stream of mud, representing a border that separates the known from the unknown that the community enters reluctantly, with either fear or vengeance. When Carmelo goes to rescue Guzmán from his long stay at Rosa's house, the boys cross the river with difficulty. Carmelo carries Guzmán across: "like a two-headed giant they crossed the moving stream. Carmelo fought the pull of the soft mud on his ankles, which like an insistent mouth tried to suck him down to the bottom. Guzmán closed his eyes against the call of the water" (44). Their combined strength can barely resist the pull of the water and the seductive Rosa; even as he leaves, Guzmán easily imagines the current carrying him back to her naturally, proving that he is ultimately unable, or unwilling, to return to the regulatory limitations of the town. Although Guzmán visits many liminal spaces over the course of the story, visiting and observing various outsider figures (including Marisol and her parents in New York), Rosa's is the only place where he has a real "sense of ease" (35) and seems willing to stay put.

Rosa clearly resists preserving the boundaries that the community lives by, transgressing most odiously, in their view, by allowing Guzmán, her pseudoson, to live with her as a lover and thus challenging their normative definitions of motherhood. But the narrative of her story (whether it is Guzmán's, Ramona's, Marisol's, or a blend of these storytellers) actually validates her transgressions and recognizes them as part of a collective resistance to the remnants of Spanish colonialism on which the town's social normativity rests. Marisol's story focuses especially on Rosa's bewitching beauty and on the alleged deviancy of her behavior, as if to further dismantle the shackles of the island's first colonizers by whose codes Salud still abides. When she describes Rosa bathing outdoors on three separate occasions she emphasizes her whiteness (22), the dark hair piled on her head (41), and her breasts rising from the water (44). The repetition of this image also suggests that the storyteller wants to memorialize Rosa, to contain her in this moment of beauty and desire, and to move her beyond the boundaries of her time and place (1940s Salud) into the present (1960s New York). Rosa is also remembered as an integral part of the island's natural landscape: her home contains "the beauty of the Island all concentrated into a few acres with river, valley, hill, and turquoise-blue sky" (91), which contrasts sharply with descriptions elsewhere in the novel of the pain and disease that result from working the cultivated sugarcane fields. The image also conjures a fertile and productive landscape, with aromatic and healing herb gardens (96).[29] This memorialization of Rosa, which is also a memorialization of Puerto Rico, is an antidote to exile, providing a space of comfort and home not just for Guzmán when he later relates stories to Marisol but also for Marisol herself, who has, from talking to her uncle and listening to her mother's stories, often felt "deprived" of the alternative life she did not get to live in Puerto Rico. She sometimes feels that she, too, "should have grown up there" and "been able to play in emerald-green pastures, to eat sweet bananas right off the trees" (222). These moments of nostalgia contrast with the novel's mostly harsh portrayal of the reality of life in Salud, and evoke the exile's artificial memory of a lost home rather than the actual experience of it. That is, moments of nostalgia are presented as precisely that: necessary narratives that alleviate the pain of dislocation and imagine belonging elsewhere, but that do not close the gap between real and fictional memories.

PUERTO RICO AND THE UNITED STATES: LONGING AND COLONIAL AMBIGUITY

Ortiz Cofer's *The Line of the Sun* is concerned not just with the rhetoric of remembering and bringing Puerto Rico into the mainland but also with the island Puerto Ricans' longing for the U.S. mainland. Although the novel implicitly critiques the United States for its economic impact on the island, the United States remains an attractive and inevitable destination for islanders, exerting a seductive pull on the outcast figures of Salud who want to escape their insular rural town. Proving that it is geographical distance and the power of stories that enable fictions of the promised land, the narrative voice—as always, mediated from a distance by Marisol and her own migrant perspective—yearns for America: "Guzmán imagined himself walking on a white carpet of snow in a city of light, his heart leading him to the place where she [Rosa] lived. Together they would explore that wonderful new world where everyone had television sets and drove big cars" (148). In reality, of course, the narrator is keenly aware of the dislocating experiences of loss in Guzmán's and Rosa's actual exile. As Guzmán wanders around Salud on one of his last nights there, gazing at and exploring the hometown that has repeatedly rejected him, we are already prompted to read Puerto Rico as a distant memory: "There were still others whose memory he would take with him, so that in the cold rooms he would occupy for many years the remembrance of these lives would eventually guide him back to his birthplace like a beacon in a foggy night" (111). Similarly, we know before Rosa does that "in later years, in colder climates, she would recall her days in the valley through her senses, the smells of certain herbs and flowers, rainwater" (96). Anticipating cold exile in the North, the narrative voice acknowledges the necessity of some kind of national longing for home and land; appropriately for the ambiguously placed characters of the story, this longing alternates and moves between a longing for the island and the mainland.

Marisol's longing for Puerto Rico produces a story that traces migrant journeys between the island and the mainland. Through her storytelling she occupies liminal spaces: the narrative switches from third to first person as she inserts herself in the second half of the novel. By the end, she is explicitly present as the narrator, but interrogates that very presence by questioning her acquisition of storytelling material. Throughout the novel, reading itself has been presented as something shameful that is done in secret: Carmelo, the priest, Marisol's Puerto Rican grandfather, and even Marisol's little brother all engage in private and hidden acts of reading. It is therefore not surprising that Marisol's own ambitions to relate her story in writing are problematized: she consciously turns to writing as her chosen career and begins her translations of Puerto Rican life from "the land of suburbia" (282) only toward the end of the story. And although she belongs in American suburbia she still vacillates anxiously between her roles as Puerto Rican biographer, autobiographer, historian, niece, and daughter.

Suburbia thus functions both as a place of belonging and unbelonging: it is a new home from which writing occurs, and a nowhere space of permanent exile. Describing life in their new suburban house, and acknowledging her mother's role in the storytelling process, Marisol says, "my mother told me her story throughout the long, lonely first season of our newest exile" (286), creating a communal storytelling experience out of the conditions of Puerto Rico migration and displacement. It is thus only at the end of the novel that storytelling becomes situated as a collective and therefore potentially resistant process, with "Ramona . . . weaving her stories into a rich tapestry . . . [as] I held the threads for her" (286). Marisol vows to one day "put it all together," the "puzzle" of Guzmán's life. She adds, "Perhaps I would start . . . I would tell . . . I would tell . . . And I would tell" (287). The conditional tense delays the storytelling moment, emphasizing the *potential* of her autobiographical voice that for now remains biographical. Ambiguously, she also claims that despite her telling, the story "is not, nor will it ever be, finished" (286), and that it "did not end happily. . . . It continued through my mother's letters and in my imagination until one day I started writing it for him" (290). But her conscious and intentional decision to be Guzmán's biographer—a transgressive narrative act in itself—allows her to begin writing and building a place of belonging on the mainland.

With the novel's focus on transgression and transgressive storytelling, we see important implications for both reframing legacies of colonialism on the island and validating Puerto Rican belonging on the mainland. On the island, the characters' transgressions resist authoritarian colonial presence and challenge the boundaries that maintain those hierarchical structures of power, creating an alternate dynamic by which the two nations intersect. On the mainland, this challenge to power structures— as well as Puerto Rican migration and presence—problematizes Puerto Ricans' second-class or foreign status, and reimagines the United States' narrative, cultural, and ideological identity as part of a larger transnational Americas.

The Meaning of Consuelo

Ortiz Cofer's second novel, *The Meaning of Consuelo* (2003), shows how the dynamic of colonial power on the island creates a deep-rooted citizenship of unbelonging for Puerto Ricans and turns their stories into narratives of national exile. One of the most revealing moments in *The Meaning of Consuelo* comes at the end of the story when the protagonist and narrator, Consuelo, departs Puerto Rico alone on an airbus for New York, but is never seen to arrive on the mainland. This final image is interesting in part because it seems to uproot the character without quite setting her back down anywhere, denying her any real belonging. The image also denies us the promise of collective storytelling that could function as an imaginary space of belonging. Although the story is of course told, it seems to lack the imagined community of storytellers and listeners that *The Line of the Sun*'s narrative voice consciously evoked. Without this foregrounded activity of storytelling, the activity of nation building and deconstruction also remains concealed. As such, then, the process of story construction and the writing of personal and political memories and histories that are part of a nation's crafting of itself are not explicitly suggested within the narrative structure. Thus the text's potential for resisting the colonial dynamic between Puerto Rico and the United States by reimagining both nations as part of a broader transnational space of the Americas remains more implicit than in *The Line of the Sun*.

The two novels share some important elements but are also markedly distinct. Like Marisol, Consuelo, the eponymous heroine of the second novel, narrates the stories of the socially excluded and marginalized figures around her, in part out of a voyeuristic fascination with their otherness, and in part as a way to understand her own transgressive desires. And although the text is not implicitly autobiographical, it does attempt to locate a space of home from which a national Puerto Rican voice can write its history, thus echoing Ortiz Cofer's own status as a U.S. Puerto Rican writer. While both novels focus on Puerto Rico, the second one is located entirely on the island, ending in its final pages with a description of a migration to the mainland, but with no actual narrative of arrival and no explicit evidence of collective storytelling. In the end, *The Meaning of Consuelo* departs significantly from *The Line of the Sun*'s presentation of Puerto Rico as a space of belonging that can be re-created nostalgically as home from the mainland. Instead, the contradictory discomfort of American suburbia that the first novel establishes—a new home but also a space of exile—is extended, in the second novel, right into the island, where it becomes commodified and commercialized. In *The Meaning of Consuelo*, that commodified space becomes an integral part of the Puerto Rican geopolitical landscape itself, and indeed, of Puerto Rican history. What, then, are the implications for a transnational imaginary when the colonial power has established a commercialized subaltern space? It seems unlikely that such a space will produce resistance: only a limited resistance can take place because the commercialized subaltern identity represents a repetition of (rather than a departure from) U.S. economic dominance. The novel thus asks whether any kind of subaltern resistance to the legacy of colonialism is even possible. Frequently in the novel, it seems, acts of resistance end up becoming part of the system of colonial capitalism on the island. However, while possibilities for communal resistance are often thus co-opted, the novel offers one example of a transgressive figure, Consuelo's sister, Mili, whose disappearance at the end of the novel represents a collective Puerto Rican displacement that disrupts and ghosts the U.S. mainland, forces it to recognize the consequences of its own presence on the island, and thus refigures the colonial dynamic between the nations as more of a trans-American collective. Moreover, the relaying of Mili's story itself (by Consuelo) also represents a transgressive act of storytelling that disrupts U.S. presence.

COLONIZATION AND MIGRATION

The Meaning of Consuelo is explicit about the impact of the island's status as a territory of the United States, suggesting that the commodified exile that its Puerto Rican characters experience is a part of that legacy that continues in perpetuity. In particular, Puerto Rico's exilic space becomes, in the novel, a landscape of carnival—by definition a rootless and decentering event—that is commodified by the colonial presence that still textures the island. Puerto Rican geography, then, is reimagined as a migrant exilic space rather than a solid rooted home. Meanwhile, the United States remains an attractive destination for Puerto Ricans, beckoning islanders to its shores with promises of improved socioeconomic standards of living. In fact, toward the end of *The Meaning of Consuelo*, in a reversal of stereotypical tropes, the United States (rather than the island) is presented as a place of beauty that one would long for nostalgically. Descriptions of its natural landscape imagine an unspoiled terrain, the "startling beauty of the state [of Vermont], green like our island, and mountainous, but *more pure* in its topography" (151, my emphasis), while photographs of its cities hold the promise of self-made belonging: "there was . . . comfort in the monochromatic shadows and designs of American cities, in the patterns one could rearrange and interpret."[30] Despite this, however, the United States retains its fictional status, never quite materializing for Consuelo as she only reads about it in books and in Patricio's letters. The characters' experiences of home are thus based not on settlement but in an expectation of migration to a fictional space that is preceded by a commodified process of unbelonging on the island. In this respect the novel illustrates Flores and Yudice's claim that the current mass migration of Latinos to the United States has reconceptualized America into "a cultural map which is all border."[31] In this second novel, then, Ortiz Cofer depicts the ambivalence of Puerto Rican national and cultural identity by mapping the island's ongoing experience of exile back onto its own geographical and cultural landscape, and by problematizing the ways in which that landscape can ever be recalled through narrative, because its narrators' opportunities for storytelling production are inevitably co-opted by the same system that has colonized the nation. In turn, U.S. national identity is forced to face the debris of its own cultural and political presence on the island: as the United States directs its gaze southward toward Puerto Rico, it faces a hyperbolic and manufactured version of itself.[32]

The novel tells the story of Consuelo Signe's childhood and young adulthood growing up in 1950s suburban San Juan, and the dynamics of her political, cultural, and domestic environment: the growing American presence on the island, the social constraints of traditional Puerto Rican behavioral codes, her parents' ailing marriage, and her psychologically disturbed sister, Mili. Like Marisol, Consuelo is obsessed with categorical outsiders who openly challenge the cultural and social status quo—Mili, Patricio, and María Sereno—and whose resistance of normative ideologies seeps into the United States. Ortiz Cofer's depiction of 1950s Puerto Rico in *The Meaning of Consuelo* describes, again and again, an environment undergoing rapid and sudden social, cultural, and topographical changes due to the United States' cultural, domestic, and political influences. When Consuelo's parents argue back and forth about American technological advances on the island (her mother is against them, her father in favor), we see how the changes brought about by American businesses on the island affect the psyche of domestic family space, too. As Consuelo describes it, in terms that express the aggressive violation of a natural landscape, "the plan was to transform our beautiful but primitive tropical paradise into a welcoming resort for mainland tourists, and subsequently into an attractive investment opportunity for industrialists seeking cheap labor within American borders. The first item of business was a highway through the annoyingly curvaceous central mountain range" (24).

Specifically, American "progress" on the island is depicted as a violating act, manifested through the minutiae of spatial, geographic, and psychological experiences of exile that the island residents undergo. Consequently, their own relationship to the land is ambiguous: at times they are natives, at other moments, tourists. Some of the text's most troubling and ambivalent moments show Consuelo and her family as outsiders to the very topography of their own homeland. The family's middle-class status that allows them to buy a car and take Sunday drives around the island, for example, also offers them a new kind of knowledge about their island. Although they move through and absorb the physical landscape at their leisure, their recreational activity also renders them geographic outsiders to the place. Sometimes Mami points out things about the island "as if we were turistas" (22), and sometimes Papi starts "a guided tour" where he points out the new factories, shopping centers,

caring, the collective disapproving and fascinated gaze of all the women, who, going about their daily work, stare "unashamedly" at María, "smiling in a superior way or raising an eyebrow at one another" (3). When María finally purchases his shaved ice cone, he sucks it with a jarring eroticism: "He'd lick it with his long pink tongue" (4). In a place where "the community rules were strict" (4), María's discomforting crossing of gender boundaries exposes him to ridicule and ostracism. Even though he is routinely invited into the women's homes as their manicurist, his presence there remains secretive, and for much of the story he is isolated, albeit apparently unaffected by his outsider status.

Consuelo and Mili are intrigued and confused by the spectrum of otherness that María presents. Although they are not permitted to talk to him in public, he does enter their house to paint their mother's nails while their father is out, leading them to wonder, "was he friend or foe?" (6). That is, the contours of their suburban space are remapped depending on who is present, and thus the complex limits between prohibition and permission become constantly reshaped. When María visits their house to give their mother a manicure (11) the kitchen temporarily becomes a small domestic space of carnivalesque resistance against the soulless decor of suburbia. In this world María, who can "transform himself from man to woman, the ultimate clown's trick" (6), becomes magical and exciting rather than threatening, and is figured, albeit briefly, as potentially empowered, and empowering those around him. In his trickery of transgression he holds up the porousness of the limit, and highlights the constructedness of center and margin, although such undoing remains contained because it is enacted only in small moments, in a controlled space. As with all carnivalesque moments, the question is, does the carnival present a significant inversion of hierarchies, or is it constrained by the forms of social control that licensed it? What is the efficacy of a transgression that has to take place in a sanctioned space? And who exactly sanctions this space?[33]

Ultimately, María cannot survive long-term in this suburb and is essentially removed: he has a fall, spends time in the hospital, and reappears only toward the end of the story. By then, it is clear that the United States can and has created a larger sanctioned space of carnival on the island, rebuilding for María a center within which he can safely and continually "transgress." Consuelo and her mother visit him there, in the huge hotel in San Juan, the "Queen of the Sea" (147), which has been renovated to resemble a luxury ocean liner. Initially, Consuelo is disgusted and repelled by the "Hollywood-inspired snazziness of the place" (147), and the trumpeted parody of excess. Then, however, she sees María Sereno at work there, dressed in a white cabin mate's parade uniform, looking stunning and giving manicures. Her mother reports that he is doing very well at the job and that "the tourists just love him" (148). In this overturned world of parody, mimicry, and artifice, María has become an exoticized object, apparently freed from the constraints of his Puerto Rican upbringing.

While María gives Consuelo a manicure, he tells her funny stories in which "the bizarre became so common that I expressed disbelief out loud, and he said to me that I had not been looking closely enough, or I would have known by now that being 'normal' is a rare thing. We laughed until we had tears running down our faces at the things he told us" (148). Such laughter, in this setting, is carnivalesque, a complex "festive laughter," write Stallybrass and White, that "is not an individual reaction to some isolated 'comic event' but 'the laughter of all people.'"[34] According to Mikhail Bakhtin, this laughter is universal, ambivalent, triumphant, deriding: "It asserts and denies, it buries and revives."[35] This laughter is produced by, directed at, and belongs to the people, evoking a community that can, it seems, revel in its own otherness, and in its own undoing of center and margin. And indeed, before his disappearance María Sereno, in his "daily spectacle" jiggly walk through the neighborhood, proudly wears a halter top made out of a T-shirt with the symbol and motto of Governor Muñoz Murín's party: "The message was clear: the journey of our island into the future had begun, and the common people would be leading the way" (133). It appears, then, that "the common people" will be empowered in this new carnivalesque landscape.[36]

In Ortiz Cofer's text, however, the political and economic dependency of Puerto Rico on the United States limits the efficacy and empowerment of the carnival space. Any communal resistance that emerges out of this space is constrained by the boundaries of that space, where its "transgressions" and acts of emergent and new collective ideology can be monitored and managed. Not only is the carnival space temporary and sanctioned, but it also becomes commodified and commercialized. Most significant, then, María's Puerto Rican transgressions become translated into a capitalist venture that can be sold and marketed for a profit, representing not real resistance but a repetition of U.S. economic dominance. In his home-space of carnival, María himself becomes a consumer product and occupies a landscape that has been permanently exiled from itself. In fact, the text closely weaves María's marketable transgressions with the island's growing cultural and economic changes;

Consuelo points out that around this time, class status on the island was beginning to blur, and cultural history was becoming undone. Her own parents, for example, express concern at how new fashions in dress among adolescents defy social boundaries and "might indicate a regression to the lower social strata" (101). She explicitly connects the blurred boundaries of class to a transfer of power at the national level: "An era was ending on the island: Spanish colonial customs were fading into the background as American culture saturated the airwaves" (101). Thus the United States has replaced Spain in determining the national identity of Puerto Rico, shifting it politically and culturally into a carnivalesque playground where exile and otherness become marketed as consumer objects. Problematically, the tourist industry that offers María a market for his creativity is emblematic of the systemic colonization that structures the very terms of exile in the first place, rendering it not just domestic and personal but also political and national.

Like María Sereno, Patricio, Consuelo's homosexual cousin and neighbor, remains a categorical outsider to the residents of the suburb, and, like María, he ultimately finds a space on the island and later on the mainland where his talents, formally markers of fearful transgression, become marketable commodities. In Old San Juan he and his friends create turista paintings that perpetuate the chamber of commerce's depictions of Puerto Rico as "La Isla del Encanto, the enchanting vacation island where the U.S. dollar was the common currency" (63). As a child Patricio's playful yet resistant behavior represents the subaltern practice of "talking back" to imperial powers. He creates elaborate puppets out of papier-mâché, which he dresses in bright bits of fabric from Consuelo's mother, who gets them from the dresses that she alters for the American "tourist ladies" at the Golden Palms Hotel (14). Consuelo and Patricio routinely act out skits and plays with their puppets, their child's play allowing them an introspective look at their culture's evolution under the Americans. Their cast of characters includes a maid doll, a custodial doll, and other support players, who "often pretended not to understand the turistas" (15), rich American women who speak broken Spanish. The children get their cues from stories they hear from the adults, but their parodic entertainment is also an example of the limited power of the subaltern's mimicry: it simultaneously empowers the native because he controls the situation and illustrates his imprisonment on his own turf. In their skits, the conflicts peak "as the turista puppets become more and more frantic and their Spanish more broken, until, finally, the manager puppet enters in his green suit wearing his painted-on face-wide smile, to mediate" (15). Although the puppet natives can mock the tourists' broken Spanish, and turn them into others (they mispronounce Mrs. Smith's name as la Misis Smit [42]), the puppet manager's smile is fixed and his identity frozen: he has no language with which to express his outrage, and no place from which to express it. His role as a mediator also problematically places him in between the tourists and the staff, in limbo, complicit with maintaining a status quo that perpetuates the system of colonization and its everyday practices.

Later in the text, in an even more explicit attempt at talking back, Patricio captures two tiny lime-green chameleons that can change to gold, brown, blue, and almost red, "according to where you put them" (46). He names them Lucy and Desi, and makes them a tiny glass palace that he calls the "Golden Palms Lizard Hotel and Lounge." Inside he creates a small pond out of an old souvenir ashtray of his mother's and "plants" a plastic palm tree adorned with the words "PUERTO RICO ENCHANTS ME" in gold (47). His clear parody of the American tourist industry on the island, with its capture, display, and commodification of the island's beauty, is a political act that he approaches with almost detached scientific curiosity: it re-creates a miniature version of colonizing strategies that he, Patricio, cannot normally control. Chameleons, of course, both redefine transgression and embody it. Their transgressive behavior—changing colors—is not prohibited, but is permissible, natural, and even to be expected, so in a sense, it cannot really be labeled "transgressive." However, by changing colors the chameleons appear to cross limits, challenging the boundaries of what should be possible. They function in the text as a trope for the subaltern voice because they represent the possibilities of transgression: creatures that practice passing, blending into their environment in order to survive. They suggest that unstable and shifting identities might be the new norm in Patricio's and Consuelo's changing world, but ultimately, the experiment demonstrates the violation of colonization. Despite the luxurious surroundings and free meals that Patricio provides for his lizards, including backgrounds of various colors, "the chameleon couple who had not changed colors since moving into their crystal palace" are listless and remain just a "greenish grey" (56). Their response to capture and to the ease of a life filled with modern conveniences is to freeze in time and place, becoming, in this world of tourism, souvenirs that at best only represent a memory of the island by commodifying it.

NARRATIVE RESISTANCE: LIMITS AND POSSIBILITIES

Consuelo's own central transgression—her production of narrative storytelling—represents one of the text's most important possibilities for Puerto Rican resistance. But unlike Marisol, Consuelo does not describe the places from which stories can be narrated, and in this novel both orality and writing become highly problematized in terms of their ability to convey history and write a personal and national memory. In Puerto Rico's exilic terrain it becomes progressively harder to locate the material that can texture a story about one's home on the island, that can be told from afar, and that can thus create a sustaining memory. In other words, like the island, the storyteller's voice (Consuelo's) appears solitary rather than collective. While *The Line of the Sun* describes the place from which the narrator will write her stories of Puerto Rico—Marisol's bedroom with a desk built into the wall and a window facing an oak tree—this novel remains ambiguous about locating the act of storytelling itself. Moreover, just as Marisol's anxiety about "colonizing" Guzmán's voice for the purposes of storytelling colored her narrative, so, too, does Consuelo's act of storytelling carry within it certain questions about the disempowering implications of representation. For Consuelo especially, the act of written representation risks objectifying her subject.

In the novel orality initially appears to be powerful enough to sustain memories, pass down histories, and therefore disrupt U.S. identity on the island. At her grandparents' house, Consuelo listens eagerly to her Abuelo's stories about the Taino Indians, "Abuelo's familiar voice, a sound like distant thunder heard from the safety of one's bed, . . . put me in a trance" (36), in particular focusing on the features of orality: the presence of the storyteller, the sounds of his voice, and the powerful effect of hearing it. She presses her ear close to his chest, "so I could feel the deep vibrations of his voice," and places her palm on his throat as he enunciates each word (37). Part of the power of orality, then, lies in its physical production of story, and its performance at the moment of telling, especially in the multiple sensory experiences that it creates for the listener. Consuelo feels the storyteller's voice tangibly, turning orality into a physical as well as auditory experience. The scene is important, as she learns about the storyteller's power to control events, rewrite history, create affective memory, and, through story, own the space. However, any resistance offered by these performances diminishes in light of the colonial framework that produces them. Even inside the grandparents' house, a pueblo dwelling full of ancestral ghosts and history (in contrast to the family's rental house in San Juan), Abuelo's stories are interrupted and monitored by Abuela, who, fearing the radical nationalist (anti-American) messages embedded in the grandfather's stories, shoos the children away from the storyteller with promises of television shows.

Clearly, the novel figures television as the modern version of storytelling: a machine that will gradually replace the living presence of the oral narrator. And with the loss of the immediate and authentic presence of the storyteller comes the loss of Spanish as an originary language. The American shows that Consuelo and Mili watch, such as *Perry Mason* (26), are dubbed, a form of translation that tries to hide the presence of an original language (English) by layering over it with a new language (Spanish). The new language becomes the copy that functions as an original, but it does so ineffectively, because the viewer can see that the mouths moving on the screen and the sounds coming out of it are not in synch. In this context the original language of oral storytelling, Spanish, is replaced by a dubbed Spanish, which is itself a poor copy of the new originary language, English. Thus, with the advent of television, storytelling is displaced, and the political and cultural influences of urban Puerto Rico begin to map themselves onto the rural areas of the island as well.

Even without television, the collective voices of Puerto Rico's nationalist supporters are continually deconstructed with counternarratives. For every rhetorical stance taken by a character about the "defacement of nature" (25) there is a response about the progress of technology, and for every mythical legend told about the survival of the Tainos there is a counternarrative about the fabricated idealism of those legends. When Abuelo speaks lyrically about the island's original landscape, that of a "nurturing mother" whose bounty was plentiful, and warns that "nothing could grow through cement and steel" (56–57), Papi retorts that "people who believed such romantic nonsense should quit their jobs and go live in the hills" (57). The effect is that stories about the island's authentic identity appear constructed and idyllic. American national identity continues, therefore, to write itself upon the island's landscape on several levels: topographically (blasting a hole in the mountainside), ecologically (the smell of factories erases the smell of nature), linguistically, and of course culturally, by framing new stories and commodifying memories.

In addition to the commodification of orality, the text presents writing and literacy as commodity fetishes that (in the context of the island) empower the writer but disempower the subaltern space. As in *The Line of the Sun*, reading, literacy, and writing are considered shameful acts shrouded in secrecy, and unlike the collective aspect of oral storytelling, written narratives here create separation and isolation, undermining any possibility of community. When Patricio and Consuelo communicate by letters after his move to New York, they both seem to write from and toward a vacuum, "corresponding in two different languages" (152). Consuelo in fact treats her own letters as "secret" journals (173) and notes, "It was as if I were sending them into a void, since I could not really think of the strange, cold place where he had vanished as real" (96). But like Marisol, Consuelo's immersion in the written word is traced with a sense of transgression; even her acquisition of English allows her to cross limits right in front of her parents. She reads the English-language books that Patricio has left behind after his departure for the United States, becoming addicted to the "intoxicating trips to places that were mine alone to experience" and the realization that she can "read about topics that my parents would find scandalous, . . . in front of them" (64–65).

The written word thus clearly offers possibilities for transformation and reinvention. When Patricio writes to Consuelo from the United States, he does so under the pseudoname "Patty," masking his own identity by posing as her female American pen pal. The written word's unreliability here allows for a double transgression, suggesting that part of the commodification of literacy in the novel involves realizing its empowering potential. Ultimately, Consuelo is "a lover of the word" (154) and recognizes that "words were the key to power and freedom" (155). The masking that written words enable allows her to transgress silently and secretly while continuing to pass as a dutiful obedient daughter.[37] As she passes she gathers ammunition that will fuel her creativity, allowing her eventually "to gain control of hours and, soon, of whole days of my life" (65). Although the story does not explicitly point toward Consuelo's future as a writer, the implication is that her secret transgressions and her sense of dislocation preempt her solitary migration to the United States and her eventual writing down of her experiences. But the story also shows that in the context of the island, the very production of words that empower Consuelo problematically disempowers others. As if to further emphasize the island as a space of unbelonging and the tensions of writing in such an environment, the novel shows how representations of Puerto Rico are inextricably bound up in consumerism.

One such instance is Consuelo's visit to La Perla, a shantytown on the outskirts of San Juan that represents a kind of geographical ghetto of poverty. In this transgressive space, Consuelo feels herself enveloped by carnival: here, overturned social and moral values rule. Consuelo becomes, once again, a tourist figure on the island, negotiating the space for herself and the reader as she "tours" it (162). In La Perla, marginality is sanctioned and legitimated. It is the grim urban underbelly of the island, a contrast to the capitalist Puerto Rico that the Americans have created on the other side of the wall that separates the ghetto from the rest of San Juan. It is a noncommodified space that could disrupt the United States' own narrative of identity on the island, but Consuelo's immediate reaction to it is one of narrativization that instead threatens to objectify it.

In these scenes the narrative voice draws attention to Consuelo's privileged position as a visitor and potential storyteller, as she sits on a hillside and comes up with similes and metaphors to describe her surroundings. When she imagines the houses on stilts as "women holding up their skirts to cross a puddle, brown women with skinny legs wearing pastel colors," her friend Lucila responds, "Is that what you do with your time, niña, think of pretty words to describe ugly things?" (166). Lucila's response highlights the gap between representation and action. Suddenly, we are forced to question the use of stories to represent the aesthetic beauty or abject poverty of a place, even as Consuelo continues to produce metaphors ("I looked back and saw the wobbly birthday cake of La Perla" [166]). What are the ethical and political implications of Consuelo's romanticization of La Perla? As a tourist, Consuelo becomes a voyeur, outsider, and interpreter, and is also complicit in its continued poverty. Her teacher, who has brought her here, confirms this by saying that they are all "accomplices" in supporting a government that remains indifferent to La Perla's needs. It is ironic and significant that this late trip to La Perla evokes in Consuelo a feeling of love for the island where she recognizes for the first time, in "the raw misery and startling beauty," the yearning that poets and composers have long felt for the island (168). The visit suggests that beauty in Puerto Rico can only be experienced by the tourist-figure, that the memory and representation of that beauty can only be produced from afar, and that such representation is inherently problematic because of its colonial overtures.

The La Perla episode thus illustrates how narrative representation, and the production of story, memory, and national identity, can become acts of commodification. Of course, the central story that Consuelo tells—that of her sister, Mili—is so transgressive that it appears to be the only one in the novel that resists commodification, even though it is at the same time scandalous enough to incite a certain voyeurism (or objectification) on the part of the reader. Like Consuelo's narrative production, the story of Mili clearly shows the possibilities and limits of radical transgression on the island. Like Patricio and María, Mili is marginalized by those around her, but unlike them, she disappears at the end of the story and is mourned as if dead, becoming not only the text's central tragic figure but also a significant metaphor for Puerto Rican displacement. Rather than commodifying her exile, the narrative illustrates, through Mili, the alienating and frightening depths of the colonized psyche. Mili's teachers diagnose her with schizophrenia, echoing Yudice and Flores's assertion that "Latino affirmation is first of all a fending off of schizophrenia, of that pathological duality born of contending cultural worlds, and perhaps more significantly, of the conflicting pressures toward both exclusion and forced incorporation."[38] In the text, "fending off" schizophrenia means acknowledging its transgressive potential and at the same time attempting to control, manage, or place its deviance—in other words, recognizing both the limit and the entire space that it traverses. Latino "affirmation" thus emerges out of an understanding of contradictions, in which the colonized psyche becomes a site of ambivalence, a location of simultaneous boundaries and movement. In Mili herself, national experiences of straddling and duality become represented through illness, and dis-ease becomes a literal disease that reaches beyond the island. As a sacrificial figure, Mili becomes the collective site that absorbs the nation's disease and offers up an alternative version of affirmative Latino identity.

Before Mili's disappearance she claims to hear voices and noises, and speaks in an invented language, which, although systemically consistent, is "alarming" to Consuelo (52) because it cannot establish any coherent means of communication with her social environment. Like the other misfit characters, Mili moves between two worlds, in her case, of sanity and insanity, disturbingly highlighting a state of exilic limbo and instability as a new kind of norm. When later in the text she is accused of "inappropriate behavior, touching games with boys" (80) by her teachers, her otherness challenges not only social beliefs about the body but also about morality, and its display further emphasizes the porousness of borders set down by the community. Her very instability, in fact, is defined by established cultural discourses: her paternal grandmother, we learn, also had periods of insanity during which she "went after men" (91). Progressively, though, as her family keeps Mili's illness a "secret" from the community, it seems to grow. She becomes more trapped in her "inner world" (93), almost a "monster" (95), recalling the traditional categories into which women who stray beyond the norm must be placed in order to control the visibility of their transgression.

But most significant is the fact that unlike the other outsiders of the story, Mili refuses to be re-placed in a new setting. While María's and Patricio's transgressions ultimately become normalized, that is, accommodated into commodities that in a sense reintegrate and rehabilitate them into society, Mili's transgression persists as transgression, and remains a symbolic reminder of the island's ambiguous identity. It refuses to be diluted, translated, or diminished into anything else, and lingers as a ghostly presence, disrupting U.S. national identity on the island because of its unlocatability. And although Consuelo's story of Mili risks objectifying her, one could also argue that this very risk appropriately places the story where it best belongs: within (and as part of) the long history of colonization, in which memories and representations of Puerto Rico are always compromised by unbelonging, migration, and exile. Ultimately, the novel shows how this exile is an integral part of the neocolonial experience. The story, after all, does get told, and through the telling it uncovers and also troubles some of the invisible normativity that has determined both nations' cultural and moral codes. With the memory of Mili's schizophrenia and unresolved disappearance, then, Consuelo moves her story toward the United States, writing Puerto Rico's resistant unbelonging into the United States' own national and cultural identity and reimagining an interpenetration of the Americas that recalls but also moves beyond the dynamic of neocolonialism.

4 / Memoirs of Resistance: Colonialism and Transnationalism in Esmeralda Santiago's *When I Was Puerto Rican, Almost a Woman,* and *The Turkish Lover*

Esmeralda Santiago, like Judith Ortiz Cofer, writes from and about the liminal space between colonized Puerto Rican islanders and postcolonial mainlanders, uses her stories in order to return to and interrogate the space of the island, and shows how the production of narrative confounds and resists the colonial framework of the United States. Clearly, the island's status as a Commonwealth and unincorporated territory of the United States determines, to a great degree, its anomalous political status, its legislative subordination to the United States, and its residents' binational identity.[1] As such, Santiago's three memoirs raise questions about U.S. Puerto Rican belonging and displacement, and make us rethink national identity by imagining Puerto Rican identity and space as a part of the United States. In Santiago's work, particularly the later memoirs, the dynamic of colonialism and racialized citizenship that we saw in Judith Ortiz Cofer's novels is also further marked by the stigma of perceived Puerto Rican cultural and social deficiency, as the protagonist Negi's subordinate class position contributes to her acute sense of illicit and cultural unbelonging on both the island and mainland.

While Ortiz Cofer depicts the island ethnographically in both her novels, implicitly demonstrating the effects of U.S. imperialism, in Santiago's memoirs, the island's colonized identity (for both islanders and diasporic Puerto Ricans) is more explicitly written from within the subaltern's psyche.[2] It also becomes clear even early on that as a subaltern, Santiago's presence and creative ambitions on the island and the mainland are marked by others as strongly illegitimate. Over the course of her memoirs, which explore how legacies of political and cultural colonization on the island haunt the mainland and connect to her experiences of personal dislocation, she thus attempts to take possession of her environment, her writerly voice, and her transnational identity. Although scholars have tended to criticize Santiago's memoirs (particularly the first one) for their apparent assimilationist drive, I contend that Santiago's process of belonging occurs not through assimilation, which assumes as its premise that she is a cultural outsider in the United States, but by troubling normative definitions of U.S. identity and ultimately imagining herself as a binational U.S. Puerto Rican citizen. Here I read all three of Santiago's memoirs progressively to argue that in constructing this blended self, she engages in transnational decolonization, rather than figuring the cultural, topographical, and geographical erosion of Puerto Rico under the auspices of U.S. globalism, as Ortiz Cofer did. Through my interpretation of "place" in the memoirs as an intersection of physical location (land, geography) and cultural practices and experiences, I demonstrate how her personal dislocation is rooted in legacies of political colonialism and how resistance—even decolonization—can come out of her spatial, physical, and psychological experiences of unbelonging.[3] And while her first memoir seeks to separate the two nation-spaces, at the end of the last memoir Santiago sees herself in an ambassadorial role, alluding to a shared heritage between mainland and island Puerto Rican artists and imagining herself as a citizen of both spaces. As in Ortiz Cofer's work, one implication of this transnational citizenship is to shift both nations' history and dynamic of colonialism, and enable a new understanding of nationhood.[4]

In offering this reading of Santiago's memoirs, however, I want to first address both the negative critical responses to her work and some of the defenses of it.[5] Santiago's first memoir, *When I Was Puerto Rican*, has garnered the most attention; Maria Szadsuik points out (although she does not necessarily concur with the idea) that because Santiago shows the bright successful story of the American dream come true, she has been accused of complicity with the ideology of the majority culture. But even Szadsuik, who places Santiago on a spectrum with Chicana and Mexican American writers Cherrie Moraga and Sandra Cisneros, argues that while these writers respectively respond to the majority culture through active negation and withdrawal strategies, Santiago writes assimilation.[6] Lisa Sánchez González, looking at *When I Was Puerto Rican*, contends that Santiago's writing comes across as allegorical and representative of Puerto Rican experience, but denies the structural inequalities that most working-class Boricua women endure in the diaspora.[7] While Sánchez González does note Santiago's depiction of poverty, colonialism, and gender oppression, she argues that the epilogue undoes the memoir's implicit critique of colonial racism-sexism. In addition, she finds that the memoir overall presents the United States and Puerto Rico as simplistic tropes: "the Island (Puerto Rico) represents outgrown, retrograde communal and family values, while in the final instance America . . . is celebrated as the utopia of the mature female protagonist's liberatory exile," and concludes that the work is politically "insufficient."[8] Marta Echano similarly acknowledges the memoir's potential for "armchair cultural voyeurism" and admits that publishers have learned to profit from this kind of "ghetto" testimonial, but sees this process as inevitable when geonational identity becomes destabilized, as it does in the work. She notes that Santiago is simultaneously cast as "other" by mainstream America and as Americanized by Puerto Ricans, and rendered both as outsider and insider, hero and traitor. Together with Julee Tate, who argues that the memoirs should be read not as allegories but as one woman's personal journey to the center, Echano wonders whether Santiago can in fact ever speak only for herself when "ethnic" narratives are so often read as collective allegories.[9]

One of the most interesting responses to both Santiago's work and, implicitly, to Sánchez González's criticism of it comes from José L. Torres-Padilla, who reads Santiago's unpopularity with both island and mainland Puerto Ricans as evidence of an essentialist perception of identity that is still active in parts of the Puerto Rican community. For these critics, Santiago is presumably helping along cultural imperialism's annihilation of some kind of Puerto Rican inner authenticity. In defense of her work, though, Torres-Padilla looks at Santiago's own interview statements, where she positions herself as "in-between" cultures, and argues, counter to the essentialist reading of identity, that once an immigrant has lived in the United States, his or her "cultural purity" becomes compromised.[10] Ultimately, Torres-Padilla reads Santiago's memoir as the latest in a series of literary texts that embrace Puerto Rican identity as an ethnicity rather than a nationality, an interpretation that moves in the direction of my own reading of Santiago's memoirs insofar as it displaces U.S. Puerto Rican identity-formation from any particular geographical location.

Building on these various critical voices, it should be clear that my reading of Santiago's work, focusing as it does on each memoir in turn, answers many of the critical objections made above. Looking at all three memoirs in progression allows us to read them as Santiago's various and repeated attempts at self-writing, and as the result of almost a decade of literary unfolding. We can, in other words, trace a broader trajectory of transnational identity-formation that requires us to rethink readings of her first memoir in isolation. The memoirs together clearly complicate and nuance the rags-to-riches story and the terms of Santiago's (and Negi's) success in ways that the first memoir alone does not. Because my analysis sees the United States and Puerto Rico in the works as blended rather than as simplistically opposed nations, it addresses the concern that the United States is presented as a utopia of the American dream. When I argue, as I do later on in this chapter, that Santiago legitimates her presence on the mainland through the activity of writing, I understand Puerto Rico not as a space that she has left behind, but as a space that converges with the United States in order to enable literary and creative production. In particular, my reading of the first memoir's prologue and epilogue below, which examines them as framing devices, also answers Sánchez González's concern that the latter is merely a "quick tally" of successes.[11] Most important, my exploration throughout this chapter of the relationship and "gap" between the United States and the island, and consequently, between Santiago-the-author and Negi-the-protagonist, is itself a study of the ambivalence (and anxiety) that comes, for Santiago, with marketing and representing her story for U.S. audiences. To an extent, she is continually marking, measuring, and blurring the distance between the two selves and nations, and thus troubling the notion of the United States as the utopian site of an uncomplicated success story.

From early on Santiago's desire to write is undermined by her understanding that as a poor Puerto Rican migrant, her ambition for artistic expression and belonging on the mainland is perceived to be illegitimate. Thus the texts trace the problematic relationship between writing and legitimacy. In one scene early on in *Almost a Woman* Santiago describes having to translate and interpret for her mother in the welfare office. As the welfare officer asks pertinent questions, Mami has to admit that she is not married to either of the men who have fathered her many children. Initially, there is an awkward hesitation over the word "illegitimate," as Negi does not understand it. When Mami asks what the legitimacy issue has to do with getting welfare, Negi translates, "burning with shame."[12] Later on, Negi looks up the word and thinks, "Illegitimate meant born of parents who were not married. But the way the social worker's lips puckered, illegitimate sounded much worse" (44). This scene shows Negi's sudden comprehension of her own vulnerable position in society, and her understanding that her very existence and place in it, as defined through the law and the state's discourse, is a transgression of socially accepted norms and codes of conduct—she is illegitimate—and that this transgression is considered shameful. As Negi recalls the social worker's lips "puckering" she sees how transgressive acts threaten and trouble the boundaries of the body politic (national, familial): the social worker's own body responds viscerally and interprets the status of illegitimacy as a physical (as well as social) rupturing of normative values.

This scene is important for understanding how Santiago's memoirs, in presenting the subordination of Puerto Rico's economic and political affairs to the United States, also by implication address the cultural unbelonging of Puerto Ricans on the mainland. Santiago is not just trying to recapture her lost homeland or create a space of home through her writing. More specifically, in the memoirs homelessness is also expressed as an illegitimate state that has been incurred through the colonial relationship between the United States and Puerto Rico. In other words, for Santiago, the legacy of island colonialism has to an extent determined the cultural otherness and state of unbelonging that Negi experiences on the U.S. mainland. For her, then, the process of resisting colonialism is also a process of legitimating Puerto Rican presence in the nation. Santiago's autobiographical voice, in negotiating its place in the literary canon, provides such a strategy of decolonization and belonging. And while with all autobiography we know that autobiographer and protagonist are the same self, and that despite any fictional elements in the work and any attempts to separate the two they share the same body, in Santiago's case the narrative implications of this are complicated by questions of national identity and class. The autobiographer Santiago has undergone a transformation from her former poor Puerto Rican self into a U.S. mainlander and a commercially successful author: the U.S. autobiographer's body pens and creates her Puerto Rican islander body, known variously as Negi, Chiquita, and Es throughout the memoirs.[13] The separation of protagonist and autobiographer that we see particularly in the first memoir is also a separation of United States and Puerto Rican nation-spaces, while the moments of connection between Negi and Santiago in the later books signal Santiago's evolving transnational identity.

When I Was Puerto Rican: Dislocating Foundations

Santiago's first memoir is located almost entirely in Puerto Rico; the bulk of the story takes place on the island, creating a narrative return to a childhood home-space that contrasts quite starkly with the later memoirs' landscapes of urban and rural mainland United States. The memoir attempts to portray a foundational narrative space that would allow Santiago to belong to at least a fictional, if not real, version of home. But while in some ways the text does convey a distinct nation-space, this sense of a separate nation is also undermined by our knowledge that it is written as a memory from afar (from a space of migration), and also by the fact that on the island itself, Negi and her family are continually subject to experiences of internal migration as they move back and forth between rural and urban spaces. Thus, although the narrative account imaginatively transports Santiago (and the reader) back to an idyllic space of childhood, this return is also continually troubled by two things: the narrative's structure (the prologue/epilogue framing device), and the embedded trauma of migration and colonialism on the island itself. Furthermore, in this memoir the United States' colonial presence in Puerto Rico accounts for the inseparability of U.S. Puerto Rican nation-spaces and identities. This means that Negi's resistant decolonizing strategy (trying to remove the United States from Puerto Rico) is inherently ambivalent, as it also involves a fracturing of her own subaltern identity. It is not until the later memoirs, set on the mainland, that national identity is reframed as transnational and this ambivalence becomes resolved.

Various factors in the memoir demonstrate the ambivalence of Santiago's colonized psyche. The prologue and epilogue structure seems not only to separate her U.S. and Puerto Rican identities but also suggests their inseparability because the experiences she relates are remembered through a lens of migration and dislocation that blends both nation-spaces. The author-protagonist also writes Puerto Rico as a home that no longer exists and that will invariably be lost over the course of the story, as it is remembered from within and as part of the United States. In addition, even on the island Negi's own illegitimate Puerto Rican body is written as inherently fragmented and exiled from itself and its location, while the move to New York toward the end of the story represents a physical migration that throughout has been foreshadowed by the text's representation of political and migratory dislocations on the island. Thus, in keeping with the colonial dimension that informs Negi's psyche, the memoir shows how national foundations are essentially dislocated, and how the possibilities for community building and belonging on the island are often subject to the tensions of U.S. imperialism.

The prologue, instructionally titled "How to Eat a Guava," initially seems to be a reexperience, through the taste, texture, and smell of a guava, of the Puerto Rico of the narrator's childhood. For Santiago, the fruit's very presence in a New York supermarket suggests the fine line between the two home-spaces: there is some sense of amazement at the guava's very being, at its crossing of cultures and spaces, that is clearly a microcosmic representation of the writer's own larger cultural and national border crossings. She immediately recalls the last guava she had on "the day we left Puerto Rico," with a detailed description showing that she wants to understand not just the moment of crossing from island to mainland but also to know and reexperience the moments before everything changed.[14] In a recollection that seems to infuse the present moment with the past, she remembers that the guava "was large and juicy, almost red in the center, and so fragrant that I didn't want to eat it because I would lose the smell" (4). But her memory of that last day in Puerto Rico is in fact a memory of anticipating loss because she knows what she will no longer have ("lose the smell"). Thus even in recollection Puerto Rico can only be experienced as a transitional and temporary space from which future migration will take place. At the end of the brief prologue, the narrator returns to "Today" and puts the overpriced fruit back on display. It is only barely able to transport her back: "It smells *faintly* of late summer afternoons and hopscotch under the mango tree" (4, my emphasis). She sensibly remarks that "this is autumn in New York, and I'm no longer a child" and pushes her cart away "toward the apples and pears of my adulthood" (4). Here, in the opening to her first memoir, we learn of this autobiographer's ambiguous position: as a successful writer firmly belonging to the here and now she can use her narrative space to re-create and return to her childhood Puerto Rico, thus blurring, in fictional and imaginary terms, the two nation-spaces, while at the same time separating them just as she separates her autobiographical self from the island child of the story.

The book's epilogue shows a similar ambivalence about the relationship between protagonist and author. The memoir's story itself ends with Negi's audition for Manhattan's magnet Performing Arts High School, which she is sure she has failed. She writes regretfully that despite everyone's efforts to help her, "I had failed the audition and would never, ever, get out of Brooklyn" (266). But then the epilogue begins, "A decade after my graduation from Performing Arts, I visited the school. I was by then living in Boston, a scholarship student at Harvard University" (269). With this we learn that the protagonist not only gets into the high school of her choice but also goes farther than anyone imagined was possible. Although the details are not yet filled in (as they are in the next two memoirs), this leap across time attempts to provide closure. Whether the effort at closure is successful (and desirable) is debatable.[15] What is important to note here, though, is that because the gap between the end of the story and the start of the epilogue functions as a void, we can also read this "gap" or separation between the two nations and identities as a liminal space, a borderland area within which the process of transnational identity-formation can begin.

Other aspects of the memoir also show how colonialism blurs national identities. In particular, Negi's Puerto Rican body is disrupted even before her migration to New York, emphasizing the island's ambiguously codependent relationship with the United States within its own borders. While her autobiographer's body asserts its presence solidly in the text's framework, the protagonist's body she remembers within the story is culturally, psychologically, and politically dislocated. Her early memories of home speak of frequent migration and displacement, reiterating the anxiety about community rootedness on the island. The first narrated memory of the family's house in rural Macún is one of many that clearly establishes Negi's uncertainty, from a very young age, about her cultural identity, and about the spatial markers that seem to determine it: she is split between the jíbaras (country dwellers) and the urban residents of the island. Descriptions of Macún recall strong connections between body and land (49, 59) and re-create a world where roots do connect the land to a community (46) and where narrative production itself seems to strengthen patriotic ties to the island (12, 18). But such connections are fragile and at the mercy of frequent internal migrations, particularly from rural to urban spaces.

This connection to land is thus undermined by the family's frequent, often-abrupt moves between the city of Santurce (a suburb of San Juan) and the country.[16] The rootedness of the rural community is threatened by the island's shift toward industrialization and the consequent disharmony within familial circles. For example, initially Negi describes her mother, Monín, as part of the island's natural landscape. As a very young child Negi imagines her mother's dress as part of fecund and ripe nature, the "yellow and orange flowers of her dress blending into greenness: a miraculous garden with legs and arms and a melody" (8). The earth and the mother's body are brought together harmoniously; each nourishes and sustains the other's ability to provide grounding for the narrator. But later on in the story, after a hurricane worsens the family's financial situation and the government fails to help rebuild the barrio (110), Monín takes a factory job outside the house, breaking an unspoken "taboo" and suffering ostracism from the neighborhood women (122). As Negi embraces her mother before Monín leaves for work, she feels only the "harsh bones of her undergarments" and seeks the familiar fragrances of oregano and rosemary, only to come up with scented American perfumes: Cashmere Bouquet and Maybelline (113). The effects of imperialism on domestic and familial spaces could not be clearer: Mami's "natural" island body is subject first to the effects of the United States' economic directives on the island, and later, to the internal (and eventually external) migration that displaces subaltern figures in search of employment.

In the toxic environment of Santurce Negi also explicitly demonstrates the psychological effects of these continual dislocations by seeming to split her body and mind. Throughout all three of her memoirs Santiago describes this kind of escape as a response to traumatic events and experiences, imagining watching her own body from afar so vividly that she seems to separate her physical self from her psychological self (39). This splitting of self is significantly expressed as a journey of the body, a movement away from the physical self that ruptures and ungrounds her, and in political terms represents even further fragmentation of her Puerto Rican national identity. It is a defense mechanism, a way of survival in reaction to her surroundings.[17] When Negi imagines leaving her body behind during times of stress, she does so in order to psychologically survive what her physical body must endure. For example, during a humiliating put-down at school she imagines escaping: "I didn't hear [the teacher]. I left my body standing in front of her, suffering spitballs and whispered insults. I sent the part of me that could fly outside the window to the flamboyán tree in the yard" (139). Her body leaves the site of beatings and poverty, extends itself in an imaginary flight, and then watches events unfold from a distance, bringing itself into the middle of a more healing and sensory natural environment. She writes that in the tree, "the orange flowers covered me as I sat in their midst" (139). This psychological flight represents a minute moment of empowerment for a character who is otherwise acutely aware that the presence of power is continually "located elsewhere," at the level of family, community, and nation.[18] Like Soveida's response to abuse in Face of an Angel, Negi's psychological repression of these difficult experiences is translated into spatial responses to place: as a socioeconomically marginalized young girl she displaces herself psychologically through imaginative flight.[19]

Although her "flight" is a form of escapism that prevents her from directly facing difficult events, in terms of her political identity formation such responses are also empowering. Classic understandings of repression read it as an evasive response, a "pushing away" of experience, but it is important to remember that what is displaced (dispersed, deferred, repressed, pushed aside) remains, significantly, still there: as Bammer notes, "*Dis*placed but not *re*placed, it remains a source of trouble, the *shifting ground* of signification that makes meanings tremble."[20] For Negi, the eventual formation of a creative consciousness begins in this very process of displacement that troubles the grounding framework held in place by the island's institutional systems. In other words, Negi's psychological repression is also a form of resistance that shifts the cultural norms of her nation-space. In this first memoir, this becomes evident through Negi's response to U.S. presence on the island, a response that demonstrates how her geographical and personal experiences of migratory displacement are part of a longer legacy of Spanish colonial history too.

In a sense, then, Negi's personal responses to her environment must be read in light of the broader political context of the memoir. In a chapter often cited by critics, entitled "The American Invasion of Macún," Santiago describes how the identity and history of the island in the 1950s are swept under U.S. cultural practices. The cultural and political takeover becomes clear when "The Americans" come to Negi's school to explain dental hygiene and recommend healthy foods to the islanders. It should be noted that in some instances the narrative does critique U.S. cultural norms on the island and valorize Puerto Rican ones. The spatial representation of the United States in Puerto Rico, for example, marks it as a separate and foreign entity that does not belong on the island: it is a "flat and shadowless" world (74). Similarly, some of the humor of the scene—the claim that with American food the children will grow up "as tall and strong as Dick, Jane, and Sally, the Americanitos in our primers," and the comically huge set of teeth with pink gums that one of the experts unveils (64)—belies the distribution of power in the room: because the recommended food on the charts is not native to the island, the mothers appear to resist the dietary recommendations, simply deciding that they will eat "like Americans" only when real hunger strikes (68). But despite these examples of collective resistance on the part of the islanders, it is also clear that such community has emerged out of an oppositional stance against the Americans, and that its expressions of identity often remain tongue-tied or quiet. Later on, Papi's explanation of events to Negi, "that's part of being an imperialist. They expect us to do things their way, even in our own country" (73), becomes muted through the child's perspective. Again and again, the colonizer's lesson is simultaneously rejected and absorbed, mirroring the ambiguity of this dimension of the United States and Puerto Rico's relationship.

Even Negi's largest gesture of resistance, her rejection of one of the "American breakfasts" she is served at school, shows how the island's cultural and political identity is in many ways already inseparable from that of its northern neighbor. The Puerto Rican cafeteria servers, teachers, and children around her appear enthusiastically to welcome the new breakfasts of powdered eggs and processed orange juice (Negi's friend Juanita exclaims, "This is great!" and "Wow!" [76]), and imagine that American food is healthier than island food ("here are some salchichas Americanas, so you can put some meat on those bones" [75]). Negi alone refuses to eat, instead playing with the food on her plate, taking all the different colors and "creating yellow mountains through which shimmering rivers of grease flowed, their edges green, the rolled-up balls of white bread perfect stones along strips of brown earth studded with tiny black flecks, ants perhaps, or better yet, microscopic people" (76). This miniature anti-imperialist gesture, in which she rejects cultural colonization and embraces her own cultural nationalism, transforming American food into a Puerto Rican natural landscape, is magnified later on when she throws up the food she has eaten. When she is admonished by the school lunch matron, Mrs. García, and told that without it she would "go hungry every morning" (82), she screams, "I've never gone hungry!" because "My Mami and Papi can feed us without your disgusting gringo imperialist food!" (82), sending a wave of shock and silence around the cafeteria. The episode points both to the force of Negi's resistance and the futility of it: while she publicly rejects the food and makes a bold statement, she is alone in doing so. Most significant, she must direct her attack against gringo imperialist food at another Puerto Rican (Mrs. García), suggesting that the very lines that would demarcate a distinct island nation-space are blurred. In trying to destabilize American cultural norms, then, she must also take down her own island, reminding us that in such a landscape, there is no absolute space from which to practice acts of resistance that are not already part of the systemic imperial framework.

Finally, one of the most important ways in which Santiago suggests that Puerto Rican nationhood can be simultaneously part of and apart from the United States is through her experience of migration to the mainland. Specifically, she tries to identify the political boundary that divides the United States and Puerto Rico and the geographical point at which one nation begins and the other ends. In all the memoirs she mourns the losses of childhood and home and at the same time understands that the very trauma that defines that experience of loss also resists its complete or whole narrativization. Thus she returns repeatedly to her moment of arrival in New York as a thirteen-year-old girl, as if trying to really capture the moment of migration that determined her official shift in national identity. What I term her arrival narrative, featured in all the memoirs, is described as an experience of physical, psychological, and geographical dislocation: even though the original undoing of "Puerto Rico" began on the island itself, the actual move to the mainland represents an obvious rupture. This watershed moment is thus narrated as central, motivated by her autobiographer's desire to locate the moment of physical migration from one nation to another. Ultimately, Santiago narrates it as an inevitable and final culmination of the internal migrations that have moved Negi back and forth, throughout her childhood, across Puerto Rico itself.

The description of the voyage to New York is most detailed in this first memoir, describing the flight itself in terms that imagine migration—the crossing itself—as stillness: "we floated in a milky whiteness that seemed to hold the plane suspended above Puerto Rico. I couldn't believe we were moving" (214). The most remarkable cultural, physical, and psychological moment of transition in Negi's life is thus experienced—and remembered in narrative—as a process of immobility, suggesting that the very nature of this shift in national identity—the stepping over of a national border—eludes experience as movement. The moment of crossing that would denote difference and change vanishes before Negi can grasp hold of it. In one sense, she seems disempowered: while she apparently stands still, the world moves beneath her, changing her location and displacing her irrespective of her desires. But at the same time, her hold on Puerto Rico brings the island into the mainland, troubling the United States' presence in Puerto Rico and its delegitimation of the island's geography, population, and culture. This scene of external migration to New York thus symbolizes the entire memoir's representation of colonization as a process of unbelonging, and anticipates the ones that follow, where she will begin to articulate a citizenship of belonging based on the interpenetration of Puerto Rico within the United States.

Almost a Woman: Rewriting Nation on the Mainland

In New York, Negi's status as a Puerto Rican in the United States renders her a second-class (albeit legal) citizen, whose ethnic identity becomes racialized because of how her body is ascribed as foreign. Santiago clearly establishes the ways in which Negi becomes displaced and othered because of the inescapable darkness of her skin and the "hostile culture and environment" (337) of the mainland. For example, despite years of education in Manhattan, when she leaves the city and visits small towns with her acting group, she suddenly cannot "pass" unnoticed. Describing the experience as one of violation, she writes that often "I was the darkest person in the room, and the stares I drew felt like darts" (240). She realizes that racially, her in-betweeness defines her "unbelonging": "I wasn't black, I wasn't white. The racial middle in which I existed meant that people evaluated me on the spot. . . . Their eyes flickered, their brains calibrated the level of pigmentation they'd find acceptable" (242). In these newly threatening spaces of the United States, her national and cultural identity ceases to matter; instead, the mainstream marks her body as racially but ambiguously foreign: "I was simply too dark to be white, too white to be dark" (242).

How, then, does Negi challenge the perception of cultural otherness that comes out of this rhetoric of racialized citizenship? As part of the mass exodus created through migration from the island, she begins, in her new space, to develop a geopolitical U.S. Puerto Rican identity in transit. And as Puerto Rico recedes in her memory, she begins to forge a transnational identity on the mainland that can, through writing, engage with and challenge her subordinated citizenship status. The development of this transnational identity means that although Negi experiences her physical and geographical break with the island as traumatic, the rupture is not absolute. While the large shifting of Puerto Rico's population from the island to the mainland displaces Puerto Rican cultural identity, it also reconceives that nation within the boundaries of the mainland, writing, in other words, Puerto Rican nationhood into U.S. nationhood. In what follows I explore the ways that Negi's acquisition of English and oral/literate facilities in her new language change her body's experience in place. This apparent act of acculturation into the U.S. mainstream (learning English) is tempered by the ways in which Puerto Rico's fragmented yet disseminated presence troubles normative cultural and national discourses. Similarly, I argue that her formal education in dance can be interpreted as a physically creative act that, like learning English, also renegotiates her body's "place" in the United States and enables her to eventually assert her presence creatively as a writer.

Before exploring the development of such resistant identity-formations, the memoir establishes how the island's displaced and ambiguous identity is manifested on the mainland. Santiago begins the narrative with a recollection of the family's frequent moves both before and after their migration to the mainland, underlining the disruptive cultural rootlessness that fractures the core of Puerto Rican geographic nationhood. Even as an adult she moves easily and packs lightly: "Each time I packed my belongings, I left a little of myself in the rooms that sheltered me, never home, always just the places I lived. I congratulated myself on how easy it was to leave them, how well I packed everything I owned into a couple of boxes and a suitcase" (2). She occupies spaces like a visitor, unable to put down roots and resisting making memories or connections based on place, but in leaving a little of herself in each place, she also slowly fractures herself. In the moment of leaving a place, therefore, she reexperiences a rupture that recalls the original violence of departure from Macún to Santurce, and from the island to the mainland. This also establishes a pattern for the future: a repetition of the nomadic legacy that permeates and defines the colonized psyche and that is embedded with an undercurrent of violence.

As in the first memoir the narrative's very structure exacerbates Negi's displacement by suggesting that some of Negi's most formative memories of Puerto Rico are fictional. On the second page of *Almost a Woman*, Santiago invokes the relationship between protagonist and autobiographer, just as she did in the prologue and epilogue of *When I Was Puerto Rican*. Here she describes an important moment of her return visit to Puerto Rico as an adult, but she has fast-forwarded to this moment in time, because chronologically it does not occur until years later near the end of *The Turkish Lover*, where she narrates the visit in more detail. In *Almost a Woman*'s description of the visit, she returns to Macún, "the spot where my childhood began and ended" (2). She says, "I stepped on what was left of our blue tiled floor and looked at the wild greenness around me" and recalls certain memories associated with the place. But then she concludes that ultimately, "It was no longer familiar, nor beautiful, nor did it give a clue of who I'd been there, or who I might become wherever I was going next" (2). Despite the powerful memories of this exact location that have sustained her for at least eight years in the United States, standing again in the place itself fails to bridge the gap between her disparate mainland (adult) and island (child) identities.

The place, in reality, cannot work as an origin point that might collect her migratory personas into one center. In its failure, the place cannot even summon up ghosts or any presence of the lost childhood self that Negi longs for. Despite the very tangibility of the place—she is finally, finally, standing on the earth of her Puerto Rican home—Negi remains removed from the immediacy of the experience in the now. In fact, this experience is less immediate and powerful to her than the imaginary flights that over the years allowed her to journey, in times of stress and trauma, back to the landscape of Puerto Rico that was, of course, merely a landscape in her mind.

In addition, the vegetation around her former home is so overgrown that nature appears to suffocate rather than nourish, erasing rather than recalling any evidence of the family's former presence there. Negi describes the weeds chocking the dirt yard, "creepers" that have "overgrown the cement floor," and pinakoop that has "climbed over what was left of the walls and turned them into soft green mounds that sheltered drab olive lizards and chameleons, coquí and hummingbirds" (2). Most disturbingly, the land itself does not remember her, even though she has remembered it: "There was no sign we'd ever been there, except for the hillock of blue cement tile on which I stood. It gleamed in the afternoon sun, its color so intense that I wondered if I had stepped onto the wrong floor because I didn't remember our floor being that blue" (2). In fact, the entire "return" ends on this note, essentially admitting the fallibility of memory. If indeed her memories of Puerto Rico are unreliable (perhaps the floor was that blue, perhaps not), then in this retrospective moment, we know that the Puerto Rican identity that she forged from afar is similarly built on fictions. Furthermore, because this scene appears at the very start of *Almost a Woman*, Santiago has chronologically collapsed time, and given us some sense of her future before the story itself reaches that moment. In this way, the entire second volume is framed by the reader's knowledge (but not the protagonist's) that a real return home is impossible for her, and that "home" was always, at most, a temporary landing place between migrations. Thus the creation of Santiago's new transnational identity must emerge from her recognition that her national roots are based on a series of personal and collective memories, some real and some forged, that can be transplanted onto—and thus reshape—the mainland.

This reshaping of the mainland occurs in unexpected ways. Her acquisition of English becomes a way for her to relocate her Puerto Rican identity on the mainland, rather than a process of assimilation and loss, so that the apparent dissolution of Puerto Rican nationhood becomes a rewriting of U.S.–Puerto Rican nationhood. In other words, her movement into spoken English actually represents a disruption of dominant culture just as later on, her facility in written English will validate her as a writer. When she describes the difficulty of acquiring spoken English, she fragments American English and troubles dominant culture's practice of linking normative speech with nationhood. Initially, the process involves a loss of Spanish, signaling an end to Negi's absolute comfort in her former language. Juan Flores has described this as an "alingual" rather than bilingual state: occupying a linguistic in-betweenness where one lacks written and oral competence in either language, and thus becomes stigmatized.[21] Indeed, while learning English Negi admits becoming "caught between languages" (21), and endures the stillness of alingualism, rather than the limitlessness of bilingualism. In this situation, where her English is obviously still lacking, her Spanish also becomes inadequate because the words it offers up to her are both wrong (they are not in English) and meaningless in the new English-only environment.

For Negi, the experience of alingualism means inhabiting a space between the two languages where neither language is sufficiently meaningful, a third space that consists not of plurality, but of emptiness. When language, which carries national and familial traditions and is an emblem of cultural and personal identity, ceases to work as an "identity-grounding home under conditions of displacement," that is, when place and then language both fail to ground the migrant, there is only loss.[22] And if, as Massey puts it, "Language is the place where our bodies and minds collide, where our groundedness in place and time and our capacity for fantasy and invention must come to terms," then being without language—being alingual—makes it impossible to reconcile the imagination's dislocation and the body's rootedness, leaving the migrant spatially adrift and without a way to articulate a legitimate home.[23] Negi admits that her days in the English-speaking world feel like a "simulated reality" where she speaks fluent English, but mourns the "dissolution of the other me, the Spanish-speaking, Puerto Rican girl" (74). Yet once she is home after a day of moving around the world outside, she has to begin "another performance . . . this one in Spanish" (160).

In addition, the memoir describes the physical discomfort of learning a new language, as Negi and her siblings toil to manipulate their tongues and mouths around the unfamiliar sounds of English: "Our faces contorted into grimaces, our voices changed as our tongues flapped in our mouths trying to form the awkward sounds" (17). In the welfare office her body suffers fatigue and stress from the effort of translation: "I was exhausted, my palms were sweaty, my head ached as I probed for words, my jaw tightened with the effort to pronounce them" (20). But even this physical exertion becomes a symbol of resistance, as trying to speak an unaccented English at this point further highlights her Puerto Rican accent and betrays her body's historical and national affiliation.

Such expressions of linguistic and national connection to the island disrupt dominant culture, representing a troubling that is further demonstrated through her play with the phonetics of Spanish and English. Near the start of the memoir, Negi focuses on the strange disparity between written and spoken English, where words "looked nothing like they sounded" (7). When Santiago recounts some humorous episodes in which she writes down Negi's phonetic experience of the language—that is, what she hears, rather than what is actually being spoken—the effect is to dislocate the reader's own comfort with language. In other words, whether or not we are Spanish speakers, when we look at the English words on the page we lose comprehension and are forced instead to speak them aloud, in a Puerto Rican accent. We thus come close to Negi's own confusing transition into English, which, she says, "was hard for me to enjoy . . . as I focused on the words whizzing by" (7). The most significant of these moments is Negi's account of learning to sing "The Star-Spangled Banner." She sings, "Ojo sé. Can. Juice. Y? / Bye de don surly lie / Whassoprowow we hell / Add debt why lie lass gleam in" (10). At a glance, some of these written words do have meaning in English ("debt," "lie," "can," "juice"), but are incorrect in the context of the song. The reader is then required to undo, and then redo, the meaning, and to build sense out of nonsense words by speaking them aloud, that is, by moving from a literary experience to an oral one. The narrative insists, then, that we occupy a space between literacy and orality and combine the two: we speak aloud the words that we read.

It is no coincidence that while Santiago deconstructs the American national anthem and renders it almost meaningless, the Puerto Rican national anthem that appears in the first memoir is conveyed smoothly in English rather than in the Spanish in which the events of the story took place. This translation does not disrupt the relationship between words and meaning. In the first memoir, Negi learns an anthem "which said Borinquén was the daughter of the ocean and the sun," and because the song makes sense to her, she interprets it emotionally: "I liked thinking of our island as a woman whose body was a garden of flowers, whose feet were caressed by waves, a land whose sky was never cloudy" (*When I Was Puerto Rican*, 77). These lyrics valorize not only Puerto Rico's natural landscape but also the ability of language to forge a powerful cultural identity, albeit from afar, in memory. Meanwhile, the disrupted American anthem that Negi reproduces in the second memoir clearly deviates from and thus delegitimates the norm.

In this second memoir, ultimately, the most surprising and significant disruption of national identity occurs through Negi's creative engagement with dance, a skill that in her third memoir will play an important role in forging her sense of belonging on the mainland. The text frequently recalls the ways in which dancing liberates Negi and teaches her how to move her body in space (66). While her earlier flights of the body served as escapes, transporting her in imagination back to Puerto Rico, her dancing seems to bring Puerto Rico right into the mainland. Thus, in dancing, her body writes its Puerto Rican origins back onto the mainland's landscape and disrupts the narratives that have objectified it. On the dance floor, whether at school, in performance, or in a nightclub with her family, she transcends the gap between her child and adult body, and thus between her Puerto Rican and U.S. selves: "I lost all sense of time, embraced and embracing, beautiful, graceful, trembling with sensations possible only this way, *in this place*" (99, my emphasis). She explains, "For me, dance was . . . to *bring me to a place* nothing else did" (117, my emphasis). Place, here, becomes redefined as an experience, a moment of dance, rather than a fixed geographic location; place, therefore, is movement. Thus, in the same way that Negi's phonetic rewriting of the national anthem confounds the nation's articulation of its linguistic identity, so, too, does her dancing validate displacement as part of national belonging, challenging the nation's normative privileging of identity based on geocultural roots and political borders.

The Turkish Lover: From Nation to Transnation

Santiago's second memoir ends just as Negi meets Ulvi, the Turkish lover, for the first time. Her attraction to Ulvi in *Almost a Woman* is not surprising, as he offers her a sense of wholeness and promises to finally heal the rupture of migration by returning her, emotionally, to a premigratory space. With him, she says, "I was what I stopped being the day I climbed into the propeller plane in Isla Verde, to emerge into the rainy night in Brooklyn. After seven years in the United States, I had become what I stopped being the day I left Puerto Rico. I had become

Chiquita—small, little one. Little girl" (306). Thus she welcomes the chance to psychologically reinhabit the childhood nation that preceded her migration. Most of *The Turkish Lover* describes Ulvi's abusive treatment of Negi, as he tries to repress her Puerto Rican identity and she struggles to recall and legitimate the significance of her own history. By the end of the memoir Santiago is able to bring the island protagonist and mainland autobiographer together by articulating her connection to Negi, and recognizing herself anew as a U.S. Puerto Rican. First, however, the memoir works through the damaging and abusive relationship between Ulvi and Negi, which in some respects seems to reflect the structural and codependent dynamic of power between the United States and Puerto Rico.

Throughout the book Santiago clearly describes Ulvi's controlling treatment: he silences and infantilizes Negi, and tries to teach her what to think, what to say, and how to behave, forging a life full of limits for her, delineating her spaces, and controlling her movements. She becomes imprisoned on every level and finds herself under such surveillance that the limitations he imposes gradually become internalized within her as well. He restricts her intellectually, physically, culturally, and creatively, so that when she does actually visit Puerto Rico toward the end of the memoir, she is ill equipped to deal with the changes she finds there. Thus the "world" he re-creates for her—like Puerto Rico itself—is a nation spectered by the trauma of internal migrations and colonialism. Of all three memoirs, *The Turkish Lover* demonstrates most explicitly how the colonial psyche developed on the island manifests itself in this new location on the mainland. Negi's self-damaging dependence on Ulvi in part recalls the dynamic of normative colonialism, whereby geographic, historical, and cultural identities become negotiated through experiences of codependency, abuse, and displacement. In particular, her relationship to narrative and its potential to legitimate her presence in the United States become threatened. Living with Ulvi, she is unable to write in her journal or otherwise record her emotions and experiences, finding it, as she says, "impossible" because "words fled the minute I tried to express my feelings, mostly because I wasn't sure what they were."[24] This of course highlights the gap between protagonist and autobiographer, as the latter remembers and records events that the former experiences as unnarratable, beyond language, and ungraspable. Such wordlessness reflects the rupture of language both on the island and after migration to the mainland: it results in an anxious vacillation between alingualism and bilingualism. In other words, Negi's undialectical condition is psychologically induced by Ulvi's influence but also speaks to the broader personal and national history of her identity-formation as a Puerto Rican.

Part of Negi's disintegrating relationship with narrative thus involves the loss of her personal and cultural histories. One of the most damaging ways in which Ulvi displaces her is by eroding her familial and cultural connections to Puerto Rico and Brooklyn, and defining her as culturally (and to an extent, nationally) deficient. As she puts it, he "disdained my people and me" (337). For a long time he refuses to meet her family, but when he finally does, at her mother's house, he looks around at the poverty and decor with distaste, horror, and amusement (67). He attempts to erase her Puerto Rican memories and refuses to recognize the extent to which those nostalgic memories constitute, for Negi, her only comforting memory of a home-space. By the end of her seven-year relationship with him she has lost all connection to Puerto Rican culture in the United States. She notes that she cannot identify the latest Puerto Rican celebrities or musical trends, and does not know what party is in power on the island or who the governor is (258), signaling a detachment that is the result of his pattern of emotional and, at times, physical abuse. In effect, she is imprisoned spatially, emotionally, and culturally in the present as Ulvi monitors her every move, and marooned from her past as he devalues and discourages mention of it.

Negi's isolation from her Puerto Rican peers in the United States and her ambiguous legacy of dislocation mean that for much of this memoir she is too shrouded in shame to actively want to take control of her life. Santiago acknowledges that even at the time, she knew that "women were taking charge of their lives while every day I relinquished more control over mine" (186). Negi's shame at her own disempowerment, encouraged by Ulvi's snobbish disdain for her background and perpetuated by her experiences of structural and systemic racism (growing up in a disadvantaged neighborhood), is further enhanced by her continual awareness of her body as a racialized object. No matter how much Ulvi, her Pygmalion, resculpts her, dressing her in conservative outfits, teaching her new table manners, and refining her behavior, those who see her often refuse her passing.[25] For this reason, she clings to her alternate pseudoidentities as Chiquita and Essie (the name her coworkers give her), preferring to sustain this problematic acting strategy rather than "expose Esmeralda to the disdainful gaze of those who would judge me" (209). Her split identity also determines her physical identity: on the way back to the apartment from work each day she remarks that "it was such a conscious shift from Esmeralda to Essie to Chiquita that I actually felt my body contract and diminish in stature" (209).

Her public persona and the diminutive label "Es" maintain her private imprisonment. On one level, Santiago implies that her name becomes "Es" because of people's fear of the foreign sound of her name; that is, she allows it to become Anglofied and less threatening, just as in her personal life, Ulvi reduces her to an infantile plaything devoid of her particular culture and history. The memoir is not clear on how much social prejudice actually surrounds Esmeralda, but clearly she has internalized Ulvi's own harsh judgments enough to sustain whatever negative messages she gets from her public environment. With Ulvi especially, she is never allowed to forget her complex illegitimate status: that she is dark-skinned, from rural Puerto Rico and the Brooklyn ghettos, and the first child "of a teenage mother who had never married the fathers of her eleven children" (209). She thus remains illegitimate in many respects: not just because of her mother's transgressions or her own national, cultural, and social background but also because of the disempowered role that she continues to play with Ulvi, and the subservient writing of her body that the relationship entails. The shame of occupying the wrong body from the wrong place keeps her immobilized in the relationship with Ulvi.

Santiago also describes the disturbing effects of Ulvi's emotional hold over Negi's physical space and body. Over time, to survive, she retreats: "I gave the world a shadow me, a me who looked like me but wasn't, a me that could function according to the rules that would get me what I wanted and needed. I reserved the real Esmeralda in a quiet, secret place no one could reach. . . . I kept that me so hidden, that I was invisible even to myself" (210). As with the flights of escape she described in her first two memoirs, this response to trauma involves a splitting of the self (the public one is the shadow; the real one remains hidden), but unlike those earlier flights, this time the "real" self is not able to imaginatively escape to Puerto Rico because her memories of it have been co-opted by Ulvi. In this memoir, unlike the earlier ones, Santiago's narrative voice actually interprets Negi's behavior by identifying her psychological and emotional experiences of displacement as reactions to trauma. She writes, "Sometimes, in moments of stress, I separate myself, so that a part of me is an observer as the other part enacts whatever is happening" (180). Here, this interpretation and movement into the present tense does two things. First, it signals to us that the autobiographer has openly come forward, acknowledging her connection to the girl and young woman she has been writing about, in particular her ongoing connection to the body that they occupied and that she still occupies today, as she writes. In other words, the autobiographer momentarily admits the lingering effects of her colonized legacy, both personal and national. Second, however, Santiago's brief stepping out as a writer also safely brackets Negi's traumatic experiences. While she is forced during her time with Ulvi to retreat so entirely that her Puerto Rican self, with its particular history, becomes erased, almost forgotten, and definitively "invisible," the autobiographer's explicit presence reminds us that such a time has ended. Thus the line between protagonist and writer wavers, at times appearing fixed, framing and separating the character and author into separate selves, while at other times dissolving and suggesting that the autobiographer, through memory and narrative representation, shares some of the same painful legacies of her protagonist.

Santiago's eventual recording and publication of her experiences in the form of her memoir trilogy is thus an act of decolonization that breaks away from both Ulvi's intellectually imposed limitations and her own fractured history and identity. It is significant that eventually Negi not only legitimates her experiences by deciding to publish her memoirs, but that she does so under her full name, Esmeralda Santiago. The distance between traumatized subaltern subject and published author begins to be bridged with Negi's return visit to Puerto Rico—the visit she first referred to at the start of *Almost a Woman*—and her discovery that it is not, after all, her home. Although for years she sustained herself with nourishing memories of the island, they turn out to be, unsurprisingly, frozen in a time of childhood and quite unreliable, produced from within New York's unnatural "gray and shadowy" landscape (29). The most glaring changes in Puerto Rico's physical landscape are evident from the moment of her arrival, where the consumer culture emphasized in Ortiz Cofer's novels has bitten into the cultural and natural landscape. Immediately Negi sees billboards for cars, Burger King, and a large shopping mall and knows that "it was not the Puerto Rico I remembered" (273). Although the night sounds are soothing and nostalgic—"a coconut palm whispered its welcome" (277)—nothing is as she remembers it (278). The changes are shocking to her. She writes, "I had not expected Puerto Rico to have changed. The island, my sun-filled days on it, were shaped in memory like the figures I used to sculpt from Macún's orange clay. I had not counted on time being like that clay that dried and crumbled into dust, to be reshaped again" (273).

Her memories, once intact, become threatened now that she returns to their original location and understands that they originated not in a physical landscape but in her mind's landscape. Puerto Rico remains her inspiration for writing, but the real island offers a shifting and moving ground (rather than rootedness) that reminds her only of her losses. When she visits her father, who lives with his wife, Fela, in a house full of photographs of their children, she envies the display of his family life. She remarks, "Those should have been pictures of me and my sisters and brothers. . . . The house should have been the one where I grew up, where Mami and Papi had raised their children" (286). Here, one of the central losses of her life—that of her father, intricately bound up with the loss of the island—is rearticulated as the loss of a legitimate family narrative that she has never participated in, but has so often longed for. And because she returns to the island with Ulvi, the cultural specificity of Puerto Rico continues to elude her. With him, as always, her history and connection to this place are ignored even when they are right there. At the Caribe Hilton where they are staying, the pools, casino, restaurants, and English-speaking tourists make her feel as if "we could have been in any resort on any sunny coast in the *United States*" (281, my emphasis). The cultural erasures implicit in the tourist industry—its exotization of locales, its problematic overwriting of difficult history—are also enforced by Ulvi on a personal level: "*High above the ground*, within the air-conditioned rooms of the Caribe Hilton I was Ulvi's Chiquita, whose past held no interest for him" (282, my emphasis). This version of Puerto Rico, industrialized and co-opted by American consumer culture, cannot ground her.

The brief scene that began *Almost a Woman*, in which Negi returns to Puerto Rico and stands on a patch of the family's old blue tile floor, appears again in the third memoir, but this time the emphasis on the fallibility of memory is also associated with Puerto Rico's rapid industrial development, acknowledging the creeping presence and impact of U.S. industrialization on the island: "Birds flitted and chirped in the overgrown hibiscus hedge near where we once grew eggplants. Lizards slithered into the weeds and around the annatto bushes under which I used to hide, near the oregano bushes, still fragrant. . . . To my right, traffic roared toward what I assumed were the gates to the golf resort. . . . I closed my eyes and listened to the soughing leaves, the flapping wings, the chirruping, tweeting, trilling life around me. I stood immobile, listening, discarding the throb of cars and trucks, the thunder of a plane overhead" (279). Here, the natural landscape of the island connects to

Negi's memories of her past home and provides an intense connection to the earth and air of Puerto Rico: birds flit near their old eggplant patch, lizards slither around the bushes in which she used to hide, and the vegetation is "still fragrant," intensifying the present moment.

But this very experience is simultaneously undercut, defined, and disrupted by evidence of urban and suburban developments around her. Although Negi focuses and tunes out the sounds of cars, trucks, and planes, she is also forced to resituate her memories in a partly new and changing landscape. Furthermore, her return to the land is framed by her family's disapproval of her relationship with Ulvi and her social straying from the paths she was supposed to follow in life. Even as she stands "in the center of the land" and tries to absorb its significance, she overhears their old neighbor ask her mother the only important question: "Does she [Negi] have children?" (279). After she finds the blue tile floor, again, "the bluest tile I'd ever seen" although "I had no memory of it being on our floor," she looks up at her mother and sees "sorrow in her eyes" (279). The homecoming unravels not just through the place's refusal to stand still but also through the stigma of her own wanderings: in this moment, she is uprooted and alienated not just from place but also from the familial and cultural expectations that intersect with it.

The trip to Puerto Rico cements Negi's determination to leave Ulvi, clarifying for her just how disempowered she is in their relationship. Once she has left him, she begins to reengage with the cultural and social aspects of her Puerto Rican identity, valorizing her relationship with the nation and finding a way to express herself creatively in a public space. This valorization begins in an unlikely way at the end of her time at Harvard, where for her final term project she decides to set the "Song of Songs" to music and dance, and to write her own choreography. For the first time, she writes her own dance steps rather than following others' instructions for movement, creating both the movements and the limitations upon the movements. Clearly this is significant. The creation is entirely her own, but at the same time, it is contained within a framework of academic scrutiny that will give her the validation, respect, and dignity—in effect, the belonging—that she seeks. She writes: "The Song of Songs was more than my thesis. It was how I explored and conflated my interests, skills, worries, and concerns. . . . Each performance explored and expressed themes of race . . . and alienation from culture, family and lover. It was as close to a biography as I could come" (314).

This single project represents Negi's decolonization on several levels. It is psychologically liberating as it signals her move away from Ulvi's world of surveillance. The Ivy League milieu that enables the project and gives her the space to perform it represents a significant socioeconomic departure from the ghettos of her childhood. It is evidently a sign of her intellectual ability to create something new, and importantly, it represents a spatial and physical independence from the restrictions that have held her in place for the last several years: it is, of course, her own dancing body that performs the final project. It is also a public statement of creative freedom, and a collective one, because of the support she receives from fellow students and faculty members. Finally, it is a moment that encapsulates, for the reader of her memoir, the nascence of Negi's transformation into the autobiographical writer Esmeralda Santiago, that is, from the displaced Puerto Rican girl into the U.S. Puerto Rican woman. As she dances she seems to physically change: "Each word of the Song of Songs, each mudra, each step, each jingle of my ankle bells was a bit of Esmeralda, emerging. The tiles of Lehman Hall, cold beneath my feet, received the shadow me, lit by the flames in my hands. . . . After the last note of the last performance, I was a different person" (314–315). The shadow self, which had formerly been her public persona, disappears into the ground, and the real Esmeralda is born.

The connection between the newly emergent dancer, Esmeralda, and the writer, Esmeralda Santiago, becomes even more explicit after her graduation ceremony. The day itself is sad for her; she has neglected to invite any of her family because of Ulvi's dislike of them, but then also finally separates, permanently, from Ulvi the evening before. Consequently, neither Ulvi nor her family is present at her graduation ceremony. In her description of her graduation day, she emphasizes her isolation, remarking, "I turned with my classmates and looked into the faces of several thousand men and women, not one of them there for me. I cried then" (331). As she wanders Harvard Square after the ceremony she realizes "there was not a single familiar face in the hundreds of people I passed" (331). The memoir itself, however, translates this experience from a solitary one into a shared one, recollecting not just her isolation but also the transition to writing that the event prompted. After the ceremony she impulsively buys herself a graduation gift: a pen, the most expensive purchase she has up until then ever made for herself. She persuades herself to buy it after holding the pen, feeling that "it *belonged* in my hand, solid and real, warm" (332, my emphasis). She is aware of how the writing implement serves as an extension of her body—and potentially, through memoir writing, as a tool that might heal that body—and also recognizes that "with use, the patina would become richer; the nib would flow across a page with familiar authority and weight" (332). The pen thus heralds the birth of an authorial presence that will heal the stigma of her cultural deficiencies and racialized citizenship, and begin to legitimate her experiences, her literary recording of them, and her displaced status in the United States. Then Santiago the writer steps in, bridging the distance between the two selves, and states, "I still have it. Whenever I take it in my hand to write a note, to sign my name, to make an entry into my journal, I remember the loneliness of that day" (332). Writing in the memoir-genre in particular represents Santiago's forging of a blended national identity, as she negotiates the presence of her U.S. authorial self in the recollected Puerto Rico of her childhood, and the presence of Puerto Rican geography, history, and identity in her present-day mainland location.

Negi's creative performance of the "Song of Songs" works as a prelude to the broader transnational work she envisions for herself at the end of the third memoir, where she describes her postgraduate summer plans to return to Puerto Rico to make a documentary film about Puerto Rican artisans. She is interested in the "artistic and cultural legacies of developing countries," and dreams of "living in Puerto Rico someday" and bringing expertise "to its artistic heritage" (319). She thus directly imagines herself, a mainlander, as part of the island's artistic community, but realizes that in the process she must renegotiate her own presence on the island: "I didn't want to come as a tourist or to be a leisured guest in Mami's or my sisters' homes. . . . I wanted a reason to be there other than nostalgia for home and family" (319). Her decision to immerse herself in the island's creative culture, therefore, is also a decision to erase her nostalgia for her past national identity and reframe her U.S. Puerto Rican consciousness. She notes that she looks forward to introducing her film technicians, Keith and Geno, to "*my* culture" (320, my emphasis), and hopes that her funded project will "draw attention to part of *our* artistic and cultural heritage" (337, my emphasis), imagining a documentary that will enable transnational conversations to take place.

Although the nature of memoir writing means that we always know that the creative destiny of the protagonist is to become a writer, for much of Santiago's memoirs she attempts to markedly separate the writer and the protagonist. As we follow Negi through the geographical and emotional displacements that define her, the production of the published memoir we are reading seems distant, almost impossible. But by the end of her third memoir, she has narrowed the gap between her islander and mainlander personas and, in so doing, has begun to develop her authorial voice from within a blended U.S.-Puerto Rican nation-space. In her work overall, then, the development and emergence of the protagonist as a writer goes hand in hand with the forging of a new national identity: her personal history as a Puerto Rican–islander–turned–mainlander is part of a broader political narrative through which her subaltern voice, by resisting the imbalance of colonial power, starts to trouble and question U.S. national boundaries.

As I have shown, the neocolonial relationship that underlines U.S.-Puerto Rican relations becomes, in the texts discussed in chapters 3 and 4, newly reframed as a collective and transnational relationship. This collective dynamic in turn can challenge the United States' cultural and geopolitical presence and its definition of itself as a distinct national identity to which only particular prescribed members can belong as cultural citizens. In other words, if the legacy of the nineteenth-century's manifest destiny continues to determine the United States' negotiation of its national identity through an othering of Latin American nations, then to an extent, these narratives disrupt that understanding of political and cultural citizenship. Turning next to an important but understudied Cuban American text, Himilce Novas's *Princess Papaya*, I ask how literary representations of Cuban American identity negotiate similar questions of national identity, given that there are ostensibly no relations between postrevolutionary Cuba and the United States, and that the United States has, therefore, defined itself largely in opposition to, and as separate from, Cuba.

5 / Tales of the Unexpected: Cuban American Narratives of Place and Body in Himilce Novas's *Princess Papaya*

The issues of U.S.-Latino citizenship and nationhood that I discussed in preceding chapters show in part how Mexican Americans and U.S. Puerto Ricans have experienced a particularly racialized dynamic of otherness and perceived foreignness. Cuban Americans, however, have not been subject to quite the same dynamic of "unbelonging," partly because Cubans themselves have historically tended to identify as "white" on the U.S. Census, and partly because the United States' opposition to the Castro regime has overdetermined its policies toward and reception of Cubans migrating into the country.[1] The first waves of Cuban exiles entering the United States, themselves a majority white, educated, and socioeconomically upper-class demographic, benefited from Congress's 1966 Cuban Adjustment Act, while later waves are protected by the "wet foot, dry foot" policy, which has given all Cubans seeking asylum in the United States the special status of political refugees. Consequently, Cubans have faced very few restrictions governing immigration and have enjoyed a legislative status that virtually guarantees permanent settlement in the United States to all who have escaped Cuba.[2]

Despite this, however, as I argued in the introduction, Cuban American identity formation has been significantly shaped by a sense of "foreignness" and unbelonging, both because of the United States' historical interest in the island, which long predated Castro's revolution, and because of the ongoing inclusion of Cubans in U.S. popular culture's negative interpellations of Latinos, where, as Latinos, Cubans are held responsible for the supposed erosion and devaluation of U.S. national identity. And in instances where Cubans' U.S. citizenship *is* racialized, it is frequently Cuban culture (its "unassimilable" markers), rather than body or phenotype, that becomes racialized as "other" and foreign to the integrity (and sometimes security) of the nation.[3]

The United States' intervention in Cuba's war of independence from Spain in 1898, in which the explosion of the USS *Maine* in Havana (purportedly sent there to protect U.S. citizens) legitimated the United States' entry into the war, was a defining although not solitary example of its long interest in the island. As early as 1808 Thomas Jefferson had tried unsuccessfully to purchase the island from Spain, saying in 1820 that it was "the most interesting addition which could ever be made to our system of States."[4] While this interest did not replicate Puerto Rico's colonial status, it did create conditions, over the late nineteenth and early twentieth centuries, that allowed the United States to gain a position of political, military, and economic dominance in Cuba. With a vast majority of foreign investment holdings, the bulk of imports and exports in U.S. hands, and a strong influence on Cuban political affairs, U.S. military rule and presence on the island between 1898 and 1902 ended only with the Platt Amendment, which itself formalized the United States' right to intervene in Cuban political, economic, and military affairs if necessary (in exchange for the withdrawal of American troops from all parts of the island other than Guantánamo Bay), and strongly overdetermined U.S.-Cuban relations for much of the twentieth century. In short, the United States' economic and political influence on the island pre-Castro cannot be overstated, making the postrevolutionary shift to economic sanctions and trade embargos even more startling.

Considerations of Cuban American national identity must, therefore, take into account this level of prerevolutionary cultural, economic, and political interchange between Cuba and the United States, which suggests that in some respects the two nation-spaces were blended.[5] With the closing of the U.S. embassy in Havana in 1961, however, Cuba and the United States began a long history of supposed separation. Of course, they have continued to determine one another's presence quite powerfully in the popular and the literary imagination of both nations, as each defines itself in opposition to the other. One could even go so far as to say that for both Cuba and the United States, invoking the difference from and absence of the "other" nation has long played a major role in determining national identity, whether that articulation of difference takes place in political, cultural, or literary circles. Nevertheless, despite each nation's heightened awareness of the other, this dynamic of U.S.-Cuban relations depends much more on a fictional and at times exaggerated portrayal of the other than has been evident in U.S.-Mexican and U.S.-Puerto Rican relations. Cuban migration to and subsequent settlement in the United States follows a path of no return, and in material terms often represents a complete rupture from the homeland that moves in a single direction northward, rather than in the circular back-and-forth patterns that are part of the Mexican and Puerto Rican diaspora.

What, then, are the literary consequences of this particular national identity formation, which must occur, so often, from afar? How, and with what kind of presence, can Cuban American literary production contest the national imaginary, challenge the rhetoric of national belonging, and construct a revision of national identity that reimagines Cuba as part of the United States? For Cubans in the United States, it appears that with the passing of time any real knowledge of Cuba subsides. Achy Obejas, for example, argues that while Puerto Ricans go back and forth to their island, for Cubans "there is a divorce from our island."[6] In fact, scholars find that more recent Cuban American novels are displacing earlier narratives with a series of diasporic questions, so that "second-generation Cuban writing reveals authors effecting a transition from exile to ethnic minority members."[7] Ultimately, as Isabel Alvarez Borland argues, "the Cuban American ethnic writers' search will be oriented toward issues of recovery as they set about the task of constructing a U.S. identity that very much needs to take into account their Cuban heritage."[8] The consensus seems to be that "soon it will be Cuba as an echo."[9] In other words, Cuban American literary identity is more and more based on a sense of ethnic difference rather than on a particular exilic nationalism; its unbelonging necessarily includes reconciling an "echo" of Cuba and a reckoning of "Cuban heritage" with a firm presence in the United States.[10]

In this chapter I examine how Himilce Novas's critically unexplored 2004 novel, *Princess Papaya*, takes up this conversation of Cuban American presence in the United States. Novas to a degree continues the legacy of Cuban national identity formation, which has since the eighteenth century been created largely from afar and away from the island, with a consciousness of exile, an awareness of the complexity of cultural dislocation, and the consequent evocation of an island-space that is simultaneously imagined, elusive, and physically real to its diaspora.[11] But Novas also moves in significantly new directions by considering the place and presence of Cuban ethnicity in contemporary American life, thus becoming part of a new wave of Latino/a literary production that, according to Smorkaloff, is "breaking new ground" by ridding itself of nostalgia for Cuba and engaging more actively and critically with the reality of a hyphenated and contradictory life in the United States.[12] In other words, Novas's work, in representing an ethnic consciousness rather than an exilic one, reimagines Cuba as an inherent and inseparable part of the United States and Cuban Americans as members of a collective group of U.S. ethnic minority citizens. Unlike the material reality of Mexico and Puerto Rico in earlier chapters, however, the Cuba that becomes woven into the United States' political landscape in *Princess Papaya* represents an idyllic version of socialist Cuba that never fully materialized on the island itself.

Analyzing here the novel's presentation of various locales (Cuba, New York City), its valorization of marginalized bodies, and its figuration of cyberspace and California, I argue that *Princess Papaya* imagines a new kind of frontier narrative for the nation that offers a new story of national identity. The narrative writes Cuba itself as a haunting and real presence in the United States that has traumatized the nation-state. Specifically contesting the westward-moving manifest destiny's acquisition of land and property, the text posits that the United States can be healed of (or at least alleviated from) its traumatic relationship with Cuba by taking back the physical spaces of frontier land (specifically, California) for the outcast, marginalized, and "foreign" members of the nation and privileging their belonging to it, while at the same time shifting and challenging the very markers that have defined it as a distinct and separate nation-space. As part of this healing, the new socialist community located in the United States strongly resists one of the nation's defining features of citizenship: the notion of a capitalist market economy. The novel, particularly by the end, challenges the concept of property and land as capital and espouses Communist principles, presenting a radically new challenge to contemporary notions of U.S. national identity.

Princess Papaya tells the story of a Cuban American Jewish family, the Lobos, who live in New York City. When the story opens, the oldest son, David, has been missing for the past eighteen years, incarcerated in a Cuban jail after a failed rescue mission to save an old rabbi in Havana. Roberto, the other son, runs an ob-gyn clinic—the Lobo Meyer Clinic—performs late-term abortions, and owns the Lobo Vineyard near Santa Barbara, California. Unbeknownst to his family and the reader until the end of the novel, the Lobo Meyer Clinic is a cover and front for an impenetrable state-of-the-art methamphetamine lab operated in partnership with a Cuban drug lord. Roberto is married to Kitty, an anorexic bulimic WASP, but for years has been having an affair with Ideliza Mercado, the

Princess Papaya of the title, an Afro-Cuban American Santera who lives in the Barrio. Bembé, Roberto and Ideliza's "deaf-mute, hydrocephalic" nine-year-old son, lives with his mother (43). When the novel opens, Roberto is receiving threatening anonymous phone calls in the night, and turning to Ideliza to seek her help.

Meanwhile, his sister, Victoria, a poet and writer, mourns the death of her husband, Francisco, who was in one of the hijacked airplanes on September 11, 2001, a year earlier. As the novel begins, Victoria has embarked upon an Internet relationship with a mysterious stranger named Cooper, from California. Eventually, Victoria meets Cooper in person, and learns that he is an intersexual, a Chumash from California, and that he runs rescue missions out of Cuba, including one that by the end of the novel brings the missing David back to the United States. Throughout the novel, these displaced characters occupy various problematic locations, some physical (Cuba, New York City), and some virtual (cyberspace), finally gathering in the only truly redemptive and healing place offered by the text: California. And while we might conjecture that *Princess Papaya*'s final scene of an economically self-sustaining "Marxist" system (a co-op winery in California) is only viable because it exists within the broader context of U.S. and global capitalism, it is important to note that the closing pages of the story are focused solely on this collective vision.[13] Thus, in offering even the possibility of such an operation, the novel sets up a resistant, albeit idyllic, model of collectivity that challenges normative thinking and remaps political, social, and cultural identities for Cuban Americans and Americans in the United States.

In part the novel is clearly a radical literary response to the two nations' intersecting histories, overturning, as it does, the United States' defining narratives of national identity in hyperbolic ways. In response to the United States' manifest destiny, its vilification of the island's Communist agenda, and its ongoing economic sanctions, the novel has, by the end of the story, both set up an alternative frontier narrative that envisions a Communist idyll in the United States itself and established an illicit relationship of economic exchange between the two nations whereby the United States has become dependent on Cuba. In this new frontier space, marginalized and/or foreign citizens, whether they are Juban, Afro-Cuban, or Native American, can express their belonging because of the way that cultural heterogeneity is valorized. As part of this valorization of heterogeneity, the novel specifically challenges notions of U.S. national identity that assume heterosexual bodies to be the ideal cultural norm, and that privilege biological family structures for the purposes of national reproduction and continuity. It validates, instead, an alternative national identity that interrogates not just the nation's normative practice of economics but also, in connection with this, the normative practices of its bodies, suggesting that its traumas can be alleviated best through collective rather than individually oriented behaviors.

In many respects, then, *Princess Papaya* goes farther than any of the other texts I have discussed in its radical troubling of the United States' cultural and national identity. Its privileging of intersexual rather than heterosexual desire, for example, which is most evident through the portrayal of Cooper, represents a model of syncretism and collectivity that reframes such bodies as healthy national ideals and that, in its final vision, pervades the Communist utopia with which the novel ends. This reconceptualization of heterosexual normativity also specifically confounds understandings of Cuban American and American nationalism because it taps into the anxiety about reproduction and ethnic continuity that has settled into the Cuban diaspora community.[14] In fact, according to Ricardo Ortiz, the relatively recent movement of Cuban Americans away from Miami and into other areas of the United States has silenced expressions of Cuban dissent, isolating Cubans who live away from their community's cultural centers.[15] Without a doubt, by imagining a new world where gender and sexuality are reinvented, Novas's text overturns the tradition of "foundational fictions," narratives of "fulfilled and redemptive heterosexual unions" that Ortiz suggests have empowered Cuban national identity since the nineteenth century.[16] This new frontier-world, which advocates a socialist political system over capitalist individualism, not only privileges alternative family structures but also interrogates real and virtual landscapes (Cuba, New York, cyberspace, California) and imagines U.S. identity as ethnically syncretic. While the Mexican and Puerto Rican literature I discussed in earlier chapters read the Southwest, the Midwest, and New York as part of a broader Americas, Novas's narrative ultimately abandons any long-held dreams of returning to a restored prerevolutionary Cuba, rejects the failed political experiment on the island itself, and instead builds an alternative model of Communism in the United States. In this model, California is turned into a fantastical new frontier land for U.S. Cuban American identity, and imagined as a microcosmic blend of Latin America, Native America, and Africa, where the natural landscape becomes a collective home for cultural and religious syncretism.

Traumatic Places: Cuba and New York City

Given that U.S. and U.S.-Cuban identities depend to a large extent on the construction of Cuba itself, it is important to explore the ways in which the island in *Princess Papaya* is depicted as traumatized, and the ways that the United States also suffers residues of that trauma. Most of the single chapter set on the island deals with David's experiences in jail and his rushed escape out of the country. Cuba is imagined as a jail cell, a rotten and whoreish landscape and, because of David's experiences with Dolores after his escape, a nation that exploits women's bodies as consumable and exchangeable sexual objects.[17] Although most of the novel's action takes place outside of Cuba, the island functions, as Obejas has noted when speaking about the place of Cuba in ethnic-American literature, very much as a powerful echo within the consciousness of the United States, an echo that has strong implications not only for the United States' construction of Cuba as a memory but also for its own economic and political identity. While the physical space of the island recedes toward the end of the novel, it nevertheless dominates the narrative: beyond its geographical boundaries, it exerts a disruptive presence in the United States, infiltrating the nation psychologically and economically with a traumatic residue and making the United States, in effect, a placeholder for Cuban trauma.

This Cuban trauma centers on the treatment of bodies in Cuba and is most clearly manifested in the novel's depiction of the island as a prison-space, where people are reduced to their bodies and deprived of any agency or control over those bodies. This is particularly evident in the descriptions of torture and abjection in the prison where David is incarcerated. The novel explicitly describes acts of physical violence in the jail, but together with this, also shows how the punitive system destroys the narrative structures that might make sense of this violence. Even as the horrors inflicted on the incarcerated bodies are foregrounded, then, the unrepresentability of the place and its experiences also becomes clear. In other words, in Cuba, the Cuban (or Cuban American) body remains continually at the site of the traumatic experience, rendering that experience, by definition, unnarratable: in the physical world of Cuba the tortured body can never leave or forget itself and is unable to translate that experience into narrative memory.[18]

Descriptions of the jail emphasize the reduction of inmates to their bodies and the denial to them of all forms of subjectivity and agency, as they undergo abjection, perversion, and the destruction of narrative meaning. For example, bodies are forced to consume their own waste, eliminating all boundaries that would normally accord them respect. David remembers how his former cellmate Felipe, for example, was drowned "in a hole of liquefied pig shit" (51), while David himself has "almost rotted his whole life in jail" and has been forced to eat feces and drink urine (52). In addition, prisoners are forced to act in sexually deviant ways and are then punished for these deviances with public circumcision, castration, and rape on makeshift stages "for all the guards to gape at and laugh at and clap" (52). Taboo sexual activities are violently enforced, creating a world where the social regulation of sexual practices recategorizes deviant desires as voyeuristic public performances. Finally, inmates are deprived of literacy, which itself is reduced to the physicality of the media on which symbols appear: the degradations suffered become even more traumatic by this explicit denial of narration. When David is forced by prison guards to chew and swallow paper (girly magazines, his own sister's published book of poems) "without a sip of water" (53), words and images are stripped of their semantic meaning and thus lose their potential to incite resistance, thought, or even pleasure. As mere objects to be consumed, words become relevant only as matter, and literacy becomes physical and unpalatable. Consequently, as the potential for words to retain their meaning disappears, the potential for traumatic experiences to become healed through narrative also disappears. In such a world, where all of existence is physical and all physical experiences are disempowering, resistance is only possible through escape.

Throughout the chapter the novel also positions the United States as inextricably opposed to and yet inseparable from Cuba, particularly in terms of narrative constructions of the nation. This is evident first through David's experiences. Despite his eighteen years in a Cuban jail, David has almost no firsthand experience of the island; instead, his American rescuer, Cooper, must describe Havana's landscape to him as they drive through it, suggesting that part of the control over stories of Cuba and thus over Cuba's identity-formation remains in the hands of the United States. It thus engages in a continuous cultural intervention that writes other nation's identities from afar, and, in so doing, also writes and establishes its own particular identity. But while the United States can narrate stories of Cuba, how can it integrate traumatic memories of Cuba into its own political landscape? In other words, what is David to do with the traumatic memory of his time on the island? David's decision about how to negotiate his memories of the Cuban jail suggests one of the ways in which Cuba remains actively present within the United

States. After his release, David hopes to "bury that part of his life the next day, as one would a cadaver according to Jewish law, sit *shiva* for the prescribed seven days, and only visit his memories once a year on the *yortseit* of his escape" (62). The novel posits that ideally such memories of Cuba should be treated as bodies that must be quickly buried, turning the island itself into an unseen but nevertheless material part of the United States' physical landscape. In this imaginary, Cuba and its traumatic experiences can be controlled, acknowledged, and narrated within the United States without radically disturbing it.

However, the novel's revelation that Roberto's clinic produces meth drugs for Barbudo, a Cuban drug lord, to sell all over the United States shows not only how the two nations remain connected but also how the United States has become deeply disempowered under Cuba and dependent on it for its own addictive and self-destructive behavior. In other words, Cuban traumatic memory manifests itself in the United States not merely as a representation or story of the island but also as a strong echo and legacy that implicates and infects U.S. economics, politics, and identity. The trauma of the United States' relationship with Cuba thus remains actively present through its integration into the United States' physical and ideological spaces. It is significant that the novel appeared at the height of the crystal meth scare in the United States, when the media was saturated with images of emaciated addicts and the suggestion that widespread use was destroying not the chronically morally suspect inner cities but the rural American heartland.[19] In tying Cuba to the spread of this drug, the novel imagines the traumatic Cuban carceral system symbolically moving into the geography of the United States, where rural Americans become reduced to their suffering bodies and deprived of agency. In addition, because Roberto is acting for all intents and purposes as "an emissary of Castro's fascist government who was propitiating the intoxication and addiction of American children and adults in droves across the United States" (204), the United States is in effect aiding and abetting the Cuban political and economic system by helping to prop it up financially. Thus, while Cuba in this novel does not haunt the U.S. cultural landscape as a nostalgic exilic memory, it does undermine the United States' social and economic structure by secretly managing and controlling the physical desires and appetites of the U.S. body politic. U.S.-Cuban relations thus become an integral, although invisible, reason for the United States' ill health.

The novel's other important location, New York City, is also figured as a geopolitical space in which the nation's bodies suffer from traumatic experiences, and in which the nation's response to those experiences determines how it will narrate and understand its identity.[20] For Victoria, New York City is defined solely by memories of 9/11 that permeate her waking and sleeping moments and exacerbate her sense of unbelonging to the place. She is haunted by the city landscape whose very urbanity seems to represent the event itself and its disquieting destruction of bodies. Looking out of a window before a dinner party at her brother's apartment, she can see "the transparent bloody burial site where the Twin Towers had stood before sky fire, clawed steel, and mortar had crushed her life, rent her heart" (22). She suffers classic symptoms of post-traumatic stress disorder so that any small or large tragedy, "the slightest indication of human suffering" (14), sends her into a spiral of obsessive-compulsive self-destructive behavior. With 9/11 in particular, "the body" has become an entity and a cultural practice that others determine. After 9/11, Victoria's fear of corporeality is increased: specifically, she fears that the post-9/11 body has become first and foremost part of public discourse, and thus that it belongs entirely in the public sphere. The repeated televised images of 9/11 attach specific cultural and visual meanings to it, until the memory of Francisco's body belongs not to Victoria but to the public and the media. Like the physical vulnerability of the Cuban bodies in jail, the novel's 9/11 bodies also imply, as Judith Butler writes, "mortality, vulnerability, agency: the skin and the flesh expose us to the gaze of others but also to touch, and to violence, and bodies put us at risk of becoming the agency and instrument of all these as well. Although we struggle for rights over our own bodies, the very bodies for which we struggle are not quite ever only our own. The body has its invariably public dimension."[21] In other words, the body belongs invariably and publicly to the nation and is continually subject to the nation's own narrative practices.

In the novel Victoria first learns about Francisco's death when she idly switches on the television "for company" (11) and instead gets repeated images of her husband's final moments. Even the news of his death, then, is mediated through mass media technology, making the experience of his death belong not to him or his surviving wife but again, to the nation's own writing of public trauma. In addition, that public corporeal body seems to her undeniably broken and mortal, as she imagines Francisco's body "fragmenting midair" (80), "dematerialized midair over Battery Park" (24), and "carved and readied for the fire in the emblazoned towers, charred flesh for the craving sharks in the indigo mirror underside" (10). Most disturbingly, she begins to doubt his reality, wondering, "Did *we make these people up?"* (43). Butler again touches precisely on the way in which such a loss makes the self (and by extension, I would argue, the other) unknowable, saying, "If I lose you, under these conditions, then I not only mourn the loss, but I become inscrutable myself. Who 'am' I, without you? When we lose some of these ties by which we are constituted, we do not know who we are or what to do."[22] In the novel Victoria wonders exactly this: "she, who was *she,* now that there was no longer a *we,* and *us?*" (11).

This psychological and dislocating dissolution of the self through mourning represents a radical experience of unbelonging, but it can also open up possibilities for healing through the formation of radically new communities because, as Butler notes, "mourning has to do with agreeing to undergo a transformation."[23] Unlike the carceral of Cuba, which offers little or no space for effective resistance, the novel does identify possibilities for change that can emerge from the experience of 9/11, positing, as I discuss in the last part of this chapter, a new national narrative that transforms the frontier from a location for private enterprise and economic capital into a space of collective and socialist principles. In the novel, then, 9/11 becomes the hermeneutic through which to explore the political effects of grief on the body politic and identity formation of the nation, showing quite clearly how its experiences of personal and national displacement become transformed into experiences of re-placement. Importantly, Butler describes those who endure this grief in similar terms of dislocation: they are "living in certain ways *beside* [*themselves*], whether it is in sexual passion, emotional grief, or political rage." She notes that "the predicament is to understand what kind of community is composed of those who are beside themselves."[24] The novel's diasporic and dislocated characters (Victoria and Cooper in particular) are all collectively "beside themselves" for reasons of grief and/ or sexual and political disenfranchisement, but gradually emerge out of that dislocation to form a radical community.

That radicalization of community in fact begins with 9/11's erasing of social and class lines, and its democratization of society. For example, Victoria's cyberspace persona, Penelope, is able at least initially to hide her own privileged and educated background from Cooper because of the anonymity of the medium through which they first communicate.[25] She wants to hide her pedigree, "her languages, her Oxford, her Fords and Guggenheims" (14) because, to her mind, "What can those things matter in the end if a man or a woman loses their soul?" (14). Butler concurs, writing that one effect of 9/11 was to create a "dislocation from First

World privilege," which, "however temporary, offers a chance to start to imagine a world in which that violence might be minimized, in which an inevitable interdependency becomes acknowledged as the basis for global, political community."[26] It is precisely this new world that *Princess Papaya* works toward and envisions at the end: a new national imaginary in which those who are often denied full membership in the nation become integral and central to the healing of U.S. national identity. In the novel marginalized Cuban Americans (Jubans, Afro-Cubans), together with other nominally outcast citizen-subjects, demonstrate their belonging to the United States by recasting the nation's traumatic experience (9/11) not as a justification for reactive violence, but as an originary moment where, as Butler imagines it, a new chapter redefining national identity begins to be narrated, in which violence is minimized and a global community is possible.

By thus presenting both Cuba and New York City as figurative and literal sites of trauma in the United States, *Princess Papaya* suggests that the United States is far from autonomous in terms of its national identity. In the same way that the trauma of Cuba becomes transformed into the trauma of the United States, rendering the latter dependent on (rather than independent from) Cuba, so, too, we see how 9/11 forces the United States to recognize its interdependency and transnational identity. And although 9/11 is not the only factor that leads to Victoria's eventual relocation to California and the setting up of such a community (which in miniature very much echoes, as a literary representation, Butler's vision), it is certainly a major one. In other words, the brief democratization of community that emerges from the nation's grief after 9/11 works as a preface to the more large-scale established communal democracy and undoing of market capitalism seen at the end of the novel.

Scattered and Gathered Nations: Juban, Afro-Cuban, and Indian Bodies

As part of its exploration of the ways that national mourning brings about the possibility of renewed community, in turn dislocating and then relocating bodies in place, *Princess Papaya* also examines how legacies of diaspora, migration, and/or displacement shape certain members of the nation-state. However, rather than locating these normally disenfranchised citizens on the margins of society, the novel privileges them by recognizing the healing power of their bodies and cultural practices, and thus their belonging in the nation. In addition, the narrative marks dominant culture as itself ill at ease. These strategies clearly represent a challenge to normative assumptions about what the nation—and its bodies—should look and be like. The novel explores the histories of ethnically and sexually displaced characters such as the Juban Lobos family and Cooper in order to establish their legacies of marginalization, and then writes Afro-Cubans such as Ideliza and her son, Bembé, as well as Cooper's own embrace of his intersexuality, as antidotes to such displacement, recognizing their empowering role in the reimagining of national identity.[27]

As part of the revision of the nation's ideology of (healthy) citizen and (diseased) foreigner, the novel marginalizes WASP culture by representing Roberto's wife, Kitty, as suffering from psychological and cultural illnesses. She is a "hysterically calm . . . tight tulip, cool and contained" woman (106, 25), whose sterile existence and suppressed appetites render her out of place and in a sense sick, even in her own home. Analogous to the chemically fueled emaciation of a meth addict, her anorexia, for example, is presented as a symptom of her upbringing, a cultural disease that manifests itself as both a primordial and cultural suppression of desire. As Victoria explains explicitly, "*Mayflower goys . . . weren't brought up to like food—they're not supposed to give way to their senses*" (34). In most of the scenes in which she appears, Kitty is outnumbered by Cuban Americans and consequently marginalized in conversation. When Roberto and his parents crack jokes in Spanish that depend not just on a shared linguistic community but also on a shared historical and socioeconomic foundation, their attempts to translate for Kitty only emphasize her unbelonging: for example, the Spanish saying *el ojo del amo engorda el caballo*, translated as "the eye of the owner fattens the horse" or "you have to mind the store if you expect it to do well" (30), falls deaf on Kitty's confused ears. She cannot "make the leap" because "no one in her family had been a merchant for generations" (30). As a member of dominant culture, Kitty becomes in this context unexpectedly but firmly marginalized.

The novel also complicates understandings of the privileged status of dominant culture by exploring the specter of disenfranchisement within the Lobos family, showing how despite their socioeconomic success, their racially white status, and their apparently established settlement in the United States, these Cuban American Jews still carry within them a sense of foreignness and a "malaise of displacement" (130). This ethnically and historically rooted malaise, which separates them from Kitty's WASP privilege but renders them similarly ill at ease, strongly marks their relationship to U.S. national identity, in particular creating in them a primordial anxiety about corporeality reminiscent of the corporeal anxiety produced by the incarcerated nation-state of Cuba.[28] The family's legacy of prejudice and exile makes them unable to confidently establish a permanent or secure relationship between place and body, and thus unable to fully experience a firm belonging to the physical space of the nation. Roberto and Victoria's cultural ethnicity is defined through an awareness of their family's oppressed past and parodic attempts to mimic and occupy center stage in a world of WASPs—that is, through a persecuted and oppositional sense of identity. Victoria's father, with his "farcical accent from an alien tongue" (22), has made it in a world full of hurdles, "booby-trapped with people who called him Jesus Killer, hurled epithets in mock Ladino, and pillaged his father's grave looking for Dutch diamonds and gold teeth" (22–23). Even their manufactured noble lineage bespeaks the violence of conversion and colonization that lies beneath it, as Victoria notes sarcastically that the Lobo family crest— a wolf atop the Pyrenees baying under a crown of stars—that marks the antique yellow labels on the Lobo Vineyards wine bottles is both historically fraudulent and absurdly ironic: *"What family crest? The one King Fernando personally designed for the Marranos before he handed them their heads?"* (21).[29]

The text thus acknowledges real prejudice against the Lobos family, but situates it as racial anti-Semitism directed at the previous generation that now has little or no material effect on Roberto and Victoria's socioeconomic position, especially when compared to Ideliza's. However, Roberto and Victoria's sense of belonging and entitlement is nevertheless ungrounded, and anxious about the possibility of elimination. Victoria and Roberto's inherited legacy of displacement manifests itself through corporeal anxiety that precedes the events of 9/11. Victoria, recollecting her relationship with Francisco, explicitly connects her Jewish diasporic identity to her physical anxieties, acknowledging how Francisco's Spanish (colonial) heritage marked their sexual trysts: she imagines her own "surrender" under his "Spanish soul" (38). The novel also implies that the Lobos' displacement is exacerbated by the family's loss of faith, which has rendered them in many respects a scattered nation with no spiritual center. Even Victoria and Roberto's parents' names—Sara and Abram— connote a lack of collective spirituality: they are named after the nomadic Judaic matriarch and patriarch *before* the covenant with God that established Abram as the father of many nations, promised him the land of Canaan as an everlasting possession, and renamed him Abra*ham* and his wife Sara*h*, inserting godliness into their very names.[30] Somewhere along the path of assimilation from Cuba to the United States, then, Victoria and Roberto's parents, although observant in some traditional rituals of Judaism, have not given Roberto and Victoria a sense of faith.

As an antidote to the malaise and displacement of Roberto and Victoria, the novel situates Ideliza's, Bembé's, and Cooper's cultural practices, histories, and experiences as alternative syncretic systems that offer new possibilities for narrative, and in turn understand national identity in new ways. Rather than being relegated to the margins, these characters are unexpectedly among the text's most at-ease and spiritually comfortable characters. By presenting an Afro-Cuban woman and an intersexual Native American man as more spiritually and physically comfortable in their space than anyone else, and as potential healers of the nation and its citizens, the narrative legitimates new narratives of national identity that privilege heterogeneity and collectivity.

One example of this new narrative of identity lies in the connections drawn between Jews and Africans. Both Ideliza and Victoria suggest that the two groups share a common legacy of biblical diasporic nomadism: Ideliza reminds Victoria that "both our peoples know suffering . . . from long, long time ago" (153), while Victoria herself compares Ideliza's altar to Changó with the desert-wandering Children of Israel's tabernacle (152). The narrative writes Cuba itself as an ancestral nation that connects the two ethnic groups. Cuba is thus reimagined neither as an originary homeland nor as a threatening neighbor, but as a common midpoint in both groups' longer histories of diasporic movement. The narrative voice explains that Bembé (Ideliza's son/Victoria's biological nephew) and Victoria's unlikely compatibility stems from their similar cultural background: they have "a psychological culture in common" and thus, "like Bembé, so many of [Victoria's] idiosyncrasies, her predilections, her emotional triggers had been simmered in the Cuban cauldron—even if she was too young to remember and he, in his turn, too young to have been there at all—a souvenir along the scenic route of their common diaspora" (85–86).

Here, cultural practices and preferences turn Cuban ethnic identity from something constructed into something more primordial and psychological, creating common bloodlines between Africans and Jews that have been brewed, so to speak, on the island of Cuba. Furthermore, the text posits what Cuba now means in the diaspora: it is both crucial and dispensable, collecting and forming cultural norms and traditions but also serving as a stopgap and temporary shelter for the tourist migrant.[31]

It is in the United States, specifically, that the Cuban American voice can articulate these blended histories of migration to and departures from the island, creating by the end of the novel an unexpected but positive syncretism of cultures that will eventually become an integral part of the new story of the nation.

The narrative also legitimates marginalized cultural practices by showing how they alleviate Roberto and Victoria's dis-ease. When Roberto seeks help from Ideliza because of the threatening phone calls he receives, he tells her that he believes in *her* belief in Santería although he himself cannot believe (8).[32] He gravitates toward mulatta Cubans such as Ideliza because *"they own where they stand, bless the ground holy like Abraham,"* and "this native ease, this unself-conscious sense of place and permanence, grounded Roberto" (129). Here, Afro-Cubans, like Abraham but unlike Abram, own their space and through that ownership make it sacred, creating an empowering relationship between self and place that nurtures, protects, and (temporarily) heals the anxiety of the U.S.-Juban body. Roberto also interprets his own lack of faith—or rather, his experience of faith as one step removed from the source—as part of a cultural reversal of the norm that excludes him from Ideliza's powers: "Roberto understood that Ideliza was in touch with omnipotent forces he knew nothing about. The gods talked to her at the drop of a hat, yet had ignored him for almost half a century. In Roberto's book, G-d had embarked on a long *siesta* and left Ideliza's *santos* in charge. Naturally, they favored sassy mulatto Cuban women . . . over Jewish Cuban American obstetricians any day" (8–9). In other words, even institutional practices of religion have been overturned: the transcendentally signified God has retired to the margins and been replaced by the formerly marginalized Santos. Although Roberto seems blasé about his abandonment by a higher force, the narrative voice also mockingly exposes his ambivalence by carefully—just in case—not writing the full name of God. The novel thus early on shows his deep unbelonging: beneath his successful career as an obstetrician, his trophy wife, and his luxury apartment in the Trump Tower that should securely position him as a privileged member of society, he is marked by an underlying legacy of displacement that renders him chronically othered from his space.

While Roberto's dis-ease is alleviated only by Ideliza's presence, Victoria's begins to be healed through her relationships with Bembé and Cooper, which not only ease her personal corporeal anxiety but also symbolize the ways in which normatively "diseased" bodies and their syncretic practices of narrative storytelling can actually cure the United

States' bodies, identities, and landscapes. Bembé represents the necessary transformative aspect of the mourning process that allows, in Butler's terms, Victoria's identity as a 9/11 survivor to define her yet still recognize the new possibilities for community that are inherent in that transformation. Although knowing Bembé does not make Victoria forget her trauma—"it did not mean she was free of fears" (84)—he does function as a powerful remedy for her grief, making Victoria feel "physically better than she'd felt since Francisco had dematerialized midair over Battery Park" and "sharper, as when the cobweb mist begins to lift at sea" (24). With Bembé, her traumatic experiences become narratable: "She no longer felt the broad-hand, explosive fear that had swept in like a Bedouin storm a few months back. . . . The monster had changed stripes, perhaps even its native habitat and hiding place. From its new vantage point, it was no longer nameless or faceless. She could hear its ticking heart. It had a shape and a face" (90). Bembé's very physicality, in particular his eyes, at first almost blind her, then cause her to pass out, and then, when she comes to, bring her comfort: "At first contact, his aquamarine eyes shot a singular, quick-blinding, liquid laser light into her," but then later on "the weight of Bembé's balloon head and his razor-short, nappy hair scratching her legs brought her comfort. His body anchored in her space . . . a tree planted by the rivers of water" (24). The very features that might mark him as an outsider (his disability, his black skin and hair) symbolically belong in the natural landscape, grounding Victoria's body back in place.

Most important, as a "deaf-mute" (2), Bembé's body speaks and listens not through the usual senses (mouth/ears), but through a holistic language of the body that the novel posits as more healing than ordinary mediums of communication. He rejects cultural norms that might define his inability to hear or speak as a paralyzing or silencing illness, and instead has an "articulate presence" (28) that both Ideliza and Victoria comprehend. When Bembé arrives in California, therefore, he "speaks" to Victoria: he "grinned and silently declared, 'You are so beautiful, Victoria! Let's whirl around the silvery tree again!'" (127). Bembé's main function in the story, then, is to offer new and transformative possibilities for corporeal experience and narrative. The nation and its national subjects ordinarily identify themselves through established practices of either literacy or orality (such as giving speeches, pledging allegiances to symbols of the nation, and writing histories). In doing so, however, the nation also defines certain bodies as healthy (and as belonging to the state) because of those bodies' abilities to perform such practices and perpetuate national ideologies.[33] And if, as established in the previous section of this chapter, we understand that the body cannot be separated from the nation (the body, and the story of its demise, belongs to and is written by the nation), this also implies that the nation demarcates certain bodies as unhealthy, and that the feared contagion of such bodies is always-already perceived, by dominant culture, to be infecting the nation-state. In other words, normative practices of communication such as those described above define not just the nation's identity but also perpetuate normative understandings of the citizen's body that utters that identity.

Through Bembé, however, Novas transforms what would ordinarily be defined as an incapable (noncitizen) body into a powerful one, specifically privileging the power of new technology by showing how its blending of literacy and orality can transform the role that bodies play in their practices of communication and heal the nation's ailments by restoring narrative to it. For example, in Victoria's apartment, Bembé and Victoria communicate by typing on his computer. Sitting alongside one another, "talking" by typing on the screen, Bembé and Victoria create a mediated oral literacy: they perform orality because they communicate synchronously and are in one another's immediate (corporeal) presence, but, of course, their "talking" is written. For Victoria, who fears corporeality, this intimacy with Bembé is simultaneously corporeal (he sits beside her, hugs her, touches her) and virtual (the screen mediates their "talking"), and represents new possibilities for engaging the body in narrative production that can begin to heal both the displacements of 9/11 and those of her Juban legacy.

In addition to considering the transformative possibilities of narrative production through Bembé's corporeal practices, the novel explores the history of Cooper's sexually othered body, interrogating the normative cultural and sexual practices that devalued it, and then, as I demonstrate in the last section of this chapter, revalorizing Cooper's experiences and his body as curative sites that can transform both Victoria's traumas and the nation's ailments. When Cooper relates the story of his body, we learn that he was born with ambiguous genitalia, and that his mother and the doctor decided to pare down his penis as much as possible, inject him with female hormones, and make him a girl. In other words, because of cultural pressure to categorize sexual identity, they attempted to cover over his amorphous biological features with a fixed gender identity.[34] Consequently, he felt physically ostracized, uncomfortable with his body and also emotionally and even physically displaced from his homespaces. He grew up as a young girl with a strong sense of unbelonging to his own body, and as a teenager started to develop both male and female pubescent features, growing breasts and a beard, getting periods and erections, a breaking voice and spreading hips (113). During that time he ovulated once, fell pregnant, and gave birth to a baby boy who was raised by his grandmother. After an experimental shot of testosterone from one doctor he finally felt comfortable (117), but the medical community refused to let him continue with the treatment, arguing that as an intersexual rather than a transsexual, he needed to be pushed "back toward the gender [he] had been raised in" (in his case, a girl [118]). Cooper eventually conformed to societal expectations, denied his intersexuality, and posed as a transsexual in order to get the testosterone treatment. He states, "I was angry that I couldn't just be me, couldn't just be honest and say, 'No, I'm not a woman or a man, I think what I am is a somewhat masculine androgyne, and can we just turn me into that?' But that wasn't an option. So I swallowed my rage, said the right things, and got the drugs" (120).[35]

Here, several important features of Cooper's story stand out. First of all, despite his confidence, Cooper repeatedly stops his story to ask Victoria, his listener, for reassurance that he is not "freakish" (116), reminding the reader of the still-pervasive influence of dominant culture's definition of normative sexual behavior and desire. Second, his body, initially beyond categorization, was created first as female, and then as male: he has been a girl, a woman, pregnant, a birthing mother, a boy, a man, and a father, and thus, over the years, has embodied a syncretic spectrum of biological and cultural practices. Finally, it is important to note that when the medical establishment forced Cooper to choose one set of biological attributes (and their corresponding gendered behaviors) over another, it was operating under cultural expectations whereby one's personhood is largely determined by sex and gender identity. In other words, making him cross over and settle on one side provided the most reassurance that he was in fact one sex, simply born in the wrong body, and that despite his desire to be known simply as a person, he would be known and categorized in gendered terms.

In the novel Cooper's corporeal experiences come to represent the possibilities for practices of "inter" belonging to the nation. As an intersexual, his very presence undermines binary structures of male/female sexual dimorphism by moving between them unexpectedly. But as an intersexual who has also undergone constructive surgery and taken drugs that alter his natural physique, his body also undermines binary notions of nature versus technology. That is, as a site of experimental reconstruction and recrafting, his body presents a new understanding of biological nature, underscoring the fact that the "natural" human is always technologically mediated. In terms of understandings of national identity, this of course challenges notions of natural or rightful "belonging" to the nation and legitimates the construction and mediation of new stories of national identity, no matter how at odds they appear to be with presiding (naturalized) dominant narratives.[36] In addition, in presenting Cooper as an intersexual who rejects transsexuality, Novas specifically privileges *inter*sexuality as a model for national identity. While the model of "trans" (crossing over, settling in a new place) that previous chapters explored certainly deconstructs normative understandings of belonging to the nation, the model of "inter" is acutely more radical in its notions of normative sexual identity, national identity, and belonging. With it, there is movement back and forth, there is unexpectedness, there is surprise, and there is continual change. At times there is normative behavior, and at other times departures from that behavior. As Cooper remarks, he was "sometimes" a girl, and "sometimes" a boy (111).

As the novel acknowledges his struggle, it centralizes the unexpectedness of intersexuality and takes down the boundaries that regulate and stabilize gendered behavior, and, in so doing, it radically confounds the nation's normative practices. While Cooper appears on some levels to actually participate in this preservation of gender normativity (occasionally boasting about his masculinity, for example), on another level the narrative voice resists this by carefully describing his physical features as simultaneously both male and female. His body, therefore, has incorporated the unexpected, fluid practices of intersexuality, rather than the more fixed practices of transexuality. The valorization of practices of "inter" rather than "trans" is part of the novel's valorization of syncretism, whereby notions of belonging (whether to the nation or to the local community formed at the end of the story) emerge out of combining diverse cultural practices in unexpected ways. In other words, as we see by the end of the narrative, the very notion of belonging is retheorized: the most underrepresented citizen-members of the nation can now belong to various of its political, geographical, and historical/ancestral spaces at once, creating a radically new understanding of presence in the United States.

The narrative's physical descriptions of Cooper thus carefully move back and forth between normative female and normative male traits, showing how his body rejects notions of sexual and gendered stability and refuses to establish itself as either one or the other. Early on we learn that Cooper has an "unusually light frame for a man in this line of business" (rescue missions), and that his face is "as smooth as a baby's bottom," with small bones and "a carefully modulated, slightly southern voice, pitched purposely low and yet not resonant" (58). He has an "engagingly pubescent body" with "thin-haired thighs, and hairless chest with rosettes like women's nipples" (112). He is "gracious, light-footed" but also "a strapping swain emerging into manhood" (126). While the text typecasts certain normative expressions of sexual desire as feminine or masculine (Cooper's kisses are gentle, that is, feminine; yet his penetration is insistent, that is, masculine), it also strongly undermines the binary between the two, and emphasizes the fluidity of Cooper's sexual behavior. Thus Cooper's "light butterfly" kisses pair naturally but unexpectedly with his "importunate, full-blossomed member sheathed in his weathered jeans, seesawing, demanding entry with its obdurate cobra head" (150). As Victoria makes love to Cooper and strokes his constructed "fashioned penis" (120), she realizes that knowing the true history of his body has dislocated the easy—but deceptive—binary expectations through which she initially ascribed him to a particular gendered (masculine) role and biological (male) position. She remembers that "in bed he'd shown her strength, virile resolve, the whole gamut of masculine imperatives. There was no hint of femininity in him. *Or was there? Had she looked but refused to see?* . . . And, even so, what did it mean? She could only see him as he was now" (112). The fluidity of his appearance and her inability to now situate him firmly make her question her assumptions about masculine behavior ("there was no hint of femininity in him"), her perceptions of the experience ("Had she looked but refused to see?"), and also the need for such categorization ("what did it mean?"). She arrives at the surprising conclusion that while his body may be the sum of its syncretic histories, it is also, more important, a valuable site of present experiences. Seeing him only "as he was now," Victoria suspends categorical structures that would define him as male/female and natural/ artificial, and recognizes his personhood.

Middle Landscapes and Final Frontiers: Cyberspace and California

In Cooper's recounting of his experiences, where he acknowledges his desires, understands them in light of the nation's regulatory norms of gender and sexuality, and then develops strategies that resist and deviate from those norms, we see the beginnings of a narrative of healing restoration in which the corporeal anxiety and malaise that afflict some of the nation's citizens are alleviated. This narrative retheorizes dominant culture's understanding of place and belonging, interrogating the nation's normative practices of economics and bodies by reimagining California as a site of ethnically syncretic cultural living. But even before this new national ideology of interdependent and socialist principles is fully realized in California, the novel rewrites concepts of place and identity by exploring alternative possibilities for corporeal presence, community, and narrative in cyberspace.

Cuba and New York City, as physical sites of trauma, are clearly left behind when the characters go online and inhabit cyberspace, the in-between place or "middle landscape" that allows Victoria (especially) and Cooper to borrow and temporarily inhabit a virtual reality—a precursor to the very physical belonging they both experience in California, from which they can renegotiate their bodies' experiences of place and produce narratives. This middle landscape functions as a midpoint between isolation and connection, where they, as networked citizens, can occupy versions of both frontier-spaces and homestead-spaces.[37] How, then, is corporeal presence negotiated in this kind of space, and how can one belong to such a space? Here, I explore the experiences of embodiment, narrative representation, and personal/national identity formation that cyberspace enables for the characters, particularly Victoria, reading their online landscapes as sites of mourning out of which transformative new communities can emerge.

The novel's presentation of Victoria and Cooper's cyberspace relationship suggests both the empowerment of virtual identity-formation and the limitations of it. While during their Internet conversations Cooper pushes for a more physical or tangible connection with Victoria, Victoria welcomes the disembodied narrative production that cyberspace enables. Her pursuit of online disembodiment is a clear attempt to retreat from her own physicality and her interaction with other physical bodies, and to experience virtual rather than corporeal belonging. For a long time the online Cooper "made sense" to her because he "still remained incorporeal, a part of her imagination, as real or unreal as she could handle on any given day" (87). As a networked citizen talking to Cooper she is able to step beyond herself *and* remain herself, write to another person *and* write to herself, and occupy, online, a middle landscape in which she can explore the frontier *and* remain safely at home.[38] Initially, she rejects Cooper's suggestions that the two of them meet up, enjoying the incorporeal friendship not just for the convenience ("a friendship she could conduct from her Toshiba without having to shower, stare at the closet for something to wear" [33]) but also for the management of her grief online: "If she felt crowded or bereft, she need only disconnect" (33). And because for Victoria corporeal presence obstructs communication, cyberspace conversations enable not just the process of mourning to unfold but also allow her to turn this mourning into transformative narrative production. She rejects Cooper's idea of exchanging photographs, worrying that *"something could get destabilized"* because *"Right now it's pure—I mean, it's just soul-to-soul communication"* (16).

This "pure" written communication of cyberspace suggests a process of narrative production that can contain, hold, and manage traumatic memory, and thus potentially heal residual personal and national traumas (Cuba, 9/11, histories of prejudice). However, the narrative posits that such virtual belonging cannot fully resolve corporeal anxieties because even online identities operate through markers of physical presence. Cooper writes, *"I sure would be glad to meet you for real. Not that this isn't real"* (45), raising the question that is often asked in critical discussions of Internet community, that is, the extent to which we are biased, even in virtual space, toward visual and physical presence for our definitions of the real, and the extent to which that definition of the real determines our knowledge of the other. While often online "acts of creative reading . . . can and do stand in for physical presence," online readers will imaginatively flesh out a substantial audience in their mind, "with all the familial markers by which he or she might be 'known,'" making real disembodiment impossible.[39] Even Victoria's own ruminations online constantly move away from virtual reality and toward physical presence. The very virtual nature of Cooper's presence means that to Victoria, he seems to be everywhere and nowhere at once, a definitive presence even when she is away from her computer. She cannot help but imagine Cooper's body: in an unsent email she wonders, "Are you as wide and long as a lumberjack with a full square jaw? Are you a dwarf, a paraplegic, an old man reinventing his life? Are you a young man, wise, as Solomon never was, pretty as a woman in disguise?" (42). To her discomfort, she notes that "Cooper had begun fleshing out, spinning closer into view" (87). Because the Internet can conceal cultural and physical deviances, the body, in its absence, actually looms larger and even more present and significant.

By showing how even cyberspace cannot eliminate physical presence, the novel suggests that the United States' attempts to relegate Cuba to a virtual space of haunting memory cannot eliminate its physical presence in the nation; in fact, such attempts to render it absent actually flesh out its illicit presence. Similarly, cyberspace alone cannot contain or absorb national grief over the events of 9/11, although as a middle landscape it offers a temporary space for the bereaved self (Victoria/Cooper) to identify its displacement, and is a necessary route toward complete belonging in the physical space of Southern California.[40] However, when Victoria first travels to California to take care of Roberto's vineyard she plans just a temporary visit, imagining that "she would go for the ride, be a tourist . . . sojourn in southern California amidst Merlot and Chardonnay" (89). Because her "sudden wanderlust in search of a geographical cure" (89) takes her to California rather than back to Cuba, we understand that the Juban's homeland lies in the United States' resettled frontier land, a site of syncretic ideologies and cultural practices that, in line with Turner's original frontier metaphor, offer innovative new experiences and also challenge its status as a bastion of individualism. In fact, in removing the characters from their old locations and having them adapt to a new environment, Novas actually emphasizes their American citizenship. And in having them, through that adaptation, resettle California as a Marxist/socialist space, she insinuates that American citizenship must, in its ideal form, resist systems of corporate capitalism.

The novel privileges California as a site of belonging over any other physical and virtual space by showing how the characters connect to its natural beauty, its spiritual wealth, and its sacred Native American Chumash roots. Through these connections, they can build a countercapitalist social system that valorizes alternative, nonheterosexual (intersexual) family structures and thus potentially reconstructs national identity, particularly that which imagines heterosexual reproduction as key to national continuity. The physical landscape clearly heals and restores both the body and the spirit. When Ideliza arrives in California with Bembé, joining Cooper and Victoria, she immediately notices the "amazing . . . incredible country air, this earth and sky fragrance" and opens up the window to gaze "long into the rows, the vines, and tilted stalks, the Santa Ynez Mountains refractory of verdigris and purple" (129). She puts the land to work by planting an herb garden "for protection and medicine" (136) and setting up an altar to Changó inside the house. Victoria, too, finds the area "a beautiful place" and then catches herself thinking about the novelty of her connection to it: "It had not occurred to her until now that there could be a lovely place left in the world" (97). When she and Cooper take "a pilgrim walk" (97) into the physical frontier land, the setting seems especially beautiful after the dislocating traumas of place (New York, Cuba) that preceded it. Against the raw Edenic backdrop, they stand still "at the still point of the turning world, the only two people under the purple sky" (97), illustrating the ambiguity of collective corporeal presence—they are still but moving, they are alone but together—that is reminiscent of the metaphysics of presence they learned in cyberspace.

In this idyllic physical environment, the land is rendered a sacred or holy site in which transformations can occur, allowing the body to move from corporeal anxieties toward an embrace of physical human connection.[41] Now that Victoria and Cooper can talk face-to-face (rather than through cyberspace), Cooper's body, particularly his eyes, become a welcoming abode and dwelling space that Victoria can belong to: when she turns to look at him, she "eases" her eyes onto his, "a soft *landing*" (94, my emphasis) that can begin to heal the tragic memory of 9/11's aborted flights, her family's ancestral dislocation from place, and her corporeal dis-ease. This is also a home for Santería: combining faith and place, it is honored by Ideliza's *orishas*, the spirit manifestations of Santería's *Olodumare*, or God. As Ideliza points out, "this whole city, this whole *campo* and city we're in belongs to Changó" (130). Ideliza recognizes Southern California's land as holy and spiritual because of its natural kinship with Santería, reimagining it as the heart and center of a new nation. The landscape's physical beauty is thus not just aesthetic but also an important home for the *orishas* that Ideliza imagines directly onto the land, noting that it is "such a beautiful *campo*, so much green and pale yellow and open country for the *orishas* to romp around in" (131). Changó, who Ideliza says "likes to hide in trees, like that one over there, next to the fence, and smoke his good Partagas cigars" (131), here becomes a god of rootedness, connecting people to their place and working as an antidote to the legacy of diaspora and ill ease that they all carry with them.

Most important, the land's sacredness is rooted in its ancestral Chumash presence, and to the tribe's valorization of intersexual bodies, a valorization that becomes important in light of the characters' forging of a communal identity based on nontraditional family structures. We learn from Cooper's account of his sexual and gendered experiences that the Chumash originally helped restore him to his body. Where the medical community failed, the Chumash succeeded, teaching Cooper of the superior value that many tribes place upon people like himself, whom they call berdache. In contrast to the Western establishment's view of his body as needing surgical repair, then, the Indian community did not disrupt or change his body. Where the medical community finally gave Cooper drugs to tame his female hormones, fixing the botched-up mess of his body that they created for him at birth, the Chumash took him in, nursed him back to health, and gave him physical and spiritual strength. He describes the Arapaho tribe's belief that the berdache exists due to supernatural gifts from birds, the creation story of the Colorado Mohave that speaks of a time when people were not sexually differentiated, and the Omaha, Sioux, Zuni, Navajo, and Lakota myths that in various ways warn against interfering with the special powers of the berdache (121, 122). Thus, on the Chumash reservation, Cooper learns to translate his deviant body into an occulted and holy entity, rewriting it as a sacred thing that can resist dominant culture's norms with dignity and certainty.

It is appropriate that this land in Southern California becomes the setting for the novel's socialist reimagining of nation and the normalization of intersexual belonging; in addition, the fact that the Chumash so highly valorize intersexuality also gives the new social structure described at the end of the novel a powerful ancestral legitimacy. In other words, while the alternative national identity envisioned at the end presents a new version of America, it also, at the same time, echoes and returns to certain Native American values about the body, suggesting that they must become an explicit part of the United States' understanding of itself. The novel ends with a pastoral scene in California wine country that grounds the characters to the land and to one another under a new familial and socioeconomic model of community. Lobo Winery (now owned by Victoria) has become the headquarters for Ideliza's spiritual practice, and the winery is reorganized so that Mr. Hollister, the original owner who was, under Roberto's ownership, "*a serf to his own domain*" (91), is now a limited partner in the venture (and has also sworn off whiskey and joined Alcoholics Anonymous). There are on-site accommodations for the grape pickers and the sharecroppers, who because of Cooper's structural reorganization are also shareholders. At harvest time, one-tenth of the returns will go to each bracero and thus "the Lobo Vineyards [will] become the first co-op winery in all of central California, from the San Joaquin Valley all the way down to Santa Barbara" (211). In an explicitly anticapitalist move, this "curious Marxist or Christian system" recognizes that the psychic and physical health of the nation can come about only when "every worker on this land" is "a partner" and when "everyone whose sweat contributes to making Lobo wine good is rewarded for it" (211). Cooper asks rhetorically, "Why should you pay those poor people a miserly wage, exploit them, and then scoot them out of here like cat litter? . . . It's a no-brainer . . . the sort of thing César Chávez prayed about" (211). In addressing the country's relationship with its migrant farming population this Communist utopia begins to resolve the nation's problematic economic ills by imagining a healthier (socialist) economic interdependency between Latin America and the United States.

The novel, however, not only brings Latin America into the space of the United States but also imagines a broader global identity in which new models of family structure, based on a fusion of cultural identities, legacies, and traditions, are normalized. Thus, in addition to the winery's co-op structure, Cooper builds "indigenous Caribbean-style round houses" around the winery for himself and Victoria, Ideliza, and Bembé, and for the workers. Usually surrounding an African *batey*, or sacred African town center, this is "a microcosm of the way Cooper thought human cooexistence should be" (211). And although Ideliza and Bembé live in their own round house next to Victoria and Cooper's, "Mother, child, Cooper and Victoria had fallen into the habit of having almost every evening meal together in the big house" (210), showing, of course, a communal rather than a nuclear family dynamic. Cooper and Victoria themselves live together in an "unorthodox union" (206), in an arrangement that prevents their kinship from becoming reducible to biological family, and their sexual relationship to be gauged, as Butler warns, against the marriage form.

In particular, their relationship challenges normative family structures (that depend on exogamic heterosexual reproduction) because of the images of twinning that are frequently used to describe how physically similar they are. Thus, although Victoria and Cooper are not biological twins, both have "strawberry-blond hair" (58), and Cooper, like Victoria, is "thin-boned, her height, hair like hers, face smooth as a choirboy" (93). Overall they are strikingly similar, a "copper-haired couple of identical height and breadth" (146). This "twinning" reframes the sexual desire in their relationship, pushing it beyond the accepted norms prescribed by society but also permitting it. That is, they are physically similar enough for their union to suggest the possibility of tabooed incestuous desire while still allowing it, because they are not, after all, biological twins. Ultimately, this "twinning" moves Victoria and Cooper away from their particular ethnic group and toward a new community organization. Thus their coupling represents a space of nonbiological kinship: it is exogamic yet identical, pairing a Cuban American Jewish woman from New York with her physically identical partner, an intersexual Chumash man from California.[42]

At the center of this new kinship structure is Bembé, who, as Ideliza's biological son and Victoria's biological nephew, connects the Cuban American Jewish and Afro-Cuban mulatta women. As the only child in the novel Bembé might normally represent a conventionally reassuring message about the heterosexual reproduction of culture and national identity. Butler, for example, writes that the figure of the child is an "eroticized site in the reproduction of culture, one that implicitly raises the question of whether there will be a sure transmission of culture through heterosexual procreation—not only whether heterosexuality will serve the purposes of transmitting culture faithfully, but whether culture will be defined, in part, as the prerogative of heterosexuality itself."[43] Although *Princess Papaya* does situate a transmission of culture through procreation (Bembé), the group that will raise him, presented at the end of the novel, clearly breaks away from the normative understandings of family and marriage that Butler cautions against. Novas's portrait of Bembé troubles any "sure transmission" of cultural norms not only because of the alternate connections forged between him and other "family" members by the end of the novel but also because of the legacy of heterogeneity and miscegenation in Bembé's bloodline. In fact, Bembé enables the very concept of the maternal to be refigured, as he becomes Victoria and Cooper's child as much as Ideliza's.[44] By the end, then, the text has confounded the reproductive practices that would otherwise produce ethnic continuity, and Bembé, a child who will be presented with Juban and Afro-Cuban traditions and practices, becomes the site of cultural and spiritual syncretism.

With Bembé as the site of syncretism, the novel posits a new literary and national identity that centers what has previously been marginalized. The impact of this new national identity on narrative becomes clear at the end when Bembé begins to speak. Against all odds, he learns to sound out the words "Happy Birthday" for his mother. He thus starts to renegotiate the practice of oral literacy that he has, up until this point, depended on. Eventually, the novel suggests, Bembé might not need to communicate by typing on a screen alongside his listener/reader. Instead, his physical body alone will produce meaning, reiterating the novel's mediation of technology as ideally enabling an extension of, but not replacement for, the body. In the same way that Victoria and Cooper no longer need to communicate online once they have established physical contact, so, too, we can infer that when Novas finally gives Bembé a purely oral voice, she imagines that the future body of America will empower itself with the immediate presence of speech.

It is appropriate that by the end, orality has become a possible form of communication in this particular space: the African *batey* with its indigenous round houses on a decentralized "Cuban" collective farm. Orality, compared to literacy, emphasizes the physical presence of the speaker, and, in so doing, can also highlight the speaker's physical deficiencies and/or disabilities (which in themselves may obstruct oral communication). However, giving such bodies speech enables them to practice a politics in which their physical presence—in its non-normative "deficient" form—is legitimated. Thus, in giving the Afro-Cuban Bembé oral speech, Novas validates the physical presence of particularly diasporic and "othered" Cuban-Latino bodies in place and on the land. In this way the novel imagines the future citizen of America as a member of a new nation-space, one that borrows from Africa, Native America, and most of all Latin America in order to construct a U.S. national identity based on a frontier story where (healing) collective and socialist principles are valorized over (destructive) capitalist ones.

The postscript that follows illustrates how these issues of Latino nationhood and citizenship play themselves out in current debates about immigration, in which Latino unbelonging is frequently articulated through a rhetoric of criminalization. Specifically, I explore how the legal and cultural layers of "otherness" through which dominant ideology often interprets and reads Latinos/as, and in effect criminalizes Latino presence in the United States, become unraveled in these literary works and thus challenge contemporary immigration debates in important ways. That is, the postscript offers a case study in how the literary works I have explored throughout this book can challenge the terms through which contemporary political debates are framed.

Postscript. The Illegal Aliens of American Letters: Troubling the Immigration Debate

Halfway through Helena María Viramontes's 1985 short story "The Cariboo Café," the nameless Anglo-American owner of the café watches the arrest (which he has facilitated) of three undocumented Latino workers and remarks, "I don't know. I didn't expect handcuffs and them agents putting their hands up and down their thighs."[1] His comment exemplifies both the moment at which undocumented Latino/a workers become criminalized by the disciplinary powers of the nation and the bewildered response that witnessing this moment of criminalization evokes in the observer. The scene takes place toward the end of the café owner's monologue, after a group of "illegals" from the factory across the street run into his café to hide, as he puts it, "like roaches when the lightswitch goes on" (71). As they run in they look at him, assessing the danger of the space, but when he just goes on stirring his chili they continue into the bathroom. When the agents arrive in pursuit, however, the owner nods them toward the bathroom, essentially turning in the workers. Before this particular scene and throughout his internal monologue, the owner has voiced a number of contradictory beliefs: espousing platitudes that clearly demonstrate and perpetuate negative stereotypes of Latinos/as, pragmatically defending his right to nevertheless serve them in the café in order to make a living, and movingly struck by the similarity between one little migrant boy (Macky) and his own long-deceased son, JoJo. He automatically adopts the ideology of the dominant culture, categorizing these workers and other Latino/a refugees and migrants as "illegals," "bad news," and "weirdos" (69), but when the moment of their arrest comes, he finds that he cannot quite comprehend the scene, and realizes that he has actively participated in the criminalization of these workers. Despite his prejudiced assumptions that they are not quite fully human because of their undocumented status on the U.S. side of the border, he finds that they look unnatural as actual criminals. In particular, the older one looks "silly in the handcuffs on account of she's old enough to be my grandma's grandma." After the invasive and constraining treatment of her body, this woman "looks straight at [his] face" (72), silently shaming him for his role in her arrest.

What is important in this scene is the way that it carefully illustrates the process that often turns undocumented Latino/a workers in the United States into criminals. Because the café owner knows the law, he knows to interpellate them as illegal. In addition, his feelings of prejudice add a layer of cultural and racial "otherness" to their geopolitically illegal status; the moment when he turns them in is perhaps less about their illegal status in the nation and more about his own level of discomfort with their otherness and unbelonging. But to see them actually treated as criminals—an act that confirms his prejudice toward them—makes no sense to him. In fact, that act of criminalization by the police in itself seems to humanize them. His "I don't know" suggests an essential dilemma, as his blurred vision of these Latinos/as—likely criminals, yet perhaps innocent humans with full, complex lives—becomes, for a brief moment, clarified. Within the realm of the story this clarity is short-lived, as the events later climax in the violent shooting of an unidentified refugee woman (from El Salvador, Nicaragua, or Guatemala) that is precipitated by the owner's call to the police.[2] However, the story remains significant in the political point that it makes: demonstrating throughout (not just in this scene) how certain Latino/a groups become criminalized, and deconstructing that criminalization of Latinos/as.

The ways in which the narrative challenges normative political views is evident elsewhere in the story, both in the ways it humanizes the various "displaced" (65) Latino/a characters and in its problematic conflation of U.S. and Latin American ideological discourses and authorities into one space. Even the café owner recognizes Macky's innocence, showing a strong sentimental, almost paternal attachment to him, deciding he is "a real sweetheart like JoJo. You know, my boy" (70). The story's focus on the attachment between children and their parents, particularly the refugee woman's emotive plea to the Lord when her five-year-old son, Geraldo, becomes a "disappeared" in her home country, is obviously intended to move even an unsympathetic reader into recognizing the faces of these otherwise faceless "illegals," and acknowledging the humanitarian, ethical, and geopolitical questions that are at stake in the nation's practice of border enforcement. The opening section, in which Sonia and Macky, the two illegal migrant children, are lost at night in an unidentified U.S. city, demonstrates not only their basic poverty and determination ("Mother would work . . . until they saved enough to move into a finer future where the toilet was one's own and the children needn't be frightened" [65]) but also the way that their movements through a frightening urban landscape appear to turn them into criminals with criminal intent. Although clearly innocent, their constant fear of the "polie" and *la migra* (65), and the nation's geopolitical articulation of this space, renders them guilty of a "crime" of displacement.

Similarly, the story's final section, narrated by the refugee woman, shows not only how the disciplinary system creates criminals by hunting down displaced migrants but also shows, in some detail, the history that lies behind the "criminal's" presence on this side of the border. We learn that once the woman's son disappears, she is essentially homeless, without a nation to call her own: "These four walls are no longer my house, the earth beneath it, no longer my home. Weeds have replaced all good crops. The irrigation ditches are clogged with bodies. . . . Is this our home? Is this our country?" (75).

The woman's narrative, told in fragments that collapse time and place between her home country and the United States, is both moving and disturbing, as she confuses Macky for her lost (and dead) son, Geraldo, and blends the United States' aggressive treatment of illegals with her memories of disciplinary and sanctioned brutality in Latin America. In the final scene of the story, Viramontes illustrates the violence of nationalism, where the traumas the woman has suffered in Latin America seem to be re-created in the space of the café. Holding Macky, whom she believes to be Geraldo, she sees the police coming toward her with "their guns taut and cold like steel erections," waving them "like a flag," and vows "I will fight you for my son . . . I will fight you all" (78). The "you" here is all Americans, both those in the present time and place and those of her Latin American nation, so that in the woman's imagination and in the story's literary imaginary, the United States becomes part of an ongoing and extended narrative about Latin American national history and politics.[3]

Viramontes's story, although written in 1985, continues to show quite vividly how the geopolitical rhetoric of the mainstream measures the state of illegal presence and citizenship in the Americas. This rhetoric, which assumes that the nation's political borders must separate those who are of the nation and those who are outside of it, determines the recent political climate in the United States in which narratives of border enforcement, immigration, and illegality have become the most popular sound bites in almost any debate about Latinos/as. And what often starts off as a discussion about illegal Latinos/as in the United States also comes to refer to legal Latino presence as well. In such discussions, the threat to national security, especially after 9/11, seems to form the basis upon which legislative decisions are made and popular discourse is established. In addition, recent immigration stories in the news media also show the ways that the nation's measure of citizenship sometimes interprets cultural otherness as a threat to national identity. At times, too, such evidence of non-American (U.S.) cultural practices, or sometimes even just bodily presence, although not inherently illegal, is rendered potentially criminal.

While Mexican undocumented workers most obviously fit this rhetorical strategy, legally established U.S.-Latino communities of both Mexican and other national origins (such as Puerto Rican and Cuban) can also become interpellated as culturally threatening to the integrity of the nation's identity, and thus, implicitly, to its security, becoming pawns in a broader national argument about the value and identity of American citizenship and character. Clearly, Viramontes's story not only illustrates this collapse between geopolitical and cultural otherness but also, as I have shown above, radically challenges dominant culture's portrayal of Latinos/as as a homogenous and illegal presence. The story shows how my prior discussions of illegitimate cultural and sometimes even political unbelonging coalesce, in mainstream popular media, into a fear of foreignness and a rhetoric of illegality that at times imagines *all* Latinos/as as criminals. The story's challenge to such images, then, is to bring together U.S. and Latin American spaces, reframing the immigration debate by mapping the United States and its southern neighbors as one collective area, and changing the space itself so that its citizens and its foreigners can no longer be so easily differentiated. This literary validation of Latino presence in the United States is politically significant, as it addresses both the geopolitical and cultural "otherness" by which Latinos/as—en masse—are frequently rhetoricized and creates an alternative rhetoric through which Latino presence can be understood.

In the current political climate, recent attempts at legislating Latinos/as make it evident that it has become a crime to be "un-American" in terms of both citizenship and culture. Recent bills in Arizona, such as the new immigration law (blocked at the time of this writing by a federal judge), have been interpreted as a straight-out "attack on [all] Latinos," and a symbol of hostility directed particularly at the state's Latino population, most of whom are legal, longtime residents.[4] Key provisions of the law would require the police to determine the status of people they lawfully stopped and also suspected of being in the country illegally. The law, based on racial profiling, would also make it a crime to lack immigration documents. Such a law, if it ever does come to pass, obviously assumes any Latino presence to be, potentially, a criminal presence. Inflammatory rhetoric by proponents of this law uses not only terms such as "aliens" to identify illegal immigrants but also talks of the "onslaught" of "enemies" to the nation-state. In an article in the *Washington Times*, for example, Jeffrey T. Kuhner writes that the federal decision to block the law suggests that "America cannot protect its national sovereignty," and that it is "no longer a real nation-state capable of defending its geographical boundaries, cultural identity, and national interests."[5] Here, the border itself seems to spawn criminals, and geopolitics is used in order to maintain the integrity of both the nation's security and cultural identity: geographical borders are there to protect the nation from those with criminal intent, even (and especially) when the "crime" consists of cultural difference. And at a Tea Party rally at the Mexican border in August 2010, in which activists gathered to advocate a more secure border and more border enforcement, Mexicans in particular were described as criminals even before they crossed the border. Sheriff Joe Arapaio, who addressed the crowd, noted that "the problem could be solved if the Border Patrol was given permission to track down migrants on the Mexican side before they crossed."[6] According to this, then, Mexicans with any intent to cross must plan to do so illegally, and are inherently criminal in this intent. Another border security advocate's remark—"We don't like illegals hiding under bushes while our kids wait for the school bus"[7]—goes even further in criminalizing Latinos/as, imagining invisible predators ready to pounce on and spoil an iconic American scene of innocent children waiting for the bus—in other words, rendering American spaces unsafe and its citizens in danger.

Although the language used in these examples represents only one segment of the population, the sentiment behind it remains an active part of even more centrist U.S. popular discourse, and in that sense contributes to a real and ongoing national imaginary that perpetuates the idea of all Latino presence in the United States as somehow suspect and troubling. For example, following on the heels of the proposed immigration law, Arizona's former state superintendent of public instruction Tom Horn proposed a law (later signed by Governor Jan Brewer) that aimed to ban the teaching of ethnic studies in Arizona schools. Proponents of the law argue that the classes are creating "future activists" by brainwashing students with anti-U.S. propaganda.[8] A clear example of the way in which extremist views can become implemented into legislation and then determine public opinion, the law specifically makes any class promoting solidarity among a specific race or ethnicity illegal, with the penalty of up to a 10 percent hold on the school's funding. Its existence (it came into effect on December 31, 2010) raises interesting questions both about the climate that generated it (proponents have a heightened sense that America is "under siege"[9]) and the climate that the law itself will create (Latinos/as believe their own community to be "under siege"[10]). How, though, does it connect to notions of U.S. nationhood? Opponents of the law immediately understood it to target Mexican American and Latino studies in Tucson in particular, and, more broadly, the Latino population at large in the state. As one stated, "There's a fierce anti-Latino sentiment in this state."[11] The law has been interpreted as trying to put "Latinos in their place" because, as Eugene Robinson points out, as the number of Latinos/as in Arizona continues to rise (about 30 percent of the state's population is Latino/a), the demographic shift has induced culture shock among some who see the "old Anglo power structure" lose control. Robinson adds that this "angry anti-Latino spasm in Arizona is only partly about illegal immigration, which has fallen substantially in the past few years. It's really about fear and denial."[12]

Specifically, Subsection A of the bill's amendments disallows schools from having, in their programs of instruction, any courses or classes that may: promote the overthrow of the U.S. government; promote resentment toward a race or class of people; are designed primarily for pupils of a particular ethnic group; and advocate ethnic solidarity instead of the treatment of pupils as individuals. But the amendments also include a clause that explicitly permits "courses or classes that include the history of any ethnic group and that are open to all students" (unless the course/class violates Subsection A), "courses or classes that include the discussion of controversial aspects of history," and "instruction of the Holocaust and any other instance of genocide, or the historical oppression of a particular group of people based on ethnicity, race, or class."[13] The language of the bill has been criticized as ambiguous and contradictory, perhaps because it allows the teaching of inclusive U.S. history but forbids making connections between past and present, essentially preventing discussion of the legacies that history still imposes on contemporary culture. For our purposes, what is most significant is the wording of the four clauses of Subsection A. Looked at in isolation, these clauses articulate an imaginary Latino/a subgroup, perhaps a rising youth culture, of potential criminal intent. The amendments, which could become part of the state—and to an extent, the nation's—anti-Latino rhetoric, warn away from collectivity, separatism, and the creation of an oppositional ethnic identity, and, most important, from attempting to overthrow the U.S. government, as if the criminal desire to overthrow it may already exist. In this way, the legislation and the debates surrounding it represent a vilification of Latinos/as that turns even—and especially—legal and/ or established communities into a suspicious and threatening collective body of potential criminals.

Several critics note that majorities have supported Arizona's immigration law, and that many state legislatures could pass similar bills— ones that "whitewash" their public education—in the years to come.[14] Peter A. Brown's piece in the *Wall Street Journal* in late December 2010, for example, believes that public sympathy simply does not lie with illegal immigrants, and that such public opinion is crucial but resistant to efforts to legalize the undocumented: "The American public probably is not behind, and certainly not by the margin that would be required, to lead to such a large change in policy—creating a path to citizenship for illegal immigrants."[15] The emphasis in immigration debates continues to focus on the problem of illegal Latinos/as rather than on any attempts to integrate them (even those who have been U.S. residents for many years), suggesting the extent to which the nation's sense of self rests on a need to identify its foreign residents and then to refuse their cultural presence in the land. The recent failure of the proposed Dream Act in fact typifies this attitude. The proposed legislation, which passed the House of Representatives but failed in the Senate in mid-December 2010, would have opened the door to military service and higher education for young people whose parents brought them to the United States as children without proper documentation. It stipulated that if they finished high school, showed good moral character, and served at least two years in the military or earned a college degree, they could earn citizenship.[16]

An editorial in the *New York Times,* which anticipated the Dream Act's failure in the Senate, remarks that although the act represents the best hope for "legalizing any significant number of Americans-in-waiting" whose lives are in limbo through no fault of their own, the nation's political climate, with regard to the immigration debate, is "poisoned" and "wretched," focusing solely on border fear and lockdowns.[17] And a still-ongoing debate, at the time of this writing, about birthright citizenship, in which lawmakers from various states are challenging the standing interpretation of the citizenship clause of the Fourteenth Amendment (granting citizenship to all persons born in the United States), and possibly forcing the issue all the way to the Supreme Court, clearly illustrates the ways in which anti-Latino immigration debates have moved into broader conversations about American citizenship and national identity. But although immigration hard-liners imagine waves of migrants illegally crossing the border in order to give birth in the United States, the reality is more complicated. Such "anchor babies" are rare; instead, many immigrants who arrive to give birth in the United States are frequent border crossers with valid visas who intend to take advantage of better medical care in the United States.[18] Lacey points out that some migrants are in fact invited to cross the border by U.S. commercial interests, such as the electronic billboard on the Mexican side that advertises the services of an American doctor and asks bluntly, "Do you want to have your baby in the U.S.?" Again, we see how Arizona has taken the lead in what is "essentially an effort to redefine what it means to be an American": one advocate of the change in law even defends his position by commenting, "We're just saying it takes more than walking across the border to become an American citizen. It's what's in our souls."[19] Once geopolitical definitions of nationhood give way to this kind of sacred and unattainable construction of the "real" American character, it becomes clear that the criminality of illegal aliens lies not just in their undocumented presence within U.S. borders but also in their deep-rooted foreign, un-American identity.

Doris Meissner, the former head of the Immigration and Naturalization Service (now known as Immigration and Customs Enforcement), agrees, admitting that although border violence is down, "it's not about numbers . . . it's about the real and perceived impact immigrants are having on the country . . . and underneath it all, the kind of cultural issues of how much immigration is changing us."[20] The anxiety about Latinos' cultural impact, of course, stems back many years, as sociologists and economists noted even in the 1990s the ways in which Latinos/as who "assimilated" in the United States did not fit the classic "melting-pot" model, but instead, became middle-class Americans without losing their ancestral identity.[21] In fact, Tom Horn's defense of his Arizona teaching bill's amendments makes it clear that the traditional assimilation model of early twentieth-century (mostly European) immigrants to the United

States still represents the conservative ideal of nationhood, as he explains that "we should be teaching these kids that this is the land of opportunity, and if they work hard they can achieve their dreams and not teach them that they are oppressed."[22] Latino resistance to this sort of complete assimilation, which imagines a meritocracy where individualism is rewarded with socioeconomic success and oppression belongs only to the past, represents, to certain voices in the mainstream, the threat posed by the presence of another nation—and its various cultural practices and identifications—within the United States.

Despite (or perhaps partly due to) both legislative measures and rhetorical patterns in popular discourse that seem driven to "other" Latinos/as, however, a strong outpouring of literary production embraces Latinidad and legitimates the cultural and geopolitical presence of Latinos/as in the United States. The texts I have discussed in the previous chapters, in other words, demonstrate the ways in which the "strong transnational connections" between most U.S. Latino groups and their Latin American countries of origin create a new "Latino nation" born in the United States,[23] a nation that reframes both the geopolitical and cultural identity of the United States. While some popular discourse has thus tended to regard Latinos/as as potentially criminal or at least culturally illegitimate, these U.S. Latino/a literary works imagine a collective U.S./Latin American geography in which such political, legal, and cultural distinctions become discredited, and in which cultural otherness is thus legitimated. Although they do so in different ways, the texts ask us to reconceptualize the United States in light of its history with and in Latin America, so that this history continually displaces the cultural identity of U.S. nationhood: a nationhood that we know, from the discussion in the introduction, has long conceived of itself in terms of spatial identity.

The Mexican American narratives discussed earlier, then, obviously redress popular discourses about undocumented workers because of their focus on the geographical and political border between Mexico and the United States. In Denise Chávez's works the healing of the Southwest's diseased topography not only reenvisioned it as part of Mexico but also legitimated the cultural practices of Soveida's and Rocío's communities. Ana Castillo's *Sapogonia* also embedded Latin American nationhood within the United States, demonstrating the process by which the nation's normative ideology disciplines its migrants, and resisting that maneuver with a new mestizo geopolitics. In *Caramelo* mestizo geopolitics similarly deconstructs the U.S.-Mexico border as part of a broader new nation-building project. The Puerto Rican and Cuban writers

demonstrate an equally urgent need to legitimate the cultural otherness that defines the characters' experiences in the United States. Both
Judith Ortiz Cofer's novels and Esmeralda Santiago's memoirs position
the United States' neocolonial relationship with Puerto Rico as one that
continually identifies Puerto Rican geography, history, politics, and
culture as suspect: the U.S. citizenship conferred upon Puerto Ricans
at birth, in other words, does not guarantee them a cultural birthright.
In fact, particularly at the time during which the stories are set, any
evidence of cultural otherness is seen as an abuse of their political status as U.S. citizens. Both redefine the terms of that cultural birthright:
Ortiz Cofer's texts do so by revealing, and reveling in, transgressions
against the normative practices of U.S. and Puerto Rican culture, while
Santiago validates her own authorial presence, and uses that new authority to imagine a collective, rather than neocolonial, U.S.–Puerto Rican
relationship. Finally, Himilce Novas's novel turns U.S. Cuban political
history on its head, imagining a postrevolutionary present and future
in which the United States' long involvement with and deep connection
to the island makes the two nations inseparable. In the novel Cuba, now
part of the United States, manifests itself as a socialist nation within
the United States, in effect legitimating the ideological roots of Castro's
Cuba, and consequently reframing the entire dynamic of U.S.-Cuban
relations since the 1960s.

Thus, while today's political climate often "others" Latinos/as in
legal and cultural terms, these literary works establish cultural legitimacy, showing how the United States and Latin American nations have
long been inseparable and integral parts of one another, and making
any declamations of pure or soulful American citizenship and identity
fictional, or, at the very least, themselves suspect. The texts selected for
this book demonstrate what Chicana critics and writers in particular
hoped for and anticipated in the 1980s and 1990s: the coming together
of art and politics in such a way that each can determine, affect, and
inspire the other. In 1993 Cherríe Moraga predicted that "by the
twenty-first century our whole concept of 'America' will be dramatically altered" because of a growing Latino population whose "strong
cultural ties, economic disenfranchisement, racial visibility, and geographical proximity to Latin America discourages any facile association into Anglo-American society."[24] Although she speaks specifically
about Chicanos as an "internal nation whose existence defies borders
or language, geography, race," her broader argument applies to all
Latino/a writers, as she calls for the need to produce and commit to an

art of resistance that can transform consciousness, refuse assimilation, and redefine America.[25] She says, "Our task is to write what no one is prepared to hear,"[26] asking that Latinas learn to see themselves less as U.S. citizens and more as members of a larger "world community composed of many nations of people." Such transnational imagining, of course, no longer gives credence to the geopolitical borders of the nation-state.[27]

The books also herald the beginning of a reinforced focus on understanding U.S. Latino/a literature as the expression of a nation-within-a-nation, and thus on seeing that literature as a powerful indication of a new direction for the reinterpretation of American literary, political, and cultural identity. Even as anti-Latino legislation was being proposed, opposed, and circulated in 2010, for example, Ilan Stavans and a group of prominent U.S. Latino/a literary critics and scholars put out the significant keystone *Norton Anthology of Latino Literature*. As its reviewers have noted, the timeliness of the hefty volume, which brings together almost 2,500 pages of U.S. Latino literature, indicates that "the Latino community isn't just thriving, but is providing answers about what it means to be American."[28] For those willing to engage with it, it provides a political, historical, and literary context for Latino life in the United States, explicitly showcasing the United States' early and ongoing connections to Latin America, and legitimating Latino cultural and political presence as part of the fabric of U.S. nationhood. In a radio interview marking the publication of the anthology, Stavans reiterates that "there is no America without Latinos" and that "in the United States today we're all Mestizos."[29] Of course, the publication of such an anthology does not in and of itself render anti-Latino legislation any less real, or the effects of anti-Latino rhetoric any less materially damaging to the community. But it does represent, in both its contents and the fact of its existence, the anxiety of a nation divided: as Stavans remarks, "the tensions that you hear in this country between the group that wants to resist immigration, and the group that wants to embrace it, is really the tension about how America should be in the future."[30] In other words, if, as Sandra Cisneros has stated of U.S. Latino/a writers, "we're the illegal aliens of American letters,"[31] then Latino literature has to become an integral part of any discussion of literary and national identity in the United States, as a presence that in redefining assimilation, continues to trouble the cultural space and definition of the nation.

Notes

Introduction

1. *Gourmet*, June 2009, 14.
2. Ibid., 64.
3. Ibid., 67.
4. *Gourmet*, August 2009, 14.
5. As Ruiz notes, "Martí's 'Nuestra América' has become emblematic of a truly transnational, hemispheric interdisciplinary discourse" ("Nuestra América," 663).
6. Stavans, "Introduction," lxv.
7. In this imaginary of a hemispheric Americas, the United States has to "understand itself as a territory within the Americas" (Sandín and Perez, "Introduction," 10). Sandín and Perez's introduction to their edited collection, which explores practices of Latino/a literary theory, argues that U.S. Latinos/as are reimagining what constitutes the United States. The idea of viewing the United States as part of the Americas is more often expressed in critical work on the history of U.S.–Latin American cultural, political, and economic relations than in any literary critical material.
8. For example, in the Mexican American texts analyzed in chapters 1 and 2, "place" refers most obviously to physical location and geography, while also symbolizing more figuratively the social and cultural dynamics of that nation. In the analyses in the chapters that follow on U.S. Puerto Rican and Cuban American literature "place" is sometimes evidently physical (urban and natural landscapes, dwellings, and so forth) but also indicates cultural and/or bodily experiences that allow one to belong (or not belong) to that physical location, and also to an imagined community (a nation-space, a collective of some sort) and a narrative experience.
9. Bammer argues that displacement is a formative experience of the twentieth century ("Introduction"), and other human geographers variously note that place, with its multiple metaphorical meanings and identities, is often assumed to be natural, and thus remains relatively unexplored. There is general agreement among critics both that place needs to be understood as socially constructed and that among social

constructions, history has been privileged over geography. See Massey, "Double Artic-
ulation"; Abramson, "Mythical Land"; Olwig, "Recovering"; Tuan, "Place"; Harvey,
Justice; Lefebvre, *Production of Space*; Soja, *Postmodern Geographies*; Soja and Hooper,
"Spaces That Difference Makes"; and Hayden, "Urban Landscape History."

10. Soja and Hooper nevertheless note that there is a recent "renewed interest in the
relatively neglected, "undertheorized" dimension of space" ("Spaces That Difference
Makes," 183).

11. See Comer (*Landscapes of the New West*) for a fascinating reading of Gloria
Anzaldúa's respatialization of the borderlands area, and Villa (*Barrio-Logos*), who
argues that the "spatial practice" of American rules of the land affects Chicano social
identity in the United States. Martha Cutter also notes that ethnic and immigrant
texts written since at least the early twentieth century (if not before) often put into
question the idea of a firm national boundary "demarcating America" ("Editor's
Introduction," 5).

12. Brady, *Extinct Lands*, 7.

13. Juan Flores, in "The Latino Imaginary," argues that there are three ways in
which Latinos have been interpellated: demographic (an instrumental, homogeniz-
ing method that produces alarming popular truisms about the numbers of Latinos in
the United States, for example); analytic (tabulates the diversity of Latino groups and
experiences; depends on socially constructed statistical evidence); and imaginary. The
"imaginary" rendition of Latinos—one that I believe the literature I look at performs,
to an extent—consists of an aggregate of lived experiences and historical memory, and
foregrounds the origin-nation's history and presence. The Latino imaginary produces
Latino identity as a productive and positive thing, and creates, ultimately, a new map
of the Americas (ibid., 613).

14. Rebolledo, "Tradition and Mythology." For further discussion of southwestern
Chicana writing, see chapter 1. Given my reading of place above, where land is never
just land but also a site of cultural (un)belonging, it should become evident why I
explore women writers in particular. Although I am not implying that male writers
do not produce literary texts that also invoke a strong connection between geography,
natural/urban landscape, and cultural belonging (Rudolfo Anaya's seminal *Bless Me,
Última*, Piri Thomas's *Down These Mean Streets*, and Oscar Hijuelos's *Our House in
the Last World* are just some examples), my interest lies in the ways that contemporary
Latina writers, in their reclamation of the literary word, are also performing a reclamation of the nation through cultural, geographical, and political spaces.

15. Brennan, "National Longing for Form," 49. See also Bhabha, who writes that
"counter-narratives of the nation . . . continually evoke and erase its totalizing boundaries" and "disturb those ideological manoeuvres through which 'imagined communities' are given essentialist identities" ("DissemiNation," 300).

16. Flores, "Latino Imaginary," 608.

17. Saldívar, *Border Matters*, 19.

18. See Ramón Saldívar's *Chicano Narrative*, 3, originally cited in Said, *Orientalism*, 59.

19. Sandín and Perez, "Introduction," 2.

20. De la Campa, "Latin Americans and Latinos," 166.

21. Oboler, *Ethnic Labels*, xii–xiii. While emphasizing how important it is to
acknowledge distinctions, asking how such diverse populations, nationalities, races,

classes, histories, languages, and experiences of incorporation even came to be categorized as a single homogenous group in the early 1970s, and considering the limitations of the term "Hispanic," Oboler also notes that it can ensure the community access to much-needed resources, and help make demands from the ethnically based policy structure of the U.S. government (ibid., 4).

22. Concannon, Lomelí, and Preiwe, "Introduction," 4.

23. Stavans, "Introduction," liv.

24. Hayes-Bautista and Chapa, cited in Oboler, *Ethnic Labels*, 4.

25. For this, see especially Caminero-Santangelo's excellent discussion of the possibility or viability of a collective panethnic Latino identity (*On Latinidad*), and Oboler's important analysis of the way that historically, Latin Americans, now "Hispanics," were critically imagined as foreigners within the nation-space ("So Far from God"). While forthcoming chapters mostly use terms distinct to the national origins of the writers or characters, I hope that my occasional necessary use of the term "U.S. Latina" will be understood in the manner in which it is intended: as a carefully considered choice that, for me, still resonates more positively than "Hispanic."

26. Oboler, *Ethnic Labels*, 165.

27. De Genova, "Legal Production of Mexican/Migrant 'Illegality,'" 62. De Genova also notes that persistent revisions in immigration law itself since the 1960s (when Mexican migration escalated dramatically) play an important role in producing a legally vulnerable, undocumented workforce of "illegal aliens" (ibid., 61). Mae M. Ngai similarly argues that the 1924 Johnson-Reed Act, the first law to establish numerical limits on immigration, helped to produce the "illegal alien" as a new legal and political subject (*Impossible Subjects*, 4–5). Arturo J. Aldama further posits the idea that such categories of "illegal alien," assigned because of one's physical and linguistic characteristics and appearance, seem to "legalize violence against your person and community" ("Millennial Anxieties," 21).

28. Rosas, "Thickening Borderlands," 336.

29. Rosaldo, "Cultural Citizenship," 259.

30. Rosas, "Thickening Borderlands," 337.

31. Ibid. Oboler also remarks that we are now looking at a contemporary reemergence of racial profiling that is justified as necessary to ensure "national security" ("Redefining Citizenship," 9).

32. A fascinating example of this "thickening borderlands" can be seen with the Texas Virtual Border Watch Program, a real-time interactive Internet site launched in November 2008. In it, anyone who wants to participate in the U.S. border control can register and have access to a network of webcams and sensors feeding live streaming video, observing the border between the United States and Mexico. Once you are logged in, you can use a hotline to alert the authorities about any activity perceived as "suspicious." An alert is then sent to the Texas Border Sheriffs Coalition, which decides whether to take further action. Clearly, this program (purportedly created to fight drug trafficking and crime) allows the American public to produce and write the "immigrant" and "the criminal," creates a distinction between lawful Americans and foreigners, and makes the border material and relevant (and "thickened") across the nation. For instance, Koskela cites an example of a suburban mother in New York who regularly commits to virtually patrolling the border while her baby daughter naps ("'Don't Mess with Texas!'" 54).

33. Chávez, *Latino Threat*, 3.

34. After 1848, a regional political economy developed in the Southwest, which relied on the active recruitment of Mexican migrant workers. Over the late nineteenth century, U.S. employers increased the permanent (and unregulated) importation of Mexican labor, until in the early twentieth century the creation of the special police force—the Border Patrol (1924)—began to discipline and police Mexican workers in the United States. The selective enforcement of law, and the Bracero Program, however, coordinated with seasonal labor demands by U.S. employers, creating a "revolving door" policy whereby mass deportations became concurrent with an overall, large-scale importation of Mexican migrant labor (De Genova and Ramos-Zayas, *Latino Crossings*, 40).

35. Chávez, *Latino Threat*, 31. For a discussion of the ways in which Mexicans have historically been rendered into second-class citizens, see Oboler, *Ethnic Labels*. For a discussion of the ways that Mexicans in the nineteenth century were criminalized, and in the 1930s were excluded from citizenship and belonging, see Camacho, *Migrant Imaginaries*. For more on the argument that Mexican Americans have long been racialized, see Gómez, *Manifest Destinies*.

36. Chávez, *Latino Threat*, 27–29, 42.

37. De Genova and Ramos-Zayas, *Latino Crossings*, 7.

38. Duany, "Nation and Migration," 52.

39. See Grosfoguel, Negrón-Muntaner, and Georas, "Introduction," 20; and Flores and Benmajor, "Introduction," 3.

40. Flores and Benmajor, "Introduction," 3.

41. Grosfoguel, "Divorce of Nationalist Discourses," 58.

42. De Genova and Ramos-Zayas, *Latino Crossings*, 7.

43. Grosfoguel, Negrón-Muntaner, and Georas, "Introduction," 11. See also Negrón-Muntaner's introduction to *None of the Above*, where he comments that the island has been considered "peculiar according to the standards of 'normal' national development" (1).

44. Grosfoguel, Negrón-Muntaner, and Georas, "Introduction," 12. Initially, the United States tried (unsuccessfully) to assimilate Puerto Ricans into American culture by coercion—for example, imposing English as the primary language in public institutions and banning the display of national symbols (such as the Puerto Rican flag). Any signs of collective national affirmation were regarded as subversive, and persecuted. Despite this form of domination, these policies were ineffective, leading to the United States' creation of the ELA.

45. Flores, "Islands and Enclaves," 69.

46. Sometimes the term "Puerto Rican" is "claimed as a sign of difference" (for example, cultural identity, language), while at other times "the same sign is equated with being part of the 'United States'" (citizenship, welfare entitlements) (Grosfoguel, Negrón-Muntaner, Georas, "Introduction," 16).

47. Oboler, *Ethnic Labels*, 171.

48. See De Genova and Ramos-Zayas, *Latino Crossings*, 7–8.

49. Oboler, *Ethnic Labels*, 38.

50. Grosfoguel, Negrón-Muntaner, and Georas, "Introduction," 21.

51. Aparicio, "Exposed Bodies," 166.

52. De Genova and Ramos-Zayas, *Latino Crossings*, 7.

NOTES TO PAGES 13-17 / 199

53. Gómez, *Manifest Destinies*, 157.

54. Ibid. For example, in 1960 the U.S. government established the Cuban Refugee Program to help Cubans find jobs and housing, learn English, and generally adjust to new society (ibid., 158). It is important, however, to remember that later waves of Cuban exiles into the United States (beginning with the Mariel Boat Lift of 1980) included more demographically and racially diverse members of the Cuban population.

55. After a 1995 revision of the 1966 Cuban Adjustment Act, the "wet foot, dry foot" policy allows any Cuban caught on the waters between the United States and Cuba to be sent back to Cuba, but a Cuban who makes it to dry land is allowed to remain in the United States and eventually qualify for expedited legal permanent residency status.

56. See Novas, *Everything You Need to Know*, 201–204.

57. See Lazo, *Writing to Cuba*, for an analysis of the long cultural contact between the United States and Cuba over the nineteenth and twentieth centuries.

58. Huntington, *Who Are We?*, 221.

59. Ibid., 220.

60. Ibid., 250.

61. Ibid., 249.

62. Ibid., 251–252.

63. Sanchez, "Y Tú, Que?," 48.

64. De Genova and Ramos-Zayas, *Latino Crossings*, 21.

65. Oboler argues that the experience of Latinos suggests that there is more to the sense of belonging than the formal state rules and regulations concerning birthright, naturalization, and citizenship ("Redefining Citizenship," 11). William V. Flores also notes that the country's anti-immigrant hysteria "deflects our attention from a simple reality: being a citizen guarantees neither full membership in society nor equal rights" ("Epilogue," 255). Arlene Dávila points out that it is necessary to see "the current immigration and citizenship debate as one that affects all Latinos," and to recognize the ways in which the immigration debate fetishizes citizenship "as a guarantor of privileges" in order to veil its increasing denial of civil liberties (*Latino Spin*, 10).

66. Rosaldo, "Cultural Citizenship," 255. Similarly, Juan Perea contends that "the public identification of 'illegal aliens' with persons of Mexican ancestry is so strong that many Mexican Americans and other Latino citizens are presumed foreign and illegal. When citizens and aliens look alike, then all are presumed to be alien and foreign and undermining of the national character. This is an old theme in American politics" (*Immigrants Out!*, 2).

67. Rocco, "Transforming Citizenship," 307–308. De Genova and Ramos-Zayas also point out that even after 9/11, Latinos/as have not been "redeemed" of the allegations of "foreignness," illegality, or criminality that were prominent features of their racialization in the years prior to 9/11 (*Latino Crossings*, 217).

68. Oboler, *Ethnic Labels*, 18

69. Dávila, *Latino Spin*, 11.

70. See Flores, "Epilogue," 256.

71. Castañeda, "Roads to Citizenship," 156.

72. De Genova and Ramos-Zayas, *Latino Crossings*, 1. Thomas Muller states that "it is not so much the legal status of aliens but rather their ethnic, cultural and religious diversity that is the origin of most anti-immigrant sentiment" (*New Strangers*, 115).

73. Torres, Mirón, and Inda, "Introduction," 8–9.

74. The term "cultural citizenship" may also be useful for examining the meanings and experiences of alienation, membership, and belonging of Latinos/as with respect to the national community. Initially coined by Renato Rosaldo in the 1980s in order to explore Latino civic participation in and negotiation of cultural space, the term now refers to the social practices of belonging that establish distinct spaces for Latinos/as, and that can contribute to an emergent Latino consciousness and social/political development. See Flores and Benmajor, "Introduction"; Oboler, "Redefining Citizenship"; and Castañeda, "Roads to Citizenship." Leo Chávez argues for Latino cultural citizenship as a kind of "Latino Contribution Narrative," a discourse that is silenced in popular culture beneath the one that posits Latinos/as as a threat, but which would celebrate the cultural, social, and economic contributions of Latinos/as to the United States (*Latino Threat*, 181).

75. Chávez, *Latino Threat*, 2, 22.

76. Rosas, "Thickening Borderlands," 336, 337.

77. Elenes, "Border/Transformative Pedagogies," 248. My emphasis.

78. For discussions of the 1985 issue of *Time*, see Berlant, "Face of America"; for discussions of the 1993 issue, see Brown, "Assimilation"; Berlant, "Face of America"; and Bost, *Mulattas*.

79. Oboler, *Ethnic Labels*, 29.

80. *Time*, July 8, 1985, 25.

81. Ibid., 36.

82. Ibid. In *The Latino Threat* Chávez discusses popular culture's presentation of the "hot" Latina, which assumes nonnormative sexual behavior and out-of-control fertility, both of which contribute to the immigrant threat and reconquest narratives of the mainstream (77).

83. *Time*, July 8, 1985, 36.

84. Ibid., 37.

85. Ibid., 38.

86. Ibid., 56, 57.

87. *Time* 1993, 16.

88. Into the twenty-first century we see a similar trend in newsmagazines' presentations of Latino/a presence in the United States. On February 6, 2006, *Time* ran a feature about the connection between Tuxpan, a small Mexican town, and the Hamptons, to which Mexicans have been migrating for over thirty years (Thornburgh, "Inside the Life"). The piece includes an insert map of the United States entitled "How the Influx Is Changing the U.S." with the states in varying shades of red-orange, yellow, and white, depending on the number of illegal Mexicans that enter and reside in them. Visually represented in this way, Mexican presence is depicted as a stain spreading across the nation, its impact felt everywhere. And while many voices interrupt the dominant culture's portrayal of Mexican threat to the nation— Gregory Rodriguez ("Why We're the New Irish") argues that Mexicans *are* similar to previous immigrants, eventually succeeding by assimilating and being stripped of their foreignness; Henry Cisneros ("Fence") argues that Latinos/as in general can become part of future community revitalization if they are helped socioeconomically into the middle class—many still argue for curtailing immigration (Samuelson, "Hard Truth").

89. Beebe writes, "Territory and boundaries . . . are not ontological givens, but rather cultural productions needed by the state in order to become a nation" (*Nation and Region*, 6).

90. "Here and Now." Vicki L. Ruiz also notes that visa overstays rather than dangerous border crossings are the preferred means of arrival into the United States ("Nuestra América," 381).

91. In terms of general public responses to Latino/a immigration, there is ambivalence: all the newsmagazines cited here include polls that report contradictory responses on the part of Americans when questioned about Latinos/as in the United States; Cornelius argues that to many native-born residents of the United States, the economic benefits of a large, flexible, and relatively low-cost supply of immigrant labor are offset by the noneconomic costs of a rapidly expanding and increasingly settled immigrant presence ("Ambivalent Reception," 165). Mae M. Ngai also agrees that unauthorized entry into the nation "remains vexing for both state and society" because undocumented immigrants are welcomed as cheap and disposable labor, and thus regarded as economically necessary (*Impossible Subjects*, 2).

92. See Saar ("Heritage of American Ethnicity") for a more detailed argument about Crèvecoeur's text as an important literary example of the rhetoric of assimilation in the United States.

93. Ibid., viii, original in Fender, *Sea Changes*, 12.

94. Manning, "Introduction," xviii, original in Jefferson, *Papers of Thomas Jefferson*, 426.

95. Crèvecoeur, *Letters*, 27.

96. However, in his infamous last letter, James, ashamed and disgusted at the turn of events in the colonies (the war), actually endorses communal living, imagining himself transformed and running away to live with the Indians, in a perfect "little society" (ibid., 215).

97. Ibid., 27. My emphasis.

98. Ibid., 43.

99. Ibid., 44–45.

100. Marta Sánchez, in her exploration of the growth of translations into Spanish of U.S. Latino/a literature written in English and published, generally speaking, in the United States, argues that the United States, now more than ever, is part of the Spanish-speaking *Americas*, and names this phenomenon a "renationalization" ("Para Español," 51, 57).

101. Transnationalism is a concept developed by social scientists in the 1990s "in order to understand the life and culture of people moving from one place to another, especially during the latter part of the twentieth century" (Kanellos, "Schematic Approach," 29).

102. Slater, "Situating Geographical Representations," 66.

103. Concannon, Lomelí, and Preiwe, "Introduction," 3.

104. McClennen, *Dialectics of Exile*, 24.

105. Raymont, *Troubled Neighbors*, 8. See also Pike (*United States*) and Grandin (*Empire's Workshop*) for discussions of U.S.–Latin American relations.

1 / Spaces of the Southwest

1. Rosas, "Thickening Borderlands," 337.

2. Chávez, *Latino Threat*, 3, 31.

3. Perea, *Immigrants Out!*, 2.

4. See the introduction for a discussion of the separation of U.S. and Latin American nation-spaces and identities.

5. Eakin, *History of Latin America*, 215.

6. King, *Border Confluences*, xii.

7. Although both the short-story collection and the novel make references to the world beyond the towns in which the stories are set (with references to nuclear contamination, the U.S. military in Vietnam, the struggle for land rights, migration, racial conflicts, and the Chicano movement), I see these references as oblique and presented in a subjectively opaque way, probably because their narrators (Rocío and Soveida) only gradually become aware of the wider world around them. Francine Ramsey Richter notes that in *Face of an Angel*, Soveida and her family do not seem particularly connected or linked to the United States at large and do not feel part of the major culture ("Romantic Women").

8. Much of the analysis that follows, in both this chapter and later ones, has some affinities with ecocritical work done by figures such as Glotfelty, "Introduction"; Cosgrove, "Prospect"; Killingsworth and Palmer, "Ecopolitics"; and Murphy, "Grandmother Borderland." Ecocritical approaches to literature—studying the relationship between literature and the physical environment—recognize that we define ourselves socially, culturally, and politically through "place"; read "place" itself as a socially produced ideological concept; and understand the environment to be a cultural construction that must be read in a material way. Insofar as "place," in particular urban and rural landscapes, is understood as a critical category, ecocriticism offers important directions not only for analysis but also for activism. In addition, authors of borderland literature have taken the lead in expanding the literary treatment of issues in environmental justice (although this is not a prominent feature of Chávez's work). While I do not want to dilute the focus of my argument—nation and ethnicity—by regarding it through a singular critical lens, attending to the geophysical aspects of these literary texts does allow us to recognize the way they resist attempts at silencing minority voices and presence in the United States.

9. While Chávez has clearly stated that her work is not directly autobiographical, and while my interpretation is not author-based, it is still worth using some of her nonfictional descriptions of the desert as a lead into her fictional narratives: both function to create a sense of the cultural and geographical transformation that her work illustrates.

10. Farah, *Literature and Landscape*, 18.

11. Ibid.

12. Many critics have interpreted Chávez's short-story collection as a kind of coming-of-age bildungsroman, in which narrative strategies reflect the fragmented nature of the Chicana developmental process. Some critics discuss the way that Rocío's emergent writer-consciousness (based on a plural and collective community, not an individualistic one) allows her to re-create her own past and creatively affirms her cultural origins and voice. See Eysturoy, *Daughters*; Kelley, "Minor Revolution"; and Browne and Harvey, "Más Tamales." Others, such as Mehaffy and Keating ("'Carrying on the Message,'") and Keating ("Towards a New Politics"), focus on the jarring narrative style of the stories, arguing that the temporal gaps and time shifts, and the

privileging of omissions, fragments, and broken voices, expose the limited representations of female identity available in masculinist discourse.

Face of an Angel, which has garnered very little critical work, is usually discussed in terms of the valorization of service and women's work. See Madsen (*Understanding*), Rebolledo ("Tools"), and Brady ("'So Your Social'") for discussions of the ennobling nature of work in the novel, and the understanding that through it women show their contribution to the community and construct an alternate sense of meaning and purpose to the social hierarchies created by economic structures. I discuss Anderson ("Displaced Abjection"), Wright ("She and I Are Molecules"), and Richter ("Romantic Women") and their work on bodies, space, and the environment in more detail in the sections that follow.

13. Rebolledo, "Tradition and Mythology," 96.

14. Ibid.

15. Ibid., 97.

16. Chávez, "Heat and Rain," 27. My emphasis.

17. Kevane and Heredia, *Latina Self-Portraits*, 40; Dunaway and Spurgeon, *Writing the Southwest*, 33.

18. See Norwood and Monk, "Introduction."

19. Candelaria, "'Wild Zone,'" 252.

20. In the first edition of the book, published in 1986, Chávez arranges the stories in an arbitrary order, but in the second edition, published in 2004, the order is chronological, beginning with the story that features the youngest Rocío, and ending with her as an emergent writer. Chávez has remarked that the collection is made up of "scenes" rather than individual stories, and there is debate among critics as to what genre they belong. Some, such as Eysturoy (*Daughters*) and Quintana (*Home Girls*), describe *Menu Girls* as a novel; others, such as Anaya ("Preface") and TuSmith (*All My Relatives*), argue that the stories are so interrelated that they should be read as a novel. Debra Castillo describes the collection as a "sequence" of short stories (*Talking Back*); Anderson views it as a set of interlocking stories ("Displaced Abjection"); Kelley describes it as a "composite novel," a hybrid of short story and novel ("Minor Revolution"); and Rosaldo reads it as a short-story cycle ("Fables of the Fallen Guy"). For the sake of convenience, I call them stories. To me, the new sequence of the stories is important, as it shows a gradual movement toward understanding the border as a material and political presence.

21. See Anderson, "Displaced Abjection"; and Wright, "She and I Are Molecules."

22. Jacobs similarly contends that the stories are concerned with smaller spatial units (such as homes) and the town as a borderland location where national and international economies coexist ("New Mexican Narratives").

23. In the earlier story "Willow Game" the most significant moment of disease occurs when the neighborhood willow tree starts to die and needs to be cut away. Rocío notes that it seems to refuse to leave the earth, and when it does, it leaves "a cavity of dirt, an enormous aching hole like a tooth gone" (13). The loss of the tree and the violence that follows in the story end Rocío's childhood, leaving her with an "immense sadness, the burning of snow in a desert land of consistent warmth" (14). In "Space Is Solid" Rocío's own sickness (her nervous breakdown) and another character's physical disability demonstrate the marginalized outcast status of the borderland body, and serve as another example of how political and national dislocation are articulated through disease and sickness.

24. Chávez, *Last of the Menu Girls*, 88, 89. Hereafter this work will be cited in the text.

25. Jacobs, "New Mexican Narratives."

26. Chapter 5, which explores Himilce Novas's *Princess Papaya*, identifies a similar valorization of alternative kinships that are not based on bloodlines.

27. Salvador complains several times that Regino is living in a "mansion" and asks rhetorically, "Since when do poor Mexicans live like kings in two-story houses? Christ, it's a mansion!" (201).

28. Of course, Regino does not speak his own story, suggesting that even in narrative, he becomes disempowered yet again. Rocío asks, "Who understands the words silence makes?" (184), because for much of the story Regino is so silent, or silenced, that there is some anxious imbalance between him and Rocío.

29. See Socolovsky, "Narrative and Traumatic Memory." Some ideas in this chapter are taken from that earlier essay.

30. There are very few full-length critical works on *Face of an Angel* (typically, critics devote a paragraph or so to it as part of a discussion of several writers together), but see Richter ("Romantic Women") for an in-depth analysis of the novel, where she discusses the nineteenth-century ideology of the feminine, its parallels with Mexican American women's experiences today, the function of writing as self-expression and memory building, and the Dosamantes's family's cultural dislocation and disassociation from their land.

31. Soveida only directly acknowledges her own experience of abuse at the hands of Luardo toward the end of the novel, when she says, "I remember him hurting Mara, and then me" (402). See Socolovsky ("Narrative and Traumatic Memory") for a discussion of the status of recovered memory in the novel.

32. Chávez, *Face of an Angel*, 3. Hereafter this work will be cited in the text.

33. One of the reiterated tropes of the novel—that the world is reducible to a domestic space, and that attaining collectivity in that space represents a possibility for broader collectives—means interpreting characters such as Oralia, Chata, and Lizzie in their broadest contexts. They all demonstrate the ways that domestic labor is not inherently undignified, only that its marginalization has rendered it so. In sanctifying such labor, they center Soveida in her space and allow her to begin to address the "off-balanced" legacies of her life. Similarly, in Soveida's "Book of Service," a collection of personal anecdotes, quotes from other restaurant workers, and recorded conversations that appear in segments throughout the text, physical labor and service are rendered transcendent and spiritual, again showing how the dislocated characters can relocate themselves in place, texture it with history and memory, and thus legitimately own their space.

34. Various houses and dwellings feature prominently in the novel: the Blue House, where Lupita and Oralia live and raise Mara; the Brown House next door, where Dolores and Luardo raise Soveida; Soveida's house with Ivan, which is the site of misery, abuse, and abandonment; the house Soveida shares with Veryl, a dry and cold space that later becomes the site of his suicide; her rented house on Manzanilla Street, where she is a reluctant witness to her neighbors' abusive relationship; her trailer, where she begins to peacefully mature; and El Farol, the restaurant. Her return to the Blue House at the end represents both a coming home and a renewal of the space.

35. Although Soveida does not dwell on Albert's or other customers' racism, she acknowledges prejudice against Mexicans and Mexican Americans even in the insular

Mexican American world of Agua Oscura. She warns Dedea, a younger waitress, that "sometimes we have to deal with stereotypical images of what people imagine Mexicans to be" (343).

2 / Mestizaje in the Midwest

1. Gabriela Arredondo (*Mexican Chicago*) and Juan R. García (*Mexicans in the Midwest*), among others, have noted the long history of Mexicans in Chicago, which is the setting for much of the two novels under consideration in this chapter. Arredondo describes how the geographic proximity of Mexico, continual new migrations, the particularities of preexisting histories between Mexico and the United States, and the "connectedness of land and histories" meant that "Mexicans in Chicago lived in dynamic, ongoing ways with Mexico." Part of Arredondo's argument in looking at historical experiences of Mexicans in Chicago, in fact, posits that during the early twentieth century, they became Mexican *in Chicago* itself, "constructing their own Mexicanness" as a response to anti-Mexican prejudice (*Mexican Chicago*, 145, 7). This idea of the construction of a nation from afar, beyond its political borders, and the impact of that nation building in the new land, is one that I am interested in throughout this project.

2. Critical responses to the borderlands have long acknowledged the impact of Chicano relocation to areas beyond the Southwest: Saldívar-Hull's phrase "the borderlands of Greater Mexico" (*Feminism on the Border*, 84), for example, suggests an extension of Mexican cultural presence into the United States in a way that might impact the United States' cultural and political self-identification. As Sergio Elizondo writes, "We understand now the Border between the United States of America and the Estados Unidos Mexicanos; now we would do well to consider that Borderlands might be a more appropriate term to designate the entire area over which the Chicano people are spread in this country. In so doing, we would also come to understand that the mere physical extension between the U.S.-Mexico border and, let us say, Chicago, is a fact of human dispersion" (cited in Pérez-Torres, "Refiguring Aztlán," 115).

3. See Rosas, "Thickening Borderlands."

4. See Rosas, "Managed Violences of the Borderland."

5. Rosas, "Thickening Borderlands," 344. Rosas's examples of intensified vigilantism in the thickened borderland include the Pentagon's contribution to the Border Patrol planning, the multiple human rights reports on the excesses of such border policing, and the work of particular community organizations that struggle against border violence and racial abuse.

6. Stavans, "Introduction," lxix.

7. Anzaldúa's description of a mestiza consciousness in *Borderlands/La Frontera*—the new mestiza develops "a tolerance for contradictions, a tolerance for ambiguity" and breaks down "the subject-object duality that keeps her a prisoner" (101, 102)—has proved influential for both postcolonial critics and border theory scholars.

8. Gabriela Arredondo's *Mexican Chicago* is an invaluable source for understanding mestizaje's usage during this time period. Arredondo notes that mestizaje was "pointedly about the project of nation building" (2), and that Vasconcelos "believed that the country could incorporate the *indio* into the *mestizo* mainstream, thus creating *la raza cósmica*" (150), in effect assimilating or extinguishing the indio.

9. Herrera-Sobek, "Gloria Anzaldúa," 267.

10. Ibid., 271.

11. Anzaldúa, *Borderlands/La Frontera*, 25. Hereafter this work will be cited in the text.

12. This could be interpreted as a reference to Moctezuma's revenge, a time in the future when there will be an opportunity for Mexicans to regain the lands that were taken away under the terms of the 1848 Treaty of Guadalupe-Hidalgo (Stavans, *Latino History*, 23).

13. The text alternates between a first-person and a third-person narration of events, itself an interesting strategy that reflects Max's own vacillating identity as exile and tourist. My reading here focuses on a hitherto unexplored part of the novel: the impact of indigenous Sapogonians in the United States—in particular, Chicago—and refers to the second edition of the text published in 1994. For my earlier critical piece that analyzes Max's status as a tourist-exile, see Socolovsky, "Borrowed Homes."

14. For a useful collection of essays on the recent transformations in immigration patterns to the United States and a discussion of the impact of this "conspicuous new geography," see Zúñiga and Hernández-León, *New Destinations: Mexican Immigration in the United States* (xiv), in particular the chapters by Durand, Massey, and Capoferro ("New Geography") and Grey and Woodrick ("Latinos Have Revitalized Our Community"), which explore Mexican migration to the midwestern areas of the United States.

15. It is important to note that although Sapogonia is fictional, Castillo cautions readers in her opening, *"This is the story of make-believe people in a real world; or, if you like the story of real people in a make-believe world,"* implying that whichever way we look at it, her fiction is inevitably paired with reality. While the novel's trope is fictional, its intent, purpose, and impact are material.

16. Castillo, *Sapogonia*, 1. Hereafter this work will be cited in the text.

17. Interestingly, Castillo signs off her prologue as *"A.C. July 29, 1985, Chicago, birthplace,"* highlighting the Midwest as her homeland (of sorts) even and despite her Chicana ethnicity. As I show later in the chapter, Cisneros, in *Caramelo*, also describes the long history of Mexican Americans in Chicago.

18. The majority of early articles on *Sapogonia* explore the relationship between the novel's male and female characters, in particular Max and Pastora. See Saeta, "Ana Castillo's *Sapogonia*"; Gómez-Vega, "Debunking Myths"; Benjamin-Labarthe, "L'Amour"; and Rochel, "Social Change." See also Gómez-Vega ("Homoerotic Tease") for a discussion of the novel's self-censoring presentation of lesbian sexuality (Pastora/Perla). Walter ("Cultural Politics"), Johnson ("Violence in the Borderlands"), and Sánchez-Pardo González ("Desire Called Utopia") focus more on the role of borders and mestiza consciousness in the novel.

19. See Walter, "Cultural Politics"; Johnson "Violence in the Borderlands"; and Sánchez-Pardo González, "Desire Called Utopia."

20. This erasure of Sapogonian identity is similar to the depiction of Guatemalan refugees in the United States in the 1983 film *El Norte*. In the film, because Enrique and Rosa pose and pass as Mexicans during their entire time in the United States, and never admit to their Guatemalan (and indigenous) origin, indigenous Guatemalan identity remains both invisible and unspeakable. In comparison, Mexican identity is understood to be more disposable and even more familiar to the U.S. mainstream.

21. Pérez-Torres, *Mestizaje*, xiv.

22. Ibid., 13, xiv.

23. Yang discusses this "instrumentalist school" theory of ethnicity, in which ethnicity is used as an instrument or strategic tool for gaining resources, noting that it is also "a means of political mobilization for advancing group interests" *(Ethnic Studies,* 46).

24. For a discussion of the systems of occupational and residential segregation that shifted Jewish American racial identity over the course of the twentieth century, see Brodkin, *How Jews Became White Folks.*

25. Anzaldúa, *Borderlands/La Frontera,* 89.

26. Cisneros, *Caramelo,* 438. Hereafter this work will be cited in the text.

27. A number of critics have explored the novel's representation of maternal relationships, its critique of society's attempts to discipline women's sexuality, and the connection between Chicana (in)visibility and Chicana bodies. See Berglund and Brown, *"Sin Verguenza";* Herrera, "Rejected and Reclaimed Mother"; Roberts-Camps, *Gendered Self-Consciousness;* and Bode, "Mother to Daughter." Several critics whose work complements mine explore the novel's transnational impact: Bill Johnson González's excellent analysis argues that Cisneros defamiliarizes the norms of English by rendering common Mexican sayings as English ("Politics of Translation"); Gutiérrez y Muhs reads the novel for its cultural content and contribution, suggesting that it inscribes Mexican cultural icons into mainstream consciousness ("Sandra Cisneros"); and Juanita Heredia discusses the novel's presentations of transnational gender identity and Mexico's Golden Age ("Voyages South and North," *"Caramelo," "Transnational Latina Narratives).*

28. See Alumbaugh, who writes, "Cisneros uses space to create Lala's migratory narrative desire and ability, which in turn enables Lala to 'bear across' her family's bilingual and bicultural stories" ("Narrative Coyotes," 55).

29. See Finnegan, *Narrating the American West,* 144–145.

30. Arredondo notes that in the 1920s and 1930s, Mexicans in Chicago constructed a "Mexicanidad" that provided "a means of coherence" and a "growing sense of national identity" that also allowed them to imagine and "claim their American identity by virtue of continental, or hemispheric, citizenship, not U.S. citizenship" *(Mexican Chicago,* 171).

31. The footnotes, as a narrative device that allows for asides and extra information, have bothered some reviewers of the text (see Haupt, *"Caramelo").* The effect, however, is to expand, enlarge, and complicate the narrative, reminding us that for every tale told, there are several untold versions. The footnotes, as margins of the text, do not have to be read: Cisneros has even said, "I ran away with the footnotes . . . some people didn't want the footnotes there. But you don't have to read the footnotes" (Birnbaum, "Identity Theory"). The footnotes do indicate that the story has no edges or borders, and is seamless, always potentially able to unravel and disrupt its own progress. They also create a space for historical, cultural, and fictional events that provide contextual backdrops to the story.

32. Sayers, *"Caramelo."*

33. Ibid.

34. Originally, in its attempt to create a unified nation, Mexico's ideological embrace of mestizaje represented, in rhetoric if not in practice, a new Mexican racial ideology that ostensibly privileged the nuances and ambiguity of racial mixture.

Arredondo notes several times that although mestizo nationalism touted racial hybridity, in reality Indians (as well as blacks) suffered discrimination and marginalization (*Mexican Chicago*, 2–3), and that although *indigenismo* appeared progressive, Indians faced only two real options: to "remain frozen in time as representatives of an imagined pre-Columbian Mexican past, or incorporate into the Mexican state only if they could be transformed into homogenous *mestizos*" (ibid., 147). Batalla, who points out that Indian subjugation dates back to colonial times and persists into the present as part of an exclusionary Westernization plan that invalidates Mesoamerican civilization (*México Profundo*, xvi), envisions a future "ethnically plural nation" in which oppressed peoples and cultures will be liberated and brought into the present, where they can democratically participate in national life. He states, "this process must take place within a democracy that not only recognizes individual rights, but also emphatically asserts the rights of historical collectivities" (ibid., 166).

35. Structurally, the novel also reflects Mexico's elusive presence, as each section recounts a different kind of attachment to the country. In Part One, Celaya's narrative of her summer visits to Mexico, she knows Mexico as both a tourist and a native, and thus becomes both an ethnographer of Mexico and an autobiographer. In Part Two, where Celaya recounts her grandmother's story in Mexico, she is her grandmother and father's biographer, their storyteller, and, of course, a historian, and because there is a historical immersion into Mexico's past, this section constructs Mexico as a center, a place of authenticity and origin. In Part Three, Celaya's adolescent recounting of her grandmother's move to Chicago, the narrator is a biographer and autobiographer of her own and other women's desires, and in forging a mestiza consciousness, she acknowledges the ambiguity of her relationship to place, realizing that Mexico both is and is not her home.

36. Celaya's attempt to know Mexico is also a desire to write down her father's life. The novel is dedicated to Cisneros's father ("Para ti, Papa") and in some respects presents a very intimate, loving, and humorous portrait of her father (her mother's voice is quieter and more silenced). Importantly, her father is the Mexican parent, the one with the more "pure," direct, and intimate knowledge of Mexico that her mother, as Mexican American, lacks. Cisneros has said that the novel was written "out of memory, and a dedication to my father and discovering him" (D, "Interview," 7). The novel can thus be read as a third-person autobiography. Saldívar-Hull writes that "Sandra Cisneros's personal background is that of a border feminist, a product of Chicago's urban barrios" (*Feminism on the Border*, 87), and Cisneros herself comments that when she was a child, her family was "constantly moving back and forth between Chicago and Mexico City due to my father's compulsive 'homesickness'" ("From a Writer's Notebook," 69).

37. Pérez-Torres points out that "the idea of borders has become central in various contemporary critical discourses" and that "the US-Mexico border remains a highly contested and dangerous area where naked power is employed in the ideological and economic service of the nation states" (*Refiguring Aztlán*, 103). He thus emphasizes the difficult doubleness of the border: that it can simultaneously be part of a theoretical discourse and continue to pose a real threat to human beings.

38. Anzaldúa, *Borderlands/La Frontera*, 108.

39. Several critics have focused on the power that Mexico holds over Mexican American writers, and in this respect, Cisneros is part of a literary trend. Genaro Padilla claims that the general sense of dislocation evident in Chicano writing has led

to an idealization of Spanish forbearers and a nostalgia for the Mexican homeland, arguing that this nostalgia stems from a feeling of alienation from the United States on the part of Chicano/a writers and thinkers, and a desire to "maintain a vital spiritual link with Mexico" ("Myth," 126, 108).

40. Suarez, "Interview." For an account of the history and sociology of Mexicans in Chicago, see Acuña, *Occupied America.*

41. As one British book review notes, *The House on Mango Street* is taught "all over America and has sold about two million copies in 11 languages, making Cisneros . . . the bestselling Latino author in the U.S." (Edemariam, "Mexican Gulf").

42. Cisneros said in 2002, "Though we know these stories, President Bush doesn't. For all his claiming to know Mexican culture, he knows nothing. So I need to write this down so President Bush can say, 'You know what, this is some American history I don't know!'" (Jones, "Latina Author"). In another interview she proclaims outright that novels represent her political side: "They're written 'to change people's minds,' she says, alluding to the mainstream" (Lopez, "Interview").

43. Rebolledo, "Tradition and Mythology," 119.

3 / Colonization and Transgression in Puerto Rican Spaces

1. See Negrón-Muntaner, "Introduction"; Flores and Benmajor, "Introduction"; Grosfoguel, "Divorce of Nationalist Discourses"; De Genova, "Legal Production"; Flores, "Islands and Enclaves"; and Oboler, *Ethnic Labels.*

2. Flores and Benmajor, "Introduction," 3.

3. Eakin, *History of Latin America*, 273.

4. Burns and Charlip, *Latin America*, 375

5. Stavans, "Introduction," lxvii.

6. See Korrol (*From Colonia to Community*) for a discussion of the way migration patterns into New York were effected through early economic partnerships between the two countries.

7. Muller, *New Strangers*, 126.

8. Yudice and Flores, "Living Borders," 57.

9. Yudice and Flores, "La Carreta," 158.

10. Flores, *From Bomba to Hip Hop*, 9. Faymonville notes that "given the colonial legacy of Puerto Rico's survival as a nation, the assertion of Puerto Ricanness in the face of U.S. imperialism can be read as an act of postcolonial resistance that nevertheless acknowledges the special position that colonial history affords Puerto Ricans in the heart of the empire, whether in New Jersey or Georgia" ("Motherland versus Daughterland," 125–126).

11. Unlike Ortiz Cofer's collection of memoir-essays, *Silent Dancing*, neither *The Line of the Sun* nor *The Meaning of Consuelo* has attracted a great deal of critical attention. However, some critics have engaged with *The Line of the Sun* in useful ways. Two early articles by Bruce-Novoa ("Ritual") and Favre ("Liminality") explore, respectively, the role of ritual and liminality in Ortiz Cofer's novel, arguing that the written word functions powerfully in it, that Marisol is a mediator between the novel's two worlds, and that she represents a new form of culture (of writing) that represents a creative cultural production. See also Faymonville ("Motherland versus Daughterland") for a discussion of the novel's portrayal of mother-daughter relationships; Kevane ("Fiction") for useful biographical

information on Ortiz Cofer; and Montilla ("Island as Mainland") and Mujcinovic (*Postmodern Cross-Culturalism*) for brief discussions of the novel's presentation of biculturalism and return migration. The most interesting recent work on *The Line of the Sun* is Joanna Marshall's, who extends her analysis of "home" in the novel by using recent translation theory to argue that the novel counters the idea of the island itself as an original "source" culture. Instead, Marshall claims, the novel shows how island culture is created through a series of translations and retranslations (through Marisol's stories), and suggests that in the novel, the Puerto Rican diaspora is part and parcel of the Puerto Rican nation ("Translating 'Home'"). To an extent, Marshall's reading of the presence of the "foreign" (language/culture) in the "original" complements my argument that both novels (particularly *The Meaning of Consuelo*) feature an island landscape and national identity that are inseparable from the United States'.

12. Foucault, "Preface," 33–34.

13. Flores, "Broken English Memories," 343.

14. Ibid., 339.

15. Foucault, "Preface," 35.

16. Although the novel is not categorically an autobiography, it shares enough material with Ortiz Cofer's memoirs to be read as a version of autobiography that has blurred generic boundaries. According to Ocasio, much Puerto Rican American literature has a highly autobiographical quality to it ("Puerto Rican Literature"), and *The Line of the Sun* is no exception. Many aspects of *The Line of the Sun* are taken from Ortiz Cofer's own life. Salud is based on the small town of Hormigueros, Puerto Rico, a semi-urban municipality in which the religious fervor of being the custodians of the sanctuary of the famous Virgen de Monserrate (visited by thousands of devoted pilgrims every year) is mixed with the contradictory moralities of a small town. Like Marisol, Ortiz Cofer's father was in the navy, leaving her at the center of her family's life as her mother did not know much English. And like Marisol, Ortiz Cofer became the translator, "the interpreter, the decision maker" early on in life (Acosta-Belén, "*MELUS* Interview," 95). Guzmán is based on Ortiz Cofer's uncle, "the wild son who drove everybody to distraction" who "knew that I had based my novel on him" (Kevane, "Fiction," 118). Ortiz Cofer's grandfather, like the grandfather in Salud, was a *mesa blanca espiritista*, "like the resident psychologist" (Ocasio and Ganey, "Speaking in Puerto Rican," 47), and of course at the end of the novel, Marisol, like her author, becomes a writer herself.

17. Flores argues that Puerto Rico has minimized talking of the violent traumas of its history – in particular, the large migration to the mainland—and believes that we must pay attention to the break that migration has caused ("Broken English Memories," 339).

18. In an interview, Ortiz Cofer says, "I wanted the novel to have a narrator, but I also wanted *The Line of the Sun* to be a commentary on story-telling" (Lopez, "Possibilities for Salsa Music").

19. Flores, "Broken English Memories," 343.

20. Marisol does not participate actively in the Salud story, of course, and even in the second half of the novel, where she tells her own story, she frequently alludes to distinctions between Guzmán and Ramona's world and her own, creating a them/us split (263).

21. Ortiz Cofer, *Line of the Sun*, 282. Hereafter this work will be cited in the text.

22. In a sense, the first part of the novel can be read as an invention, and the second half as a confession about the act of invention and creativity.

23. Faymonville concurs that Marisol experiences racial difference because, despite her attempts to assimilate, the "dominant society continues to define her as 'other'" based on "the visible racial difference inscribed on her body [that] cannot be hidden or made invisible" ("Motherland versus Daughterland," 130).

24. Bruce-Novoa argues that Marisol feels a sexual attraction toward her invented wild uncle, writing that her desire "to know and be part of the island is like her physical desire for Guzmán, an ambiguous longing for a contact that is forbidden, taboo" ("Ritual," 63). I would add that part of that taboo fascination that Marisol has for Guzmán centers around his Taino Indianness.

25. Interestingly, critics have pointed out that Guzmán serves both as a pivot for the action in the novel and as a kind of imaginative muse for Marisol's writerly imagination, even though the two—writer and subject—do not actually spend much of the novel in direct contact with one another (ibid., 62).

26. It is also worth noting the way that Marisol connects herself to the Spaniards' colonization of the native Taino tribes of Puerto Rico by remarking in several places that Guzmán, her uncle, has Taino blood in him (74, 116, 134). She lies behind his story, attempting to locate her own origins through his racial lineage, acknowledging Indian presence on the island and the mainland, and disturbing the nation's racially determined boundaries of citizenship.

27. Favre points out that Guzmán himself is attracted to, and occupies, liminal sites where he meets eccentric figures ("Liminality," 225).

28. Significantly, the men in the novel also fail to live up to cultural expectations: Papa Pepé, Guzmán's father, is described as a "meek husband" (1), and throughout men—in particular, fathers—are presented as effeminate, weak, or violent. Rafael's father, Don Juan, is a neglectful, alcoholic, and abusive figure who gives away his youngest daughter to the local powerful American family (141), and Rafael himself, as father to Marisol, remains a benevolent although largely absent figure.

29. Early on in the novel we learn of the effects of the U.S. economic presence on the island. The men in the sugarcane fields (themselves cultivated by the Spaniards) mention someone named Jesus who "had passed out on the job that morning. When they removed his shirt to let him cool off, they had seen horrible open sores all over his back. They knew at once the sores had been caused from leaks in the cylinder that he had strapped on his shoulders to manually fumigate the field the previous day. The American had introduced this economical new system" (11).

30. Ortiz Cofer, *The Meaning of Consuelo*, 155. Hereafter this work will be cited in the text.

31. Yudice and Flores, "Living Borders," 59.

32. The only critical piece on *The Meaning of Consuelo* is Kevane's analysis of the novel's reconceptualization of religious influences ("Fiction"). She suggests that Ortiz Cofer argues against the traditional institutional religious dominance of Catholicism and Pentecostalism, and presents a modern alternative religious space that allows Consuelo to empower herself without the blessings of an institution. Ortiz Cofer thus modernizes the female "gospel" that the Puerto Rican women of the novel uphold by basing it on different social outcasts.

33. See Stallybrass and White (*Politics and Poetics*) for arguments about the uses of and debates about carnival.

34. Ibid., 8, quoting Bakhtin, *Rabelais and His World*, 11–12.

35. Ibid.

36. The model of carnival is particularly apt here; as Stallybrass and White note, "literatures produced in a colonial or neo-colonial context where the political difference between the dominant and subordinate culture is particularly charged," such as Latin America, tend to have "a strong repertoire of carnivalesque properties" (*Politics and Poetics*, 11), suggesting that carnival is *the* way to practice transgressive resistance in a neocolonial setting.

37. After her sexual transgression, Consuelo imagines becoming a prostitute in San Juan, and in her fantasy dreams of making a fortune "by selling my body to *los americanos* who stayed at El San Juan Hotel, where they played for high stakes at the casino" (149). She adds that her father says that this is all these men see of the island: then "they'd go back to their mainland suburbs and say that Puerto Rico was nothing but thieves and whores" (149). As Consuelo imagines perpetuating these images of the island, she redefines her sexual transgression as a commercially successful business.

38. Yudice and Flores, "Living Borders," 60.

4 / Memoirs of Resistance

1. For a more detailed explanation of the roots of this cultural "unbelonging," see the introduction and chapter 3.

2. Although Ortiz Cofer's family moved to New Jersey in the early 1960s, their frequent return visits to the island allowed them to maintain ties with it and "provided Ortiz Cofer with sufficient material" with which to portray the island (Kevane, *Profane*, 45). Nevertheless, my point here is that such visits, even by their very definition as visits, placed Ortiz Cofer in a more objective position with regard to the island than Santiago.

3. See the introduction for a more detailed discussion of the theorization of place and national identity.

4. For an insightful and concise discussion of the intersection of ethnic studies and transnationalism studies, see Lugo-Ortiz, "Ethnic Studies"; Warrior, "Native American Critical Responses"; Radhakrishnan, "Ethnic Studies"; Rodríguez, "Ethnic Scholarship"; and Sanders, "Brief Reflections." For Latino identity, as for other ethnic group identities, there is a constant doubleness, a "paradox of being "nationals" in a thoroughly "transnationalized" economic geography" (Flores, *From Bomba to Hip Hop*, 214).

5. As well as the critical responses specifically discussed here, see also Munis's reading of the first memoir as a new kind of bildungsroman ("*Bildungsroman*"), Sprouse's discussion of Santiago's translation of her work into Spanish ("Between Bilingue"), and Marshall's excellent discussion of the role of shame in the memoirs ("Boast Now").

6. Szadiuk, "Culture as Transition," 111. Szadiuk also points out that in the first memoir, everything seems to be conceived of in spatial demarcations, noting a continuity between material and metaphorical territories that I expand on in my reading of Santiago's work.

7. See Sánchez González, *Boricua Literature*.

8. Ibid., 141, 160.

9. See also Echano ("'Somewhere between Puerto Rico and New York'") for her analysis of the way physical displacements in the memoirs influence and shape

Santiago's sense of identity, and Tate ("Plotting Her Way") for her interpretation of the first and second memoirs' reworking of gender discourse.

10. Torres-Padilla, "When 'I' Became Ethnic," 85, 89.

11. González, *Boricua Literature*, 158.

12. Santiago, *Almost a Woman*, 44. Hereafter this work will be cited in the text.

13. As Gilmore has asked, "Two questions hound women's autobiographical efforts: Can women tell the truth? Do women have lives worth representing?" (*Limits of Autobiography*, 21-22). The question of representation and truth is also relevant in Santiago's memoirs: her acknowledgments at the end of all of them address the issue of the fictional status of autobiography, and the constructedness of the material.

14. Santiago, *When I Was Puerto Rican*, 4. Hereafter this work will be cited in the text.

15. Lisa Sanchéz González objects to the epilogue's quick tally of Negi's successes (*Boricua Literature*, 158).

16. See chapter 3's discussion of the way socioeconomic factors create internal migration on the island and then preempt emigration to the mainland.

17. Adrienne Rich has noted that "the body has been made so problematic for women, that it has often seemed easier to shrug it off and travel as a disembodied spirit" (*Of Woman Born*, 40).

18. Bammer, "Introduction," xii.

19. Bammer uses the term "displacement" so that it carries resonances of both Freud and Derrida. She notes that for Freud, displacement—*Verschiebung* (literally, "pushing aside")—was central to the operation of dream-work, the process by which uncomfortable thoughts and feelings are transferred to the safe removal of representational symbols. Displacement and repression are thus related because in both something is "pushed aside." Derrida's interest lies in the idea that what is displaced (dispersed, deferred, repressed, pushed aside) is still there ("Introduction").

20. Bammer, "Introduction," xiii. My emphasis.

21. Flores, *Divided Borders*, 163-164.

22. Bammer, "Introduction," xvi.

23. Massey, "Double Articulation," 64.

24. Santiago, *Turkish Lover*, 54. Hereafter this work will be cited in the text.

25. Near the end of *Almost a Woman* Santiago directly describes herself and Ulvi as Galatea and Pygmalion, respectively (305).

5 / Tales of the Unexpected

1. Laura Gómez points out that Cubans identified as "white" in the 2000 U.S. Census 90 percent of the time (*Manifest Destinies*, 157), although it is also important to remember that later waves of Cuban exiles to the United States included more racially diverse members of the Cuban population.

2. See the introduction for more analysis of Cuban settlement in the United States.

3. See the introduction's discussion of racialized citizenship: the concept of citizenship beyond its legal definition, as a lived experience. See especially Rosaldo, "Cultural Citizenship"; Rocco, "Transforming Citizenship"; Oboler, "Redefining Citizenship"; and Dávila, *Latino Spin*.

4. Jefferson to James Monroe, October 24 1823 (*Works*, 12:320).

5. For an analysis of Cuba and the United States' economic and cultural relationship, especially pre-Castro, see Kaye, "Entre Americanos."

6. Del Rio, "Interview," 94.

7. Sadowski-Smith, "Homecoming," 268. Similarly, Borland, in exploring how the 1959 exodus relates to the creation of a Cuban American writing boom, acknowledges that each wave of Cuban exiles has a different perspective on that exile, and that while the first generation feels a "pressing reality" in terms of exile experience, the ethnic writer feels more of a "distance" (*Cuban-American Literature*, 9). Achy Obejas herself argues that exile is no longer a necessary component of Cuban American literature. While it is a defining aspect of her generation, she notes, "This is a unique moment in terms of Cuban-American history. There is a bridging generation" that already sees Cuba "more and more as an idea" (Del Rio, "Interview," 94).

8. Borland, *Cuban-American Literature*, 9.

9. Del Rio, "Interview," 94. For writers who, among other things, demonstrate this shift from exilic to ethnic, see Cristina García's *Dreaming in Cuban* and *The Aguero Sisters*, Ana Menéndez's *In Cuba I Was a German Shepherd*, and Achy Obejas's *Days of Awe* and short-story collection, *We Came All the Way from Cuba So You Could Dress Like This?*

10. For introductions to Cuban Americans in the United States and Cuban American literary production, see García, "Cuban Population"; Ortiz, "Cuban-American Literature"; and Pérez, *On Becoming Cuban*. For more literary critical accounts of Cuban American experiences in the United States, see Herrera, *ReMembering Cuba*; and Pérez-Firmat, *Life on the Hyphen*.

11. The prose fiction of the 1960s and 1970s, for example, has tended to be retrospective in its gaze and marked by a nostalgic and evocative tone, with Cuban identity "as dream . . . a part of consciousness preserved yet on hold: a realm to be evoked, not confronted in active engagement" (Smorkaloff, *Cuban Writers*, 2). In contrast, Cuban American writing of the 1990s explores issues of false memory in the diasporic construction of the island (ibid., 27). For discussions of the creation of a Cuban nationalism developed in exile, see Herrera, *ReMembering Cuba*; Fernandéz and Betancourt, *Cuba*; Ortiz, "Cuban-American Literature"; and Duany, "Reconstructing Cubanness."

12. Smorkaloff, *Cuban Writers*, 61, 73.

13. Novas, *Princess Papaya*, 211. Hereafter this work will be cited in the text.

14. In her first novel, *Mangos, Bananas, and Coconuts: A Cuban Love Story*, Novas's protagonists—twin brother and sister—embark on a sexual affair and, at the end of the story, marry. By legitimating their incestuous relationship in this way, Novas similarly confounds practices of sexuality and the sanctity of marriage.

15. In the illuminating introduction to his book, Ricardo Ortiz explores the disappearance of the Cuban diaspora in his parents' and grandparents' hometown in California, and argues that there are anxieties about the disappearance of a coherent diasporic Cuban identity because of various factors, such as the phenomenon of "marrying out" and/or assimilating into the host community. Ortiz is interested in the way this anxiety "compels an almost obsessive insistence on reproduction, always simultaneously social, cultural, and sexual" (*Cultural Erotics*, 8).

16. It is important to note the extent to which Novas's work represents a new and emerging trend in U.S. Cuban diasporic writing. In contrast to earlier waves of Cuban American literary production, recent writing (both by established authors and newer writers) has moved away from nostalgic remembrances of the homeland and toward a process of settlement in and connection to the United States as a homeland.

17. Ruth Behar notes that despite the early efforts of Cuba's revolutionary leaders to eliminate the image of women as prostitutes, "the Cuban state has always made paid sex available to political leaders, the diplomatic corps, and tourists" and that now "prostitution has returned to Cuba with a vengeance" ("Post-Utopia," 142).

18. Only in the United States does the traumatic experience and memory of Cuba have the potential to become a narrative memory, although in *Princess Papaya* Novas resists healing Cuban memories through story alone, instead, as I discuss below, figuring Cuba more actively within the United States. For critical discussions of narrative and traumatic memory, see Bal, Crewe, and Spitzer, *Acts of Memory*; Brison, "Trauma Narratives"; Caruth, *Unclaimed Experience*; Culbertson, "Embodied Memory"; and Luckhurst, "Memory Recovered."

19. In 1996 Janet Reno warned that illegal trafficking in methamphetamine "has been spreading rapidly across the United States." She added that some law-enforcement officers have called it the most lethal drug to hit the streets in thirty years (Orlandosentinel.com). In 2004 the meth battle heated up as Mexico's legal importation of pseudoephedrine was found to consist of twice as much as was needed to make cold medicine. The extra 100 tons was being cooked into meth, then smuggled into the United States across the border. Oklahoma became the first state to pass a law placing limits on sales of pseudoephedrine, followed in 2005 by more than thirty-five states passing similar legislation to curb home-lab meth production. In 2006 the U.N. World Drug Report called meth the most abused hard drug on earth: in America alone there were 1.4 million users. (see www.pbs.org/wgbh/pages/frontline/meth/etc.cron/html). Even as recently as 2011 the *New York Times* health topics websites describe meth as "a scourge of the American heartland" (http://topics.nytimes.com/top/news/health/diseasesconditionsandhealthtopics/methamphetamines/index.html).

20. In a radio interview about the novel Novas emphasizes her presentation of grief, claiming that through surviving grief Victoria can reinvent herself and learn to love again. See Novas, Interview.

21. Butler, *Precarious Life*, 26.

22. Ibid., 22.

23. Ibid., 21. One of the ways in which the anxiety of grief is articulated in Victoria's sections is through the use of interspersed italicized sentences, fragments, and comments. These appear to be lines of poetry or commentaries in which Victoria rearticulates a thought or interprets an event, as if silently, to herself. The italics offer a metatextual recounting of events, a conscious act of making meaning that signals to the reader that Victoria's life is not quite real to herself. The strategy brings together her professional writerly persona and her grief; as a poet it makes sense, of course, that she would try to practice writing events several times over, as if editing and re-editing her life and her interactions. She thus frequently "watch[es] herself" in her own apartment (11), separated and beside herself with grief—as Butler has noted—and the italicizations attempt to write her self, which seems so vaporized and transient, back into a corporeal existence.

24. Butler, *Undoing Gender*, 20.

25. For a discussion of the ways in which cyberspace eliminates geocodes, the "cultural map" that structures social life, see Mosco, *Digital Sublime*, 92.

26. Butler, *Precarious Life*, xii–xiii.

27. Significantly, in her radio interview, Novas describes Cooper himself as a "gender survivor" who, like Victoria, undergoes a rebirth and journey of self-discovery. See Novas, Interview.

28. While the family's Jewish background is important to the novel's thematics, Novas is careful not to anthropologize it. Instead, their Juban identity is presented as an unsurprising thread of Cuban ethnicity, making the novel another recent example of Cuban American literature that acknowledges the heterogeneity of Cubanness. For an insightful history of Cuba's Jews, see Levine's *Tropical Diaspora*. See Bettinger-López's *Cuban-Jewish Journeys* for a sociological and historical discussion of the diasporic status of Cuban and Cuban American Jews; see also Behar's "Juban América," where she describes the joining together of Latin American and Jewish identities as creating a "shock effect" in popular discourse because of the apparent conflict of the two images (341).

29. The characters' Jewish bodies in fact become somatic sites of violence when the text describes the presence of blue eyes in the family as "Pogrom Eyes," as well as markers of heterogeneity within the physiognomy of Jews: even before arriving in Cuba and then the United States, the family is a mixture of Ashkenazi, Sephardic, Spanish, Portuguese, and Dutch descent.

30. The addition of the Hebrew letter "Hey" comes from the spelling of God's name as "Yud-Hay-Vav-Hey," and is commonly assumed to insert godliness into the new names. Thus, although in the biblical story Abraham and Sarah remain nomadic, after the covenant they carry God with them wherever they go.

31. Marta Caminero-Santangelo makes the useful argument that the term "Cuban diaspora" is problematic because it points to Cuba as an origin and source. While the term helps "refer to the displacement of Cuban peoples and their subsequent geographic dispersal," it also reiterates the notion of Cuba as being racially and ethnically singular. Caminero-Santangelo identifies Cuban American literature's "more challenging narratives" as those that usefully situate Cuba not as a point of origin, but as a mid-point" (*Latinidad*, 100). Novas's *Princess Papaya* certainly situates Cuba in this way.

32. Similarly, Victoria's response to Cooper's belief that the dead linger on among the living is to say, "I believe you, I don't believe, mind you, but I believe you" (17).

33. See the introduction for examples of how the nation writes foreign bodies and their cultural practices as "nonbelonging."

34. Butler makes the point that the vast majority of intersexed infants are subjected to surgery that tries to assign them to a female sex, because "it is simply considered easier to produce a provisional vaginal tract than it is to construct a phallus" (*Undoing Gender*, 63). In the novel Cooper notes that his mother's decision (together with the doctor's) was based on her being a radical feminist who did not want to raise a boy.

35. Butler critiques the way that normative conceptions of gender, and the subsequent pressure on and by the medical community to surgically mark a body (in an attempt to make it look "normal"), can "undo" one's personhood and undermine that person's capacity "to persevere in a livable life" (ibid., 1). She discusses the intersex community's resistance to coercive surgery and its call for an understanding that intersex infants are part of "the continuum of human morphology and ought to be treated with the presumption that their lives are and will be not only livable, but also occasions for flourishing" (ibid., 4).

36. This privileging of constructed national identity parallels the novel's presentation of its characters as nomadic wanderers, and its spaces (Cuba, New York City) as souvenir pit stops along the road rather than places of origin. In this respect, the text seems to echo Salman Rushdie's famous statement, "roots . . . are a conservative myth designed to keep us in our place" (*Imaginary Homelands*, 90), certainly in its deconstruction of social and cultural regulations of normative behavior.

37. Internet technology has attracted broad critical responses that focus on embodiment (see Hayles, *How We Became Postmodern*; and Haraway, *Simians*), screening (see Bay, "Screening [In]formation"), the ethical and socioeconomic dimension of Internet usage (see Wilbur, "Archaeology of Cyberspaces"), and the impact on understandings of geography, class, and space (see Mosco, *Digital Sublime*; Porter, "Introduction"; and Foster, "Community"). My work here is most informed by Healy's discussion of frontiers and description of the Internet as a middle landscape ("Cyberspace and Place").

38. Foster notes that computer-mediated communication, compared to face-to-face communication, can make users more self-absorbed, and blurs the boundaries between self and other: "the self is pursued, but not entirely in blissful ignorance of the other. It is merely that the other has been relegated to a sub-strata of the self" ("Community," 26). During the communication process, the user is relating to himself or herself even while he or she is relating to others.

39. Porter, "Introduction," xii.

40. Not all the characters are "brought together under the California sky" (157). Roberto, who owns the vineyard, disappears never to return—perhaps punished because of his greed that led to his brother's lengthy incarceration in Cuba and his traitorous partnership with the drug lord Barbudo. Toward the end of the novel, Roberto is described in increasingly biblical terms that emphasize his fall from Eden ("Roberto took an irreversible turn somewhere east or south of Eden" [203]; "Roberto, now very far from Eden" [205]).

41. Cooper mentions the purification of the body in a sweat lodge, which Victoria compares to the biblical Abraham's walking of the land he claimed in order to declare it holy (97).

42. Butler notes that exogamy has its limits: marriage must occur outside the clan, but not go too far beyond a certain "racial self-understanding or racial commonality" (*Undoing Gender*, 122). Another tempting interpretation (that is beyond the scope of this chapter) would be to read Cooper as Adam and Victoria as Eve because the text is full of biblical and religious references (for example, to Cain and Abel, and to Kabalistic practice), and their own relationship is frequently cast as innocent, virginal, yet passionate. Their synchronicity might make them sibling twins, or it might suggest that they have been formed from one another (as Eve was from Adam in the biblical story).

43. Butler, *Undoing Gender*, 124.

44. We understand that Cooper and Victoria are unable to have biological children, as he says to her, "we can't have babies" (121).

Postscript

1. Viramontes, "Cariboo Café," 72. Hereafter this work will be cited in the text.

2. Roberta Fernández points out that when the café owner notifies the police, he does so out of a belief that children should be with their parents—ironically so,

given that "the author's main focus has been on the enforced separation of children from their parents as a result of police action and government repression" ("Cariboo Café," 74). Nevertheless, acknowledging this helps complicate and nuance the owner's motives.

3. For a critical piece that weaves the history of U.S. policies in Central America in the 1980s into a reading of the story, see Rodriguez, "Refugees of the South." Saldívar-Hull notes that Viramontes "is putting U.S. immigration policies and ideology on trial" ("Feminism on the Border" 219), an interesting move that complements my reading of the story's decriminalizing intent. See also Harlow's discussion of the way that immigration and deportation control dissent within a territory, and create and manipulate a discourse of boundaries ("Sites of Struggle").

4. Gorman and Riccardi, "Immigration Debate."

5. Kuhner, "Should Arizona Secede?"

6. Lacey, "Tea Party Rallies."

7. Quoted in ibid.

8. Lacey, "Rift in Arizona."

9. Lewis posits that this heightened sense of conservatism—imagining America as under siege—plays into the political mindset ("Arizona Bans").

10. Cisneros, "New and Established Writers."

11. Augustine F. Romero, director of student equity in Tucson schools, quoted in Lacey, "Rift in Arizona."

12. Robinson, "In Arizona."

13. House Bill 2281, State of Arizona, House of Representatives, 2010.

14. Reyes notes that the Texas State Board of Education recently approved textbook guidelines that give short shrift to minorities in favor of a conservative ideology ("Other Arizona Battle").

15. Brown, "Immigration Overhaul."

16. More recently, in the summer of 2012, President Barak Obama issued an executive order that takes advantage of prosecutorial decisions in deportation cases. Much like the Dream Act, the order covers individuals brought to the United States through no fault of their own, before the age of sixteen, who have lived in the country for at least five years and have no criminal record. They must have also earned a high school degree or served in the military, and be under the age of thirty. Those who meet the criteria can get deportation proceedings deferred for two years and seek work permits. However, Department of Homeland Security Secretary Janet Napolitano cautioned that the executive order does not constitute amnesty and does not provide a path to citizenship (Franke-Ruta, "Obama's Game Changer").

17. "Dream Time."

18. Lacey, "Rift in Arizona." Other recent news stories that present less typical accounts of border crossings are those reporting on the decision to reopen the border crossing (which was closed after 9/11) in Big Bend National Park, Texas. The binational focus in this park is an example of cooperation from both sides of the border, as parties involved on both sides understand that the ecosystem does not stop at the border. Although the informal border crossing that existed prior to 9/11 will be replaced by an official crossing, it nevertheless imagines a different sort of border crosser than the one popularly portrayed: in other words, border crossers with valid visas who cross into the United States as tourists or shoppers.

19. Representative Duncan Hunter, Republican of California, talking to a Tea Party rally in Southern California, quoted in Lacey, "Rift in Arizona."

20. Robbins, "Immigration Enforcement Working."

21. Rodriguez, "Emerging Latino Middle Class."

22. Tom Horn cited in Lewin, "Citing Individualism."

23. Stavans, "Introduction," lxvii, lxxi.

24. Moraga, "Art in América," 213.

25. Ibid.

26. Ibid., 217.

27. Ibid., 219.

28. Seaman, "Review."

29. Stavans, "Accents of Latino Literature."

30. Ibid.

31. Cisneros, "New and Established Writers."

Bibliography

Abramson, Allen. "Mythical Land, Legal Boundaries: Wondering about Landscape and Other Tracts." In *Land, Law and Environment: Mythical Land, Legal Boundaries*, ed. Allen Abramson and Dimitrios Theodossopoulos, 1–30. London: Pluto Press, 2000.

Acosta-Belén, Edna. "A *MELUS* Interview: Judith Ortiz Cofer." *MELUS* 18.3 (1993): 84–97.

Acuña, Rodolfo. *Occupied America: A History of Chicanos*. 3rd ed. New York: HarperCollins, 1988.

Aldama, Arturo J. "Millennial Anxieties: Borders, Violence and the Struggle for Chicana and Chicano Subjectivity." In *Decolonial Voices: Chicana and Chicano Cultural Studies in the 21st Century*, ed. Arturo J. Aldama and Naomi H. Quiñonez, 11–29. Bloomington: Indiana University Press, 2002.

Alumbaugh, Heather. "Narrative Coyotes: Migration and Narrative Voice in Sandra Cisneros's *Caramelo*." *MELUS* 35.1 (2010): 53–75.

Anaya, Rudolfo. *Bless Me, Última*. New York: Warner Books, 1973.

———. Preface to *The Last of the Menu Girls*. Houston: Arte Público Press, 1986.

Anderson, Douglas. "Displaced Abjection and States of Grace: Denise Chávez's *The Last of the Menu Girls*." In *American Women Short Story Writers: A Collection of Critical Essays*, ed. Julie Brown, 235–250. New York: Garland Publishing, 1995.

Anzaldúa, Gloria. *Borderlands/La Frontera: The New Mestiza*. San Francisco: Aunt Lute Books, 1987.

Aparicio, Frances R. "Exposed Bodies: Media and Puerto Ricans in U.S. Public Space." In *None of the Above: Puerto Ricans in the Global Era*, ed. Frances Negrón-Muntaner, 165–179. New York: Palgrave Macmillan, 2007.

Arredondo, Gabriela F. *Mexican Chicago: Race, Identity and Nation, 1916–39*. Urbana and Chicago: University of Illinois Press, 2008.

Bakhtin, Mikhail. *Rabelais and His World*. Trans. H. Hswolsky. Cambridge, Mass.: MIT Press, 1968.

Bal, Mieke, Jonathan Crewe, and Leo Spitzer, eds. *Acts of Memory: Cultural Recall in the Present*. Hanover, N.H.: University Press of New England, 1999.

———. Introduction to *Acts of Memory: Cultural Recall in the Present*, vii–xvii. Hanover, N.H.: University Press of New England, 1999.

Bammer, Angelika. Introduction to *Displacements: Cultural Identities in Question*, ed. Angelika Bammer, xi–xx. Bloomington: Indiana University Press, 1994.

———. "Mother Tongues and Other Strangers: Writing 'Family' across Cultural Divides." In *Displacements: Cultural Identities in Question*, ed. Angelika Bammer, 90–109. Bloomington: Indiana University Press, 1994.

Batalla, Guillermo Bonfil. *Mexico Profundo: Reclaiming a Civilization*. Trans. Philip A. Dennis. Austin: University of Texas Press, 1996.

Bay, Jennifer L. "Screening (In)formation: Bodies and Writing in Network Culture." In *Plugged In: Technology, Rhetoric and Culture in a Posthuman Age*, ed. Lynn Worsham and Gary A. Olson, 25–40. Cresskill, N.J.: Hampton Press, 2008.

Beebe, Thomas O. *Nation and Region in Modern American and European Fiction*. West Lafayette, Ind.: Purdue University Press, 2008.

Behar, Ruth. Introduction to *Bridges to Cuba/Puentes a Cuba*, 1–18. Ann Arbor: University of Michigan Press, 1995.

———. "Juban América." In *Autobiographical Writings Across the Disciplines: A Reader*, 331–348. Durham, N.C.: Duke University Press, 2003.

———. "Post-Utopia: The Erotics of Power and Cuba's Revolutionary Children." In *Cuba, the Elusive Nation: Interpretations of National Identity*, ed. Damián J. Fernandéz and Madeline Cámara Betancourt, 134–154. Gainesville: University Press of Florida, 2000.

Benjamin-Labarthe, Elyette. "L'Amour et la haine dans un roman chicano contemporain: *Sapogonia* d'Ana Castillo." In *Etats-Unis/Mexique: Fascinations et repulsions réciproques*, ed. Serge Ricard, 193–208. Paris: Harmatan, 1996.

Berglund, Jeff, and Monica Brown. "*Sin Verguenza*: Resisting Body Shame in *Real Women Have Curves* and *Caramelo*." In *Mediating Chicana/o Culture: Multicultural American Vernacular*, 62–73. Newcastle-Upon-Tyne, U.K.: Cambridge Scholars, 2006.

Berlant, Lauren. "The Face of America and the State of Emergency." In *Disciplinarity and Dissent in Cultural Studies*, ed. Cary Nelson and Dilip Parameshwar Gaonkar, 397–439. New York: Routledge, 1996.

Bettinger-López, Carolina. *Cuban-Jewish Journeys: Searching for Identity, Home, and History in Miami*. Knoxville: University of Tennessee Press, 2000.

———. "'Hebrew with a Cuban Accent': Jewbans in the Diaspora." In *Cuba: Idea of a Nation Displaced*, ed. Andrea O'Reilly Herrera, 107–122. Albany: State University of New York Press, 2007.

Bhabha, Homi. "DissemiNation: Time, Narrative, and the Margins of the Modern World." In *Nation and Narration*, 291–322. London: Routledge, 1994.

———. "The World and the Home." *Social Text* 31/32 (1992): 141–153.

Birnbaum, Robert. "Identity Theory: The Narrative Thread." Interview with Sandra Cisneros, December 4, 2002. www.identitytheory.com/people/birnbaum 76.html.

Bode, Rita. "Mother to Daughter: Muted Maternal Feminism in the Fiction of Sandra Cisneros." In *Textual Mothers/Maternal Texts: Motherhood in Contemporary Women's Literature*, 287–301. Waterloo, Ont.: Wilfrid Laurier University Press, 2010.

Borland, Isabel Alvarez. *Cuban-American Literature of Exile: From Person to Persona*. Charlottesville: University Press of Virginia, 1998.

Bost, Suzanne. *Mulattas and Mestizas: Representing Mixed Identities in the Americas, 1850–2000*. Athens: University Press of Georgia, 2003.

Brady, Mary Pat. *Extinct Lands, Temporal Geographies: Chicana Literature and the Urgency of Space*. Durham, N.C.: Duke University Press, 2002.

———. "'So Your Social Is Real?' Vernacular Theorists and Economic Transformation." In *Contemporary U.S. Latino/a Literary Criticism*, ed. Lyn Di Iori Sandín and Richard Perez, 209–226. New York: Palgrave Macmillan, 2007.

Brennan, Timothy. "The National Longing for Form." In *Nation and Narration*, 44–70. London: Routledge, 1994.

Brison, Susan J. "Trauma Narratives and the Remaking of the Self." In *Acts of Memory: Cultural Recall in the Present*, 39–54. Hanover, N.H.: University Press of New England, 1999.

Brodkin, Karen. *How Jews Became White Folks: And What That Says About Race in America*. New Brunswick, N.J.: Rutgers University Press, 1998.

Brown, Linda Joyce. "Assimilation and the Re-racialization of Immigrant Bodies: A Study of *Time*'s Special Issue on Immigration." *Centennial Review* 41.3 (1997): 603–608.

Brown, Peter A. "Immigration Overhaul Is Unlikely without a Shift in Public Attitudes." *Wall Street Journal*, December 29, 2010.

Browne, Neil, and Michelle Harvey. "Más Tamales, Anybody? Denise Chávez's *The Last of the Menu Girls* and the Chicana Narrative of Communities." In *Narratives of Community: Women's Short Story Sequences*, ed. Roxanne Harde, 241–262. Newcastle, U.K.: Cambridge Scholars Publishing, 2007.

Bruce-Novoa, Juan. "Ritual in Judith Ortiz Cofer's *The Line of the Sun*." *Confluencia: Revista hispanica de cultura y literatura* 8.1 (1992): 61–69.

Burns, E. Bradford, and Julie A. Charlip. *Latin America: An Interpretive History*. Upper Saddle River, N.J.: Pearson Prentice Hall, 2007.

Butler, Judith. *Precarious Life: The Powers of Mourning and Violence*. London: Verso, 2004.

———. *Undoing Gender.* New York: Routledge, 2004.

Camacho, Alicia Schmidt. *Migrant Imaginaries: Latino Cultural Politics in the U.S.-Mexico Borderlands.* New York: New York University Press, 2008.

Caminero-Santangelo, Marta. *On Latinidad: U.S. Latino Literature and the Construction of Ethnicity.* Gainesville: University Press of Florida, 2007.

Campa, Román de la. "Latin Americans and Latinos: Terms of Engagement." In *Contemporary U.S. Latino/a Literary Criticism*, 165–181. New York: Palgrave Macmillan, 2007.

Candelaria, Cordelia Chávez. "The 'Wild Zone': Thesis as Gloss in Chicana Literary Study." In *Feminisms: An Anthology of Literary Theory and Criticism*, ed. Robyn R. Warhol and Diane Price-Herndl, 248–256. New Brunswick, N.J.: Rutgers University Press, 1997.

Caruth, Cathy. *Unclaimed Experience: Trauma, Narrative, and History.* Baltimore: Johns Hopkins University Press, 1996.

Castañeda, Alejandra. "Roads to Citizenship: Mexican Migrants in the United States." In *Latinos and Citizenship: The Dilemma of Belonging*, ed. Suzanne Oboler, 143–165. New York: Palgrave Macmillan, 2006.

Castillo, Ana. *Sapogonia: An Anti-Romance in 3/8 Meter.* New York: Doubleday, 1994.

Castillo, Debra. *Talking Back: Toward a Latin American Feminist Literary Criticism.* Ithaca, N.Y.: Cornell University Press, 1992.

Chávez, Denise. *Face of an Angel.* New York: Warner Books, 1994.

———. "Heat and Rain" (Testimonio). In *Breaking Boundaries: Latina Writings and Critical Readings*, ed. Asunción Horno-Delgado, Eliana Ortega, Nina M. Scott, and Nancy Saporta Sternbach, 27–32. Amherst: University of Massachusetts Press, 1989.

———. *The Last of the Menu Girls.* New York: Vintage, 2004.

Chávez, Leo R. *The Latino Threat: Constructing Immigrants, Citizens, and the Nation.* Stanford, Calif.: Stanford University Press, 2008.

Cisneros, Henry. "A Fence Can't Stop the Future." *Newsweek*, January 26, 2009, 71.

Cisneros, Sandra. *Caramelo: A Novel.* New York: Vintage, 2002.

———. "From a Writer's Notebook: Ghosts and Voices: Writing from Obsession." *Americas Review* 15 (1987): 69–73.

———. *The House on Mango Street.* New York: Vintage, 1991.

———. "New and Established Writers Redefine Chicano Lit." *Talk of the Nation*, NPR interview, January 27, 2011.

Comer, Krista. *Landscapes of the New West: Gender and Geography in Contemporary Women's Writing.* Chapel Hill: University of North Carolina Press, 1999.

Concannon, Kevin, Francisco A. Lomelí, and Marc Preiwe. Introduction to *Imagined Transnationalism: U.S. Latino/a Literature, Culture and Identity*, ed. Kevin Concannon, Francisco A. Lomelí, and Marc Preiwe, 1–12. New York: Palgrave Macmillan, 2009.

Cornelius, Wayne A. "Ambivalent Reception: Mass Public Responses to the 'New' Latino Immigration to the United States." In *Latinos: Remaking America*, 165–189. Berkeley: University of California Press, 2008.

Cosgrove, Denis. "Prospect, Perspective and the Evolution of the Landscape Idea." *Transactions of the Institute of British Geographers* 10.1 (1985): 45–62.

Crèvecoeur, Hector St. John de. *Letters from an American Farmer.* [1782.] Ed. Susan Manning. Oxford: Oxford University Press, 1997.

Culbertson, Roberta. "Embodied Memory, Transcendence, and Telling: Recounting Trauma, Re-establishing the Self." *New Literary History* 26.1 (1995): 169–195.

Cutter, Matha. "Editor's Introduction: Transgressing the Borders of 'America.'" *MELUS* 35.1 (2010): 5–12.

D, Ramola. "An Interview with Sandra Cisneros." *Writer's Chronicle* 38.6 (2006): 4–12.

Dávila, Arlene. *Latino Spin: Public Image and the Whitewashing of Race.* New York: New York University Press, 2008.

De Genova, Nicholas. "The Legal Production of Mexican/Migrant 'Illegality.'" In *Latinos and Citizenship: The Dilemma of Belonging*, ed. Suzanne Oboler, 61–90. New York: Palgrave Macmillan, 2006.

De Genova, Nicholas, and Ana Y. Ramos-Zayas. *Latino Crossings: Mexicans, Puerto Ricans, and the Politics of Race and Citizenship.* New York: Routledge, 2003.

Del Rio, Eduardo R. "Interview with Achy Obejas." In *One Island, Many Voices: Conversations with Cuban-American Writers*, 85–95. Tucson: University of Arizona Press, 2008.

"Dream Time." Editorial. *New York Times*, September 19, 2010.

Duany, Jorge. "Nation and Migration: Rethinking Puerto Rican Identity in a Transnational Context." In *None of the Above: Puerto Ricans in the Global Era*, ed. Frances Negrón-Muntaner, 51–63. New York: Palgrave Macmillan, 2007.

———. "Reconstructing Cubanness: Changing Discourses of National Identity on the Island and in the Diaspora during the Twentieth Century." In *Cuba: The Elusive Nation: Interpretations of National Identity*, ed. Damián J. Fernandéz, and Madeline Cámara Betancourt, 17–42. Gainesville: University Press of Florida, 2000.

Dunaway, David King, and Sara L. Spurgeon, eds. *Writing the Southwest.* Albuquerque: University of New Mexico Press, 1995.

Durand, Jorge, Douglas S. Massey, and Chiara Capoferro. "The New Geography of Mexican Immigration." In *New Destinations: Mexican Immigration in the United States*, ed. Víctor Zúñiga and Rubén Hernández-León, 1–20. New York: Russell Sage Foundation, 2005.

Eakin, Marshall C. *The History of Latin America: Collision of Cultures.* New York: Palgrave Macmillan, 2007.

Echano, Marta Vizcaya. "'Somewhere between Puerto Rico and New York': The Representation of Individual and Collective Identities in Esmeralda Santiago's *When I Was Puerto Rican* and *Almost a Woman.*" *Prose Studies* 26.1–2 (2003): 112–130.

Edemariam, Aida. "Mexican Gulf." *Guardian*, December 21, 2002.

Elenes, Alejandra. "Border/Transformative Pedagogies at the End of the Millennium: Chicana/o Cultural Studies and Education." In *Decolonial Voices: Chicana and Chicano Cultural Studies in the 21st Century*, ed. Arturo J. Aldama and Naomi H. Quiñonez, 245–261. Bloomington: Indiana University Press, 2002.

Eysturoy, Annie O. *Daughters of Self-Creation: The Contemporary Chicana Novel.* Albuquerque: University of New Mexico Press, 1995.

Favre, Geneviève. "Liminality, In-betweenness and Indeterminacy: Notes toward an Anthropological Reading of Judith Cofer's *The Line of the Sun.*" *Annales du Centre de Recherches sur l'Amérique Anglophone* 18 (1993): 223–232.

Farah, Cynthia. *Literature and Landscape: Writers of the Southwest.* El Paso: Texas Western Press, 1988.

Faymonville, Carmen. "Motherland versus Daughterland in Judith Ortiz Cofer's *The Line of the Sun.*" In *The Immigrant Experience in North American Literature: Carving Out a Niche*, ed. Katherine B. Payant and Toby Rose, 123–137. Westport, Conn.: Greenwood Press, 1999.

Fender, Steven. *Sea Changes: British Emigration and American Literature.* Cambridge: Cambridge University Press, 1992.

Fernandéz, Damián J., and Madeline Cámara Betancourt, eds. *Cuba: The Elusive Nation: Interpretations of National Identity.* Gainesville: University Press of Florida, 2000.

Fernández, Roberta. "'The Cariboo Café': Helena María Viramontes Discourses with Her Social and Cultural Context." *Women's Studies* 17 (1989): 71–85.

Finnegan, Jordana. *Narrating the American West: New Forms of Historical Memory.* Amherst, N.Y.: Cambria Press, 2008.

Flores, Juan. "Broken English Memories: Languages of the Trans-Colony." In *Postcolonial Theory and the United States: Race, Ethnicity, and Literature*, ed. Amritjit Singh and Peter Schmidt, 338–348. Jackson: University Press of Mississippi, 2000.

———. *Divided Borders: Essays on Puerto Rican Identity.* Houston: Arté Público Press, 1990.

———. *From Bomba to Hip Hop: Puerto Rican Culture and Latino Identity.* New York: Columbia University Press, 2000.

———. "Islands and Enclaves: Caribbean Latinos in Historical Perspective." In *Latinos Remaking America*, ed. Marcelo M. Suárez-Orozco and Mariela M. Páez, 59–74. Berkeley: University of California Press, 2002.

———. "The Latino Imaginary: Meanings of Community and Identity." In *The*

Latin American Cultural Studies Reader, ed. Ana Del Sarto, Alicia Ríos, and Abril Trigo, 606–619. Durham, N.C.: Duke University Press, 2004.

Flores, William V. "Epilogue: Citizens vs. Citizenry: Undocumented Immigrants and Latino Cultural Citizenship." In *Latino Cultural Citizenship: Claiming Identity, Space, and Rights*, ed. William V. Flores and Rina Benmajor, 255–277. Boston: Beacon Press, 1997.

Flores, William V., and Rina Benmajor. Introduction to *Latino Cultural Citizenship: Claiming Identity, Space, and Rights*, ed. William V. Flores and Rina Benmajor, 1–23. Boston: Beacon Press, 1997.

Foster, Derek. "Community and Identity in the Electronic Village." In *Internet Culture*, ed. David Porter, 23–37. New York: Routledge, 1997.

Foucault, Michel. "A Preface to Transgression." In *Language, Counter-Memory, Practice: Selected Essays and Interviews*, ed. Donald F. Bouchard, 29–52. Trans. Donald F. Bouchard and Sherry Simon. Ithaca, N.Y.: Cornell University Press, 1977.

Franke-Ruta, Garance. "Obama's Game Changer on Young Illegal Immigrants." *Atlantic*, June 12, 2012. http://www.theatlantic.com/politics/archive/2012/06/obamas-game-changer-on-young-illegal-immigrants/258550/.

García, Cristina. *The Aguero Sisters*. New York: Ballantine, 1997.

———. *Dreaming in Cuban*. New York: Ballantine, 1992.

García, Juan R. *Mexicans in the Midwest 1900–1932*. Tucson: University of Arizona Press, 1996.

García, María Cristina. "The Cuban Population of the United States: An Introduction." In *Cuba: Idea of a Nation Displaced*, ed. Andrea O'Reilly Herrera, 75–89. Albany: State University of New York Press, 2007.

Gilmore, Leigh. *The Limits of Autobiography: Trauma and Testimony*. Ithaca, N.Y.: Cornell University Press, 2001.

Glotfelty, Cheryll. "Introduction: Literary Studies in an Age of Environmental Crisis." In *The Ecocriticism Reader: Landmarks in Literary Ecology*, ed. Cheryll Glotfelty and Harold Fromm, xv–xxxvii. Athens: University of Georgia Press, 1996.

Gómez, Laura E. *Manifest Destinies: The Making of the Mexican American Race*. New York: New York University Press, 2007.

Gómez-Vega, Ibis. "Debunking Myths: The Hero's Role in Ana Castillo's *Sapogonia*." *Americas Review: A Review of Hispanic Literature and Arts in the USA* 22.1–2 (1994): 244–258.

———. "The Homoerotic Tease and Lesbian Identity in Ana Castillo's Work." *Critica Hispanica* 25.1–2 (2003): 65–84.

González, Bill Johnson. "The Politics of Translation in Sandra Cisneros's *Caramelo*." *Differences: A Journal of Feminist Cultural Studies* 17.3 (2006): 3–19.

Gorman, Anna, and Nicholas Riccardi, "Immigration Debate." *Los Angeles Times*, July 30, 2010.

Gourmet. June, August, 2009.

Grandin, Greg. *Empire's Workshop: Latin America, the United States, and the Rise of the New Imperialism.* New York: Metropolitan Books/Henry Holt, 2006.

Grey, Mark A., and Anne C. Woodrick. "'Latinos Have Revitalized Our Community': Mexican Migration and Anglo Responses in Marshalltown, Iowa." In *New Destinations: Mexican Immigration in the United States,* ed. Víctor Zúñiga and Rubén Hernández-León, 133–145. New York: Russell Sage Foundation, 2005.

Grosfoguel, Ramón. "The Divorce of Nationalist Discourses from the Puerto Rican People: A Sociohistorical Perspective." In *Puerto Rican Jam: Rethinking Colonialism and Nationalism,* ed. Frances Negrón-Muntaner and Ramón Grosfoguel, 57–76. Minneapolis: University of Minnesota Press, 1997.

Grosfoguel, Ramón, Frances Negrón-Muntaner, and Chloé S. Georas. "Introduction: Beyond Nationalist and Colonialist Discourses: The *Jaiba* Politics of the Puerto Rican Ethno-Nation." In *Puerto Rican Jam: Rethinking Colonialism and Nationalism,* ed. Frances Negrón-Muntaner and Ramón Grosfoguel, 1–36. Minneapolis: University of Minnesota Press, 1997.

Gutiérrez y Muhs, Gabriella. "Sandra Cisneros and Her Trade of the Free Word." *Rocky Mountain Review of Languages and Literature* 60.2 (2006): 23–36.

Haraway, Donnna J. *Simians, Cyborgs, and Women: The Reinvention of Nature.* New York: Routledge, 1991.

Harlow, Barbara. "Sites of Struggle: Immigration, Deportation, Prison, and Exile." In *Criticism in the Borderlands: Studies in Chicano Literature, Culture, and Ideology,* ed. Héctor Calderón and José David Saldívar, 149–163. Durham, N.C.: Duke University Press, 1991.

Harvey, David. *Justice, Nature, and the Geography of Difference.* Oxford: Blackwell, 1996.

Haupt, Melanie. "*Caramelo.*" *Austin (Tex.) Chronicle,* October 4, 2002.

Hayden, Dolores. "Urban Landscape History: The Sense of Place and the Politics of Space." In *Understanding Ordinary Landscapes,* ed. Paul Groth and Todd W. Bressi, 110–133. New Haven, Conn.: Yale University Press, 1997.

Hayles, Katherine N. *How We Became Posthuman: Virtual Bodies in Cybernetics, Literature, and Informatics.* Chicago: University of Chicago Press, 1999.

Healy, Dave. "Cyberspace and Place: The Internet as Middle Landscape on the Electronic Frontier." In *Internet Culture,* ed. David Porter, 55–68. New York: Routledge, 1997.

"Here and Now." June 23, 2010, WBUR. www.hereandnow.org/2010/06/slideshow-border-barriers/#2.

Heredia, Juanita. "*Caramelo*: Crossing Borders in Translating Golden Age Mexican Culture." In *Critical Essays on Chicano Studies,* 137–148. Bennington, N.Y.: Peter Lang, 2008.

———. *Transnational Latina Narratives in the 21st Century: The Politics of Gender, Race, and Migration.* New York: Palgrave Macmillan, 2009.

———. "Voyages South and North: The Politics of Transnational Gender Identity in *Caramelo* and *American Chica*." *Latino Studies* 5 (2007): 340–357.

Herrera, Andrea O'Reilly, ed. *Cuba: Idea of a Nation Displaced*. Albany: State University of New York Press, 2007.

———. *ReMembering Cuba: Legacy of a Diaspora*. Austin: University of Texas Press, 2001.

Herrera, Cristina. "The Rejected and Reclaimed Mother in Sandra Cisneros's *Caramelo*." *Journal of the Association for Research on Mothering* 10.2 (2008): 184–194.

Herrera-Sobek, María. "Gloria Anzaldúa: Place, Race, Language, and Sexuality in the Magic Valley." *PMLA* 121.1 (2006): 266–271.

Hijuelos, Oscar. *Our House in the Last World*. New York: Persea Books, 1983.

House Bill 2281, State of Arizona, House of Representatives, 49th Legislature, 2nd Regular Session, 2010.

Huntington, Samuel P. "The Hispanic Challenge." *Foreign Policy*, March 1, 2004.

———. *Who Are We? The Challenges to America's National Identity*. New York: Simon and Schuster, 2004.

Jacobs, Elizabeth. "New Mexican Narratives and the Politics of Home." *Journal of American Studies of Turkey* 12 (2000): 39–49. http://www.bilknet.edu/tr/~jast/Number12/Jacobs.htm.

Jefferson, Thomas. *The Papers of Thomas Jefferson*. Vol. 8, ed. Julian P. Boyd. Princeton, N.J.: Princeton University Press, 1950.

———. *The Works of Thomas Jefferson*, Federal Edition. Ed. Paul Leicester Ford. 12 vols. New York: G. P. Putnam's Sons, 1904–1905.

Johnson, Kelli Lyon. "Violence in the Borderlands: Crossing to the Home Space in the Novels of Ana Castillo." *Frontiers* 25.1 (2004): 39–58.

Jones, Vanessa E. "Latina Author Reaches for Next Literary Level." *Boston Globe*, November 20, 2002.

Kanellos, Nicolás. "A Schematic Approach to Understanding Latino Transnational Literary Texts." In *Imagined Transnationalism: U.S. Latino/a Literature, Culture, and Identity*, ed. Kevin Concannon, Francisco A. Lomelí, and Marc Preiwe, 29–45. New York: Palgrave Macmillan, 2009.

Kaye, Jacqueline. "Entre Americanos: Cuba and the United States." In *A Permanent Etcetera: Cross Cultural Perspectives on Post-War America*, ed. A. Robert Lee, 133–144. Boulder, Colo.: Pluto Press, 1993.

Keating, AnaLouise. "Towards a New Politics of Representation? Absence and Desire in Denise Chávez's *The Last of the Menu Girls*." In *We Who Love to Be Astonished: Experimental Women's Writing and Performance Poetics*, ed. Laura Hinton and Cynthia Hogue, 71–80. Tuscaloosa: University of Alabama Press, 2002.

Kelley, Margot. "A Minor Revolution: Chicano/a Composite Novels and the Limits of Genre." In *Ethnicity and the American Short Story*, ed. William E. Cain and Julia Brown, 63–84. New York: Garland, 1997.

Kevane, Bridget. "The Fiction of Judith Ortiz Cofer: *The Line of the Sun* (1989)."

In *Latino Literature in America*, 117–129. Westport, Conn.: Greenwood Press, 2003.

———. *Profane and Sacred: Latino/a American Writers Reveal the Interplay of the Secular and the Religious*. Lanham, Md.: Rowman and Littlefield, 2008.

Kevane, Bridget, and Juanita Heredia. *Latina Self-Portraits: Interviews with Contemporary Women Writers*. Albuquerque: University of New Mexico Press, 2000.

Killingsworth, Jimmie, and Jacqueline S. Palmer. "Ecopolitics and the Literature of the Borderlands: The Frontiers of Environmental Justice in Latina and Native American Writing." In *Writing the Environment: Ecocriticism and Literature*, 196–207. New York: St. Martin's Press, 1998.

King, Rosemary A. *Border Confluences: Borderland Narratives from the Mexican War to the Present*. Tucson: University of Arizona Press, 2004.

Korrol, Virginia E. Sánchez. *From Colonia to Community: The History of Puerto Ricans in New York City*. Berkeley: University of California Press, 1983.

Koskela, Hille. "'Don't Mess with Texas!' Texas Virtual Border Watch Program and the (Botched) Politics of Responsibilization." *Crime Media Culture* 7.1 (2011): 49–65.

Kuhner, Jeffrey T. "Should Arizona Secede? Choice between Devolution and Dissolution May Be Inevitable." *Washington Times*, July 30, 2010.

Lacey, Marc. "Rift in Arizona as Latin Class Is Found Illegal." *New York Times*, January 4, 2011.

———. "Tea Party Rallies at Mexican Border: Activists Gather to Back Candidate, with Illegal Immigration as Top Issue." *International Herald Tribune*, August 17, 2010.

Lazo, Rodrigo. *Writing to Cuba: Filibustering and Cuban Exiles in the United States*. Chapel Hill: University of North Carolina Press, 2005.

Lefebvre, Henri. *The Production of Space*. [1974.] Trans. Donald Nicholson-Smith. Oxford: Blackwell, 1991.

Levine, Robert M. *Tropical Diaspora: The Jewish Experience in Cuba*. Gainesville: University Press of Florida, 1993.

Lewin, Tamar. "Citing Individualism, Arizona Tries to Rein in Ethnic Studies in School." *New York Times*, May 14, 2010.

Lewis, Charles, "Arizona Bans Ethnic Studies in Schools: Debate over Latino Influence Heightened." *National Post* (Canada), May 13, 2010.

Lopez, Adriana. "Interview with Sandra Cisneros." *Library Journal*, September 15, 2002.

Lopez, Lorraine. "Possibilities for Salsa Music in the Mainstream: An Interview with Judith Ortiz Cofer." August 1, 2006. http://www.english.uga.edu/~jcofer/lopezinterview.html.

Luckhurst, Roger. "Memory Recovered/Recovered Memory." In *Literature and Theories of the Present*, ed. Roger Luckhursts and Peter Marks, 80–93. Essex: Longman, 1999.

Lugo-Ortiz, Agnes. "Ethnic Studies in the Age of Transnationalism." *PMLA* 122.3 (2007): 805–807.

Madsen, Deborah L. *Understanding Contemporary Chicana Literature.* Columbia: University of South Carolina Press, 2000.

Manning, Susan. "Introduction." In *Letters from an American Farmer*, by Hector St. John de Crèvecoeur, vii–xxxvii. [1782.] Ed. Susan Manning. Oxford: Oxford University Press, 1997.

Marshall, Joanna Barszewska. "'Boast Now, Chicken, Tomorrow You'll Be Stew': Pride, Shame, Food, and Hunger in the Memoirs of Esmeralda Santiago." *MELUS* 32.4 (2007): 47–68.

———. "Translating 'Home' in the Work of Judith Ortiz Cofer." In *Writing Off the Hyphen: New Perspectives on the Literature of the Puerto Rican Diaspora*, ed. José L. Torres-Padilla and Carmen Haydée Rivera, 256–273. Seattle: University of Washington Press, 2008.

Massey, Doreen. "Double Articulation: A Place in the World." In *Displacements: Cultural Identities in Question*, ed. Angelika Bammer, 110–121. Bloomington: Indiana University Press, 1994.

———. *Space, Place, and Gender.* Minneapolis: University of Minnesota Press, 1994.

McClennen, Sophia A. *The Dialectics of Exile: Nation, Time, Language, and Space in Hispanic Literatures.* West Lafayette, Ind.: Purdue University Press, 2004.

Mehaffy, Marilyn, and AnaLouise Keating. "'Carrying on the Message': Denise Chávez on the Politics of Chicana Becoming." *Aztlán* 26.1 (2001): 127–156.

Menéndez, Ana. *In Cuba I Was a German Shepherd.* New York: Grove Press, 2001.

Montilla, Patricia M. "The Island as Mainland and the Revolving Door Motif: Contemporary Puerto Rican Literature of the United States." In *A Companion to U.S. Latino Literatures*, ed. Carlota Caulfield and Darién J. Davies, 51–66. Rochester, N.Y.: Tamesis, 2007.

Moraga, Cherrie. "Art in América con Acento." In *Women's Voices from the Borderlands*, ed. Lillian Castillo-Speed, 211–219. New York: Simon and Schuster, 1995.

Mosco, Vincent. *The Digital Sublime: Myth, Power, and Cyberspace.* Cambridge, Mass.: MIT Press, 2004.

Mujcinovic, Fatima. *Postmodern Cross-Culturalism and Politicization in U.S. Latina Literature: From Ana Castillo to Julia Alvarez.* New York: Peter Lang, 2004.

Muller, Gilbert H. *New Strangers in Paradise: The Immigrant Experience and Contemporary American Fiction.* Lexington: University Press of Kentucky, 1999.

Munis, Ismael. "*Bildungsroman* Written by Puerto Rican Women in the United States: Nicholasa Mohr's *Nilda: A Novel* and Esmeralda Santiago's *When I Was Puerto Rican*." *Athenea* 19.1 (1999): 79–101.

Murphy, Patrick D. "Grandmother Borderland: Placing Identity and Ethnicity." *ISLE: Interdisciplinary Studies in Literature and Environment* 1.1 (1993): 35–41.

Negrón-Muntaner, Frances. Introduction to *None of the Above: Puerto Ricans in the Global Era*, ed. Frances Negrón-Muntaner, 1–12. New York: Palgrave Macmillan, 2007.

Negrón-Muntaner, Frances, and Ramón Grosfoguel, eds. *Puerto Rican Jam: Essays on Culture and Politics*. Minneapolis: University of Minnesota Press, 1997.

Ngai, Mae M. *Impossible Subjects: Illegal Aliens and the Making of Modern America*. Princeton, N.J.: Princeton University Press, 2002.

Norwood, Vera, and Janice Monk. "Introduction: Perspectives on Gender and Landscape." In *The Desert Is No Lady: Southwestern Landscapes in Women's Writing and Art*, ed. Vera Norwood and Janice Monk, 1–9. New Haven, Conn.: Yale University Press, 1987.

Novas, Himilce. *Everything You Need to Know about Latino History*. New York: Penguin, 1998.

———. Interview. Houston Public Radio (KUHF FM), March 23, 2005. http://www.kuhf.org/upload/arts_interviews/050323Papaya.m3u.

———. *Mangos, Bananas, and Coconuts: A Cuban Love Story*. Houston: Arte Publico Press, 1996.

———. *Princess Papaya*. Houston: Arte Publico Press, 2004.

Obejas, Achy. *Days of Awe*. New York: Ballantine, 2001.

———. *We Came All the Way from Cuba So You Could Dress Like This?* San Francisco: Cleis Press, 1994.

Oboler, Suzanne. *Ethnic Labels, Latino Lives: Identity and the Politics of (Re)Presentation in the United States*. Minneapolis: University of Minnesota Press, 1995.

———. "Redefining Citizenship as a Lived Experience." In *Latinos and Citizenship: The Dilemma of Belonging*, ed. Suzanne Oboler, 3–30. New York: Palgrave Macmillan, 2006.

———. "'So Far from God, So Close to the United States': The Roots of Hispanic Homogenization." In *Challenging Fronteras*, ed. Mary Romero et al., 31–54. New York: Routledge, 1997.

Ocasio, Rafael. "Puerto Rican Literature in Georgia? An Interview with Judith Ortiz Cofer." *Kenyan Review* 14.4 (1992): 43–51.

Ocasio, Rafael, and Rita Ganey. "Speaking in Puerto Rican: An Interview with Judith Ortiz Cofer." *Bilingual Review* 17.2 (1992): 143–146.

Olwig, Kenneth R. "Recovering the Subversive Nature of Landscape." *Annals of the Association of American Geographers* 86.4 (1996): 630–653.

Ortiz, Ricardo L. "Cuban-American Literature." In *New Immigrant Literatures of the United States*, 187–206. Westport, Conn.: Greenwood Press, 1996.

————. *Cultural Erotics in Cuban America*. Minneapolis: University of Minnesota Press, 2007.

Ortiz Cofer, Judith. *The Line of the Sun*. Athens: University of Georgia Press, 1989.

————. *The Meaning of Consuelo*. Boston: Beacon Press, 2003.

————. *Silent Dancing: A Partial Remembrance of a Puerto Rican Childhood*. Houston: Arte Publico Press, 1990.

Padilla, Genaro M. "Myth and Comparative Cultural Nationalism." In *Aztlán: Essays on the Chicano Homeland*, ed. Rudolfo Anaya and Francisco A. Lomelí, 111–134. Albuquerque: University of New Mexico Press, 1989.

Perea, Juan F. *Immigrants Out! The New Nativism and the Anti-Immigrant Impulse in the United States*. New York: New York University Press, 1997.

Pérez, Louis A., Jr. *On Becoming Cuban: Identity, Nationalism, and Culture*. Chapel Hill: University of North Carolina Press, 1999.

Pérez-Firmat, Gustavo. *Life on the Hyphen: The Cuban-American Way*. Austin: University of Texas Press, 1994.

Pérez-Torres, Rafael. *Mestizaje: Critical Uses of Race in Chicano Culture*. Minneapolis: University of Minnesota Press, 2006.

————. "Refiguring Aztlán." In *Postcolonial Theory and the United States: Race, Ethnicity, and Literature*, ed. Amritjit Singh and Peter Schmidt, 103–121. Jackson: University Press of Mississippi, 2000.

Pike, Fredrick B. *The United States and Latin America: Myths and Stereotypes of Civilization and Nature*. Austin: University of Texas Press, 1992.

Porter, David. Introduction to *Internet Culture*, ed. David Porter, xi–xviii. New York: Routledge, 1997.

Quintana, Alvina. *Home Girls: Chicana Literary Voices*. Philadelphia: Temple University Press, 1996.

Radhakrishnan, R. "Ethnic Studies in the Age of Transnationalism." *PMLA* 122.3 (2007): 808–810.

Raymont, Henry. *Troubled Neighbors: The Story of U.S.–Latin American Relations from FDR to the Present*. Cambridge: Westview Press, 2005.

Rebolledo, Tey Diana. "The Tools in the Toolbox: Representing Work in Chicana Writing." *Genre* 32 (1999): 41–52.

————. "Tradition and Mythology: Signatures of Landscape in Chicana Literature." In *The Desert Is No Lady: Southwestern Landscapes in Women's Writing and Art*, ed. Vera Norwood and Janice Monk, 96–124. New Haven, Conn.: Yale University Press, 1987.

————. *Women Singing in the Snow: A Cultural Analysis of Chicana Literature*. Tucson: University of Arizona Press, 1995.

Reyes, Raul A. "The Other Arizona Battle: A New Law Makes Ethnic Studies Classes Illegal: Since When Is It a Bad Thing to Learn about Different Cultures?" *Christian Science Monitor*, June 3, 2010.

Rich, Adrienne. *Of Woman Born: Motherhood as Experience and Institution*. New York: Norton, 1976.

Richter, Francine K. Ramsey. "Romantic Women and La Lucha: Denise Chávez's *Face of an Angel.*" *Great Plains Quarterly* 19.4 (1999): 277–289.

Robbins, Ted. "Immigration Enforcement Working, Numbers Show." *Morning Edition*, NPR interview, January 4, 2011.

Roberts-Camps, Traci. *Gendered Self-Consciousness in Mexican and Chicana Women Writers: The Female Body as an Instrument of Political Resistance.* Lewiston, ME: Edwin Mellen Press, 2008.

Robinson, Eugene. "In Arizona, Just Say No to Latino Heritage." *Washington Post*, May 14, 2010.

Rocco, Raymond. "Transforming Citizenship: Membership, Strategies of Containment, and the Public Sphere in Latino Communities." In *Latinos and Citizenship: The Dilemma of Belonging*, 301–327. New York: Palgrave Macmillan, 2006.

Rochel, Juan Antonio Perles. "Social Change in Ana Castillo's Narrative." In *Women: Creators of Culture*, American Studies in Greece, Series 3, 127–132. Thessaloniki: Hellenic Association of American Studies, 1997.

Rodriguez, Ana Patricia. "Refugees of the South: Central Americans in the U.S. Imaginary." *American Literature* 73.2 (2001): 387–412.

Rodriguez, Gregory. "The Emerging Latino Middle Class." Cited in "Latinos in California: The Next Italians." *Economist*, December 14, 2006.

———. "Why We're the New Irish." *Newsweek*, May 30, 2010, 35.

Rodríguez, Juana María. "Ethnic Scholarship, Transnational Studies, Institutional Locations." *PMLA* 122.3 (2007): 810–812.

Rosaldo, Renato. "Cultural Citizenship, Inequality, and Multiculturalism." In *Race, Identity and Citizenship: A Reader*, ed. Rodolfo D. Torres, Louis F. Mirón, and Jonathan Xavier Inda, 53–261. Oxford: Blackwell, 1999.

———. "Fables of the Fallen Guy." In *Criticism in the Borderlands: Studies in Chicano Literature, Culture and Ideology*, ed. Héctor Calderón and Jose David Saldívar, 84–93. Durham, N.C.: Duke University Press, 1991.

Rosas, Gilberto. "The Managed Violences of the Borderland: Treacherous Geographies, Policeability, and the Politics of Race." *Latino Studies* 4 (2006): 401–418.

———. "The Thickening Borderlands: Diffused Exceptionality and 'Immigrant' Social Struggles during the 'War on Terror.'" *Cultural Dynamics* 18.3 (2006): 335–349.

Ruíz, Vicki L. "Nuestra América: Latino History as United States History." *Journal of American History* 93.3 (2006): 655–672.

Rushdie, Salman. *Imaginary Homelands: Essays and Criticism 1982–1991.* London: Granta Books, 1991.

———. *Shame.* New York: Anchor Books, 1994.

Saar, Doreen Alvarez. "The Heritage of American Ethnicity in Crèvecoeur's *Letters from an American Farmer.*" In *A Mixed Race: Ethnicity in Early America*, ed. Frank Shuffelton, 241–256. Oxford: Oxford University Press, 1993.

Sadowski-Smith, Claudia. "'A Homecoming without a Home': Recent U.S. Cuban Writing of the Diaspora." In *Cuba: Idea of a Nation Displaced*, ed. Andrea O'Reilly Herrera, 267–284. Albany: State University of New York Press, 2007.

Saeta, Elsa. "Ana Castillo's *Sapogonia*: Narrative Point of View as a Study in Perception." *Confluencia: Revista Hispanica de Cultura ye Literatura* 10.1 (1994): 67–72.

Said, Edward. *Orientalism*. New York: Vintage, 1974.

Saldívar, José David. *Border Matters: Remapping American Cultural Studies*. Berkeley: University of California Press, 1997.

Saldívar, Ramon. *Chicano Narrative: The Dialectics of Difference*. Madison: University of Wisconsin Press, 1990.

Saldívar-Hull, Sonia. *Feminism on the Border: Chicana Gender Politics and Literature*. Berkeley: University of California Press, 2000.

———. "Feminism on the Border: From Gender Politics to Geopolitics." In *Criticism in the Borderlands: Studies in Chicano Literature, Culture and Ideology*, ed. Héctor Calderón and José David Saldívar, 203–220. Durham, N.C.: Duke University Press, 1991.

Samuelson, Robert J. "The Hard Truth of Immigration." *Newsweek*, May 13, 2005, 64–65.

Sanchez, George J. "Y Tú, Que?" In *Latinos Remaking America*, ed. Marcelo M. Suárez-Orozco and Mariela M. Páez, 45–58. Berkeley: University of California Press, 2002.

Sánchez, Marta E. "Para Español Oprima El Número Dos: Transnational Translation and U.S. Latino/a Literature." In *Imagined Transnationalism: U.S. Latino/a Literature, Culture and Identity*, ed. Kevin Concannon, Francisco A. Lomelí, and Marc Preiwe, 47–60. New York: Palgrave Macmillan, 2009.

Sánchez González, Lisa. *Boricua Literature: A Literary History of the Puerto Rican Diaspora*. New York: New York University Press, 2001.

Sánchez-Pardo Gonzalez, Esther. "The Desire Called Utopia: Re-imagining Collectivity in Moraga and Castillo." *Estudios Ingleses de la Universidad Complutense* 17 (2009): 95–114.

Sanders, Mark A. "Brief Reflections on the Discourse of Transnationalism and African American Studies." *PMLA* 122.3 (2007): 812–814.

Sandín, Lyn Di Iorio, and Richard Perez. "Introduction: New Waves in U.S. Latino/a Literary Criticism." In *Contemporary U.S. Latino/a Literary Criticism*, ed. Lyn Di Iorio Sandín and Richard Perez, 1–11. New York: Palgrave Macmillan, 2007.

Santiago, Esmeralda. *Almost a Woman*. Reading, Mass.: Perseus Books, 1998.

———. *The Turkish Lover*. Cambridge: Da Capo Books, 2004.

———. *When I Was Puerto Rican*. New York: Vintage, 1993.

Sayers, Valerie. "Caramelo." *New York Times*, September 29, 2002.

Seaman, Donna. "Review of *The Norton Anthology of Latino Literature*." *Book-list*, September 15, 2010.

Slater, David. "Situating Geographical Representations: Inside/Outside and the Power of Imperial Interventions." In *Human Geography Today*, ed. Doreen Massey et al., 62–84. Cambridge: Polity Press, 1999.

Smorkaloff, Pamela María. *Cuban Writers On and Off the Island: Contemporary Narrative Fiction*. New York: Twayne, 1999.

Socolovsky, Maya. "Borrowed Homes, Homesickness, and Memory in Ana Castillo's *Sapogonia*." *Aztlán: A Journal of Chicano Studies* 24.2 (1999): 73–94.

———. "Narrative and Traumatic Memory in Denise Chávez's *Face of an Angel*." *MELUS* 28.4 (2003) 187–205.

Soja, Edward. *Postmodern Geographies: The Reassertion of Space in Critical Social Theory*. New York: Verso, 1989.

Soja, Edward, and Barbara Hooper. "The Spaces That Difference Makes: Some Notes on the Geographical Margins of the New Cultural Politics." In *Place and the Politics of Identity*, ed. M. Keith and S. Pile, 180–203. London: Routledge, 1993.

Sprouse, Keith Alan. "Between Bilingue and Nilingue: Language and the Translation of Identity in Esmeralda Santiago's Memoirs." *American Studies in Scandinavia* 3 (2000): 107–115.

Stallybrass, Peter, and Allon White. *The Politics and Poetics of Transgression*. Ithaca, N.Y.: Cornell University Press, 1986.

Stavans, Ilan. "The Accents of Latino Literature." *On Point*, NPR interview, September 13, 2010.

———. "Introduction: The Search for Wholeness." In *The Norton Anthology of Latino Literature*, ed. Ilan Stavans, lxiii–lxxi. New York: W. W. Norton, 2011.

———. *Latino History and Culture*. New York: Collins, 2007.

Suarez, Ray. "Interview with Sandra Cisneros." *Online NewsHour*, October 15, 2002.

Szadziuk, Maria. "Culture as Transition: Becoming a Woman in a Bi-Ethnic Space." *Mosaic: A Journal for the Interdisciplinary Study of Literature* 32.3 (1999): 109-129.

Tate, Julee. "Plotting Her Way to the Center: Gender Narrative as Utopian Passport in the Works of Esmeralda Santiago." *Brúla* 3.1 (2004): 101–112.

Thomas, Piri. *Down These Mean Streets*. New York: Vintage, 1967.

Thornburgh, Nathan. "Inside the Life of the Migrants Next Door." *Time*, February 6, 2006.

Time, July 8, 1985.

Time, Special Issue, Fall 1993.

Torres, Rodolfo D., Louis F. Mirón, and Jonathan Xavier Inda. Introduction to *Race, Identity, and Citizenship: A Reader*, ed. Rodolfo D. Torres, Louis F. Mirón, and Jonathan Xavier Inda, 1–16. Oxford: Blackwell, 1999.

Torres-Padilla, José L. "When 'I' Became Ethnic: Ethnogenesis and Three

Early Puerto Rican Diaspora Writers." In *Writing Off the Hyphen: New Perspectives on the Literature of the Puerto Rican Diaspora*, ed. José L. Torres-Padilla and Carmen Haydée Rivera, 81–104. Seattle: University of Washington Press, 2008.

Tuan, Yi-Fu. "Place: An Experiential Perspective." *Geographical Review* 65.2 (1975): 151–165.

TuSmith, Bonnie. *All My Relatives: Community in Contemporary Ethnic American Literatures*. Ann Arbor: University of Michigan Press, 1994.

———. "The Significance of the 'Multi' in 'Multi-Ethnic Literatures of the US.'" Presidential Address, March 2001. *MELUS* 26.2 (Summer 2001): 5–14.

Villa, Raúl Homera. *Barrio-Logos: Space and Place in Urban Chicano Literature and Culture*. Austin: University of Texas Press, 2000.

Viramontes, Helena María. "The Cariboo Café." In *The Moths and Other Stories*, 65-79. Houston: Arté Público Press, 1995.

Walter, Roland. "The Cultural Politics of Dislocation and Relocation in the Novels of Ana Castillo." *MELUS* 23.1 (1998): 81–97.

Warrior, Robert. "Native American Critical Responses to Transnational Discourse." *PMLA* 122.3 (2007): 807–808.

Wilbur, Shawn P. "An Archaeology of Cyberspaces: Virtuality, Community, Identity." In *Internet Culture*, ed. David Porter, 5–22. New York: Routledge, 1997.

Wright, Elizabeth. J. "'She and I Are Molecules': The Disabled Body in Denise Chávez's *The Last of the Menu Girls*." *Western American Literature* 41.1 (2006): 5–22.

Yang, Philip Q. *Ethnic Studies: Issues and Approaches*. Albany: State University of New York Press, 2000.

Yudice, George, and Juan Flores. "La Carreta Made a U-Turn: Puerto Rican Language and Culture in the United States." *Daedalus: Journal of the American Academy of Arts and Sciences* 110.2 (1981): 193–217.

———. "Living Borders/Buscando America: Languages of Latino Self-Formation." *Social Text* 8.12 (1990): 57–84.

Zúñiga, Victor, and Rubén Hernández-León, eds. *New Destinations: Mexican Immigration in the United States*. New York: Sage, 2005.

Index

About the Author

Maya Socolovsky is an assistant professor of English and Latin American studies at the University of North Carolina, Charlotte. She has published articles on Latino/a literature and Jewish American literature.

CPSIA information can be obtained at www.ICGtesting.com
Printed in the USA
BVOW030503070513

320008BV00002B/5/P